The Coming of the King James Gospels

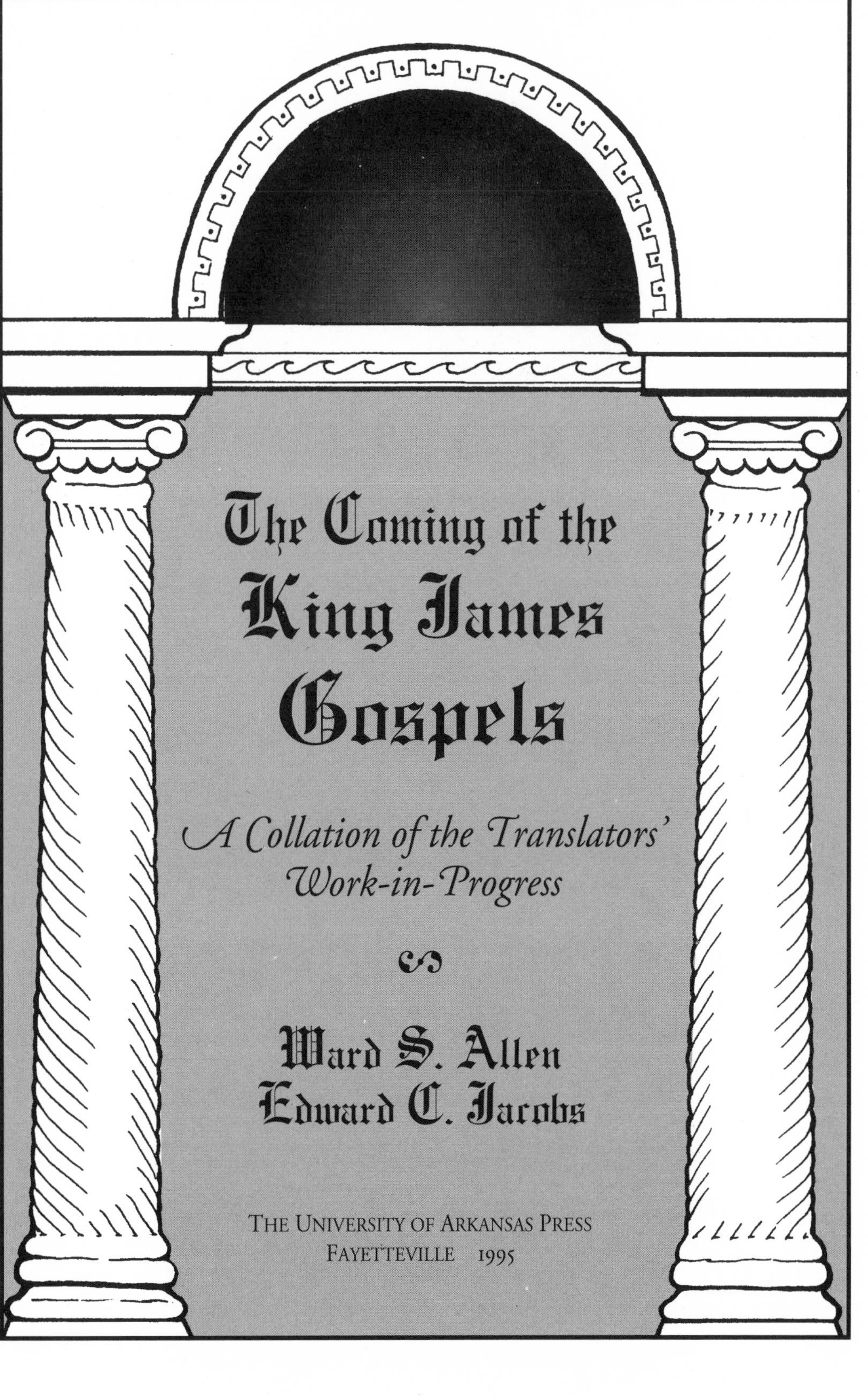

The Coming of the
King James
Gospels
A Collation of the Translators'
Work-in-Progress
Ward S. Allen
Edward C. Jacobs
THE UNIVERSITY OF ARKANSAS PRESS
FAYETTEVILLE 1995

Manufactured in the United States of America

99 98 97 96 95 5 4 3 2 1

Designed by Gail Carter
Illustrated by Liz Lester

⊗ The paper used in this publication meets the minimum requirements of the American National Standard for Permanence of Paper for Printed Library Materials Z39.48-1984.

Library of Congress Cataloging-in-Publication Data
Allen, Ward, 1922–
The coming of the King James Gospels : a collation of the translators' work-in-progress / Ward S. Allen, Edward C. Jacobs.
p. cm.
Includes bibliographical references.
ISBN 1-55728-327-3 (alk. paper). —
ISBN 1-55728-345-1 (paper)
1. Bible. N.T. Gospels. English.—Versions—Authorized. 2. Bible. N.T. Gospels—Translating. I. Jacobs, Edward C. (Edward Craney) II. Title.
BS2555.2.A45 1995
226'.052038—dc20 94-34592
CIP

To Peggy McComas Allen

&

Karen Langpap Jacobs

Contents

Preface

The curators of the Bodleian Library have kindly granted permission to quote from 'Bibl. Eng. 1602 b.1'. The photographic department has expedited the work. *The Library* has generously granted me permission to reprint some of my earlier findings published therein. A number of universities and foundations have supported this work: Auburn University, Duke University, Louisiana Tech University, the University of North Carolina at Chapel Hill, the Folger Shakespeare Library, the Southern Region Education Board, and the Southeastern Medieval and Renaissance Institute.

I owe special thanks to my close friend and colleague Professor Sam Hornsby, LaGrange College, whose interest in the Authorized Version has paralleled and encouraged my own; to Professors David Steinmetz and George Williams, Duke University, and Professor A. C. Hamilton, Queen's College, Ontario, Canada, for advice offered many summers ago during the early stages of this work; to Reverend James Lipscomb, Ruston, Louisiana, for knowledge gained during those many halcyon afternoons that we have spent reading the Greek New Testament together. To Karen Jacobs, wife and fellow Renaissance scholar, belongs my greatest thanks. Her support and special acuity have been my mainstay in this work.

Edward C. Jacobs
Ruston, Louisiana

Friends have lent me many a helping hand. Dr. Gerald Hammond, the Reverend Germain Marc'hadour, Mr. David Norton, Dr. Stephen Prickett, Dr. Craig Thompson, and Dr. Amos Wilder have taken time from pressing work for an exchange of letters over the years. Dr. Thompson's concise and sagacious account of *The Bible in English 1525–1611* led me to the Bodleian Bishops' Bible, which King James's translators had marked with their revisions, and to Dr. E. E. Willoughby's account of that Bible. Mr. David Bradshaw, Dr. Hammond, Mr. Norton, and Dr. Edward C. Jacobs have influenced the form of the instructions for using this collation. Dr. Jacobs has added to his duties as dean and teacher the tedious work of verifying the collation.

Auburn University has supplied materials and the leisure for this study. The John Simon Guggenheim Memorial Foundation made possible golden days at the Bodleian Library. Members of the Bodleian staff were generous with help and advice. Mr. Paul Morgan, Mr. I. G. Philip, Mr. D. H. Merry, Dr. D. M. Barratt, and Dr. R. W. Hunt were particularly helpful. They and the Reverend Professor S. L. Greenslade graciously entertained a stranger.

Three debts are of long standing. My parents, Clarence and Lou Willie Sykes Allen, taught me to read the King James Bible. A teacher, Donald Davidson, planted the seed of this book in an assignment to an undergraduate class at Vanderbilt University. My wife, Peggy McComas Allen, has made the Bible the central book in our home. An old man, who faced each day the stint of preparing a collation, was kept by her from giving way to impatience.

Ward S. Allen
Auburn, Alabama

The Coming of the King James Gospels

I. Background

The year 1611 holds special significance for the history of the English Renaissance. This year marks the appearance of the English Biblical translation known popularly as the Authorized Version (AV) and the King James Version. The publication of the AV concludes the first great century of modern English Biblical translations, a century which began with William Tyndale's New Testament (1525/26) and Pentateuch (1530), and progressed through the Coverdale Bible (1535), the Matthew Bible (1537), the Great Bible (1539), the Geneva New Testament (1557) and the Geneva Bible (1560), the Bishops' Bible (1568), the Rheims New Testament (1582), and the Douai Old Testament (1609–10). Not until nearly three hundred years later and the appearance of the Revised Version (1881/1885) would the English language begin to enjoy the fruits of another such remarkable century of Biblical translations, one that continues into our present day.

Excellent scholarly studies have examined these Renaissance English translations, but, generally, these studies have dwelt upon biographical facts about the translators, the historical events surrounding the translations, and the quality of the translations. Regarding the details of the work that went into these Bibles, they have had little to say, for few of the details have survived the course of time. And matters still stand so, with one major exception—the Authorized Version.[1]

The progress of the work of the AV translators is clearer for us today than it was for late-nineteenth-century scholars, such as the distinguished Bishop B. F. Westcott, or eminent twentieth-century Biblical historians, such as C. C. Butterworth, H. W. Robinson, and David Daiches.[2] At the Hampton Court Conference, January 1604, King James I commissioned a new Bible translation to replace the Bishops' Bible, the official translation for Church and State. The King hoped to supplant the popularity of the Geneva Bible, the Puritan translation whose accuracy and readability made it a vast favorite with the people, and whose often testy, sometimes threatening, marginal comments made it most disagreeable to the King. Organization for the project started quickly. By June 1604, the translators had been selected and divided into six companies—two each located at Westminster, Cambridge, and Oxford. These forty-seven or more men, of diverse personalities and shades of religious belief, included many of the best scholars and churchmen in England. The King provided fifteen rules for the work. The first rule ordered the translators to follow the Bishops' Bible and to alter it 'as little . . . as the Truth of the original will permit'. The AV was to be a careful, precise revision of the Bishops' Bible, not a new translation that would be unknown to its readers.[3]

By the end of 1604 and early 1605 most, if not all, of the six companies were at work. A letter written by Bishop Bancroft in August 1604 to Vice-Chancellor Cowell, Cambridge, attests that the two Cambridge companies had begun their assignments.[4] Rule eight directed company members to work individually on assignments and then to discuss their results together as a group. Lancelot Andrewes (Chairman, First Westminster Company), in a letter written in November 1604, speaks, in passing, of afternoon company meetings as 'our translation time'. In January 1605, John Perrin (Second Oxford Company assigned to the Gospels) resigned his professorship at Oxford to work on translating the New Testament. A letter written in April 1605 by Bishop Thomas Bilson confirms that the Oxford New Testament Company was at work. And a funeral eulogy delivered in May 1605 for Edward Lively (Chairman, First Cambridge Company) attributes his death, in part, to his intensive work on the translation.[5]

The companies began their work in the fall of 1604 and finished their assignments, most likely, by late 1607. Indeed, the First Oxford company had 'perfected' its translation of Isaiah-Malachi as early as May 1607. Review followed. Rules nine through eleven mandated that all other companies review each company's work and, if need arose, 'any learned man in the land' was to review the work. To accomplish this review, each company made and passed about copies of its work. At least three copies of the work of the First Cambridge Company (1 Chronicles–Song of Solomon) circulated during the year 1608, one being sent even to Dublin. Manuscript 98 in the Lambeth Palace Library records an intermediate stage of the work by the Second Westminster Company (New Testament Epistles). This manuscript appears to have been prepared for circulation. By December 1608, King James had ordered that 'the translation of the Bible shalbe finished & printed so soone as may be'. Hence any manuscripts of a company's work still circulating during late 1608 were to be returned.[6]

Companies probably spent, then, 1608 and 1609 reviewing, being reviewed, noting results of review, and preparing their assignments for the General Meeting. As prescribed by Rule ten, the General Meeting conducted a final review in London during the first nine months of 1610. Twelve members, two from each of the six companies, examined the finished work recorded and sent to them in three 1602 folio Bishops' Bibles. These Bibles were, no doubt, a part of the forty 'large churchbibles' that Robert Barker, the King's printer, had supplied unbound to the translators sometime between January 1604 and 10 May 1605 for use in their work.[7] Afterward, Bishop Bilson and Miles Smith from the First Oxford Company 'put the finishing touch' to the new translation.

Several important stages in the progress of the translation are now also clearer to us than to earlier scholars. A portion of the final work performed comes alive in *Translating for King James: Notes Made by a Translator of King James's Bible* (1969). In this work there is a translation of the Greek and Latin notes of John Bois. These notes cover the final revision of the New Testament Epistles and Revelation, which the General Meeting accomplished in 1610. According to Bois's biographer, it was John Bois, and only he, who took notes during these final deliberations. *Translating the New Testament Epistles 1604–1611: A Manuscript from King James's Westminster Company* (1977) provides, for the first time, an extensive look at the work of the Second Westminster Company at the end of 1607, or early 1608, when that Company had completed about two-thirds of its revision of the Epistles. These two primary sources often dovetail. With the use of Bois's notes, some of the earlier revisions in Manuscript 98 can be traced through to their final form.[8]

A third primary source exists which provides valuable evidence of the work of the translators at two different stages in the progress of the AV. That source is an annotated 1602 Bishops' Bible obtained by the Bodleian Library in 1646 for 13s. 4d., and described at the time of purchase as 'a large Bible wherein is written downe all the Alterations of the last Translacōn'.[9] This Bible is the only known one of those forty unbound folio Bibles now at hand. It is catalogued as 'Bibl. Eng. 1602 b.1'. The Bible's Old Testament annotations are a record of the revision as it probably existed in 1610 when it was forwarded to London to the General Meeting for final review.[10] The Bible's New Testament annotations are our present concern. The evidence which follows—handwriting, methods of annotation, and textual collation—argues that three scribes were responsible for recording the New Testament annotations. The evidence reveals, moreover, the presence of three causally related stages of translation which occurred sometime between late 1607 and 1610. For convenience, these stages are here identified simply as Stage 1 (S-1), Stage 2 (S-2), and Stage 3 (S-3) revisions.

II. The Text

The New Testament annotations fill margins and text in Matthew, Mark, Luke, and John 17–21. Except for five annotations scattered in the Epistles, there are no other annotations.[11] Three principal scribes, each using a different method, recorded these annotations. MT—the Matthew scribe—employs an irregular method to record annotations in Matthew and in John 17. ML—the Mark/Luke scribe—uses, by contrast, a precise method to record annotations in Mark and in Luke 1–18. LJ—the Luke/John scribe—uses a method similar to ML's for annotating Luke 19–24 and John 18–21.

Stage 1 Revisions comprise those annotations recorded in the New Testament by scribes, perhaps some of the translators themselves, near the end of 1607, or early 1608, when, in the course of the seven-year project, the Oxford New Testament Company had completed its assignment of translating the Gospels and was preparing for that review of its work mandated by 'The Rules to be observed in the Translation of the Bible'.[12] S-1 revisions fall into three sub-groups of annotations: Substitutions, Additions, and Deletions. A Substitution requires the scribe to cancel a given portion of verse and record in its place a handwritten revision, either interlinearly, or in a margin. An Addition requires the scribe to add phrasing to a portion of verse, either interlinearly, or in a margin. A Deletion requires the scribe to cancel only a given portion of verse. It is common to find all three sub-groups used in a single verse. S-1 revisions are clearly recognizable in the work of ML and LJ, who use systematic methods to record revisions; but the unsystematic method that MT uses often makes it difficult to determine if his annotations belong to an S-1 or S-2 category.

Stage 2 revisions make up a second stage of annotations. These, representing the results of the review work of 1608, have been recorded in the New Testament after the Stage 1 work. The process probably went thus: during or after the review of 1608, the Oxford New Testament Company met in 1608/09 to discuss suggested changes to their completed Gospel revisions—those in the S-1 category. Those suggestions by reviewers to which the Company agreed were recorded by the three principal scribes amid their S-1 revisions, canceling out earlier S-1 revisions when necessary. At times, these S-2 revisions reveal debate among the translators. Furthermore, it is not uncommon to spot the hand of one scribe recording S-2 revisions amid the work of the other two scribes, and occasionally other hands appear recording S-2 work amid the work of the principal scribes. S-2 work recorded amid the S-1 work of ML and LJ is identifiable because it is recorded in ways that depart from the method that each scribe used to record S-1 revisions. S-2 revisions recorded amid the S-1 work of MT are not easy to identify, again because of MT's unsystematic recording method. When we encounter a different recording hand amid MT's work, the likelihood of such work being S-2 revision is strong. But when we encounter a passage revised by MT, and then once again by him, it is not always possible to argue that the latter work falls into the S-2 category.

Stage 3 revisions comprise the third identifiable stage of the process associated with these annotations. In addition to the S-1 and S-2 revisions recorded in these annotated Gospels, it is clear from collation with the AV that revision of the Gospels was ongoing elsewhere. Such revision constitutes, then, the evidence of Stage 3 work. Exactly when this stage occurred for LJ probably differs from when it occurred for ML and MT. Estimations derived from our collation argue that Stage 1 and Stage 2 revisions of MT, ML, and LJ correspond to the AV text in the amounts of two-thirds, three-fourths, and five-sixths, respectively. If we judge the amount of work that the General Meeting accomplished by John Bois's notes, it is possible that the Stage 3 work for those portions annotated by LJ could have occurred as late as the time of the General Meeting during the first nine months of 1610. But the lesser states of the finished work found in the annotations of ML, and especially in MT, argue that the Stage 3 revisions for these two scribes must include more than the nine months of work of the General Meeting in 1610. Stage 3 revisions for MT and ML must also encompass other revisions being performed and recorded elsewhere than in the leaves of this New Testament, at about, or perhaps just after, the time that MT and ML were recording their work (1608/09), but earlier than the 1610 work of the General Meeting. It is probable, then, that the revisions recorded by MT and ML were combined with those of other parallel efforts into a version closer to that state represented by LJ's work, and then sent to the General Meeting in 1610 in one of the three large Bibles spoken of in Rule ten.

The ML Scribe

The method of ML is the clearest. (Once understood, the method of LJ is relatively easy to follow, after which the method of MT, with its uncertainties, also becomes apparent.) ML employs a small, neat, exact Secretary hand. Minuscule 'i's', 'b's', and 'w's' are clear. He controls ascenders of minuscule 'f's' and 's's'. In forming minuscule 'd's', ML usually connects the semicircular base of the letter at both points to the lower part of the ascender. ML uses one of three techniques to record S-1 revisions, depending upon whether he is recording Substitutions, Deletions, or Additions. Luke 2.12 illustrates ML's Substitution sequence (see Fig. 1). First, ML underlines with a single continuous line each passage in the verse that is to be replaced by a Substitution: 'take this for a signe' and 'childe swadled, laid'. Second, ML inserts a superscript Greek letter before the first word of each underlined passage: a nu before 'take', and a xi before 'childe'. At times, but not in this verse, ML will insert a caret beneath the superscript letter to call attention to it. Third, ML records in the margin opposite the underlined passage a second Greek letter matching the superscript one in the text. ML follows the Greek alphabet in selecting matching pairs of letters. If he finishes the alphabet, as in Luke 2.23, he usually begins the alphabet anew, as in Luke 2.24. At times, ML will use signs other than Greek letters if he is near the end of a chapter and needs only a few signs to finish textual revisions for the remaining verses. Such is the case for Luke 2.49–52 (see Fig. 2): ML uses astrological signs here. After the Greek letter (or other sign) written in the margin, ML writes the Substitution revision meant to replace the underlined passage. After the nu at Luke 2.12, he writes: 'this shall be a signe vnto you'; after the xi he writes: 'babe wrapped in swadling clothes laying' (later revised to 'lying').

The fourth and final step that ML uses to complete Substitutions is a strike-through line, a single continuous line crossing out each portion of the underlined text. The line confirms that the proposed Substitution written in the margin has been approved, thus far, as the future AV revision to replace the underlined 1602 text. Luke 2.12, now revised, reads:

> And this shall be a signe vnto you, Ye shall finde the babe wrapped in swadling clothes laying in a manger.

Study of Luke 2.19 reveals that the use of the strike-through lines in Luke 2.12 is the last step in the Substitution sequence (see Fig. 1). One passage in Luke 2.19 contains the first three steps of the sequence but does not have the strike-through line. Instead, this passage deviates from the Substitution sequence: the proposed revision written in the margin has itself been cancelled.

citie of Dauid, a sauiour, which is Christ the
Lord.
12 And take this for a signe, Ye shall finde the
childe swadled, laid in a manger.
13 And suddenly there was with the Angel a
multitude of heauenly souldiers, praising God,
and saying,
14 Glorie to God in the highest, and peace on
the earth, and among men a good will.
15 And it came to passe, assoone as the Angels
were gone away from them into heauen, the
men the shepheards sayd one to another, Let vs
goe now euen vnto Bethlehem, and see this
thing which is come to passe, which the Lord
hath shewed vnto vs.
16 And they came with haste, & found Marie
and Ioseph, and the babe layd in a manger.
17 And when they had seene it, they published abroade the saying which was told them of
this childe.
18 And all they that heard it, woondered at
those things which were tolde them of the shepheards.
19 But Marie kept all those sayings, and
pondered them in her heart.
20 And the shepheards returned, glorifying
and praising God for all the things that they
had heard and seene, euen as it was tolde vnto
them.
21 *And when the eight day was come, that
the childe should be circumcised, his name was
called Iesus, which was so named of the Angel
before he was conceiued in the wombe.
22 And when the dayes of her purification,
after the law of Moses, were accomplished, they
brought him to Hierusalem, to present him to
the Lord,
23 (As it is written in the lawe of the Lord,
*Euery man childe that first openeth the wombe,
shalbe called holy to the Lord.)
24 And to offer, *as it is sayd in the lawe of
the Lord, a paire of turtle doues, or two yong
pigeons.

The Gospel on Newe yeeres day.

Gen.17.18. mat.1.21.

The Gospel on the Purification of Saint Marie the virgin.

Exo.13.2. num.8.16.

Leu.12.6.

FIGURE 1.

The ML Scribe: Luke 2.12–24, from Bodleian Library, Bibl. Eng. 1602 b.1

At Luke 2.19 the phrase 'pondered them' has been underlined once, and a superscript chi, now voided, has been written before 'pondered', with a matching chi written in the margin, followed by the phrase 'pondering them', now also voided. The logic here is obvious: 'pondering them' has been proposed to replace the underlined 1602 phrase 'pondered them', but for some reason the proposed reading has been rejected. The 1602 phrasing is to remain in the AV—but with one slight revision. The pronoun 'them', instead of being printed in small roman type, is to be printed as the rest of the verse in black letter type: hence the insertion of the abbreviation 'Ang.', for 'Anglice' or 'Anglicize', within square brackets directly above the pronoun.[13] The rejection of this S-1 Substitution revision is evidence, thus, of S-2 revision present in these annotations. Progress of the work can thus be summarized:

1602	:	pondered them
S-1 Sub. Rev.	:	pondering them
S-2 Rev.	:	pondered them.

ML's use of the Greek alphabet in Luke 2.19 also reveals that he does not complete the fourth step of the Substitution sequence—use of the strike-through line, such as in Luke 2.12, to make final the revisions—until he has recorded all proposed S-1 revisions for the Mark/Luke text, and the revisions have been reviewed as the rules directed. For if ML had voided the proposed revision 'pondering them' and the letter chi immediately after recording them, then when he came to record the revision at Luke 2.21, he would have been free to use the chi sign again. Instead, at Luke 2.21, he uses the letter psi. The ML scribe's use of the Greek alphabet in recording S-1 Substitutions reflects the same pattern at enough other places in ML's work to validate the logic applied here in Luke 2.19 (for example, Luke 2.8, 38, and 41; Luke 3.35, 37, and 38).

In the margin opposite Luke 2.13, another sort of deviation from the Substitution process occurs which reveals the presence of S-2 revision: a second revision written above a voided Substitution. The 1602 phrase 'heauenly souldiers' was first revised to read 'the heavenly army'. Reviewers of this proposed Substitution agreed that the 1602 phrase 'heauenly souldiers' should be changed because ML has struck through the underlined 1602 phrase. But apparently reviewers raised a question about the use of the noun 'army' which the Oxford New Testament Company had put forward as part of the S-1 Substitution. The reviewers suggested, in its place, use of the noun 'hoste'. For ML has crossed out the noun 'army' in the margin and written over it the word 'hoste'. This S-2 revision remained untouched. The AV also reads 'the heauenly hoste'.

Besides these two deviations from ML's Substitution sequence that indicate the presence of S-2 revision consequent to the review process, there are also other sorts of deviation from the sequence that indicate S-2 revision. A third one involves the recording of manuscript annotations interlinearly in the 1602 text, rather than in the margin opposite the text. Luke 2.38 is typical (see Fig. 2).

ML has underlined once the phrase 'at the same' and has also struck through it with a single line. He has written above the cancelled phrase the words 'in at that'. Not only does the interlinear position of the phrase 'in at that' suggest that it is an S-2 revision, but also the recording method of the phrase does not use Greek letters as signs to locate revisions in the text.

Other evidence in Luke 2.38 argues the interlinear revision 'in at that' to be an S-2 revision. That evidence is the presence of yet another (a fourth) deviation that indicates S-2 revision: in this instance both the proposed Substitution written in the margin and the 1602 text to be replaced by the Substitution are struck through, thus creating a shortened verse. In Luke 2.38, the phrase 'vpon them' has first been revised to read 'vpon them'. The underlining of the 1602 pronoun, the use of the letter rho written before the underlined pronoun, the writing of a second rho in the margin, followed by the insertion of the pronoun 'them' in a careful print hand, and the abbreviation 'Rom' within square brackets following the pronoun—these constitute the first three steps of the Substitution revision. ML has indicated clearly that the AV is to print the pronoun 'them' in roman type. But at the fourth step of the Substitution sequence, when it comes time to approve the Substitution in the margin by striking through the underlined 1602 text, a further (S-2) revision occurs. At this stage the whole prepositional phrase appears to have been rejected, for the proposed Substitution in the margin is crossed through together with the two words in the 1602 text. Deles, one in the text over the phrase, and the other in the margin, confirm this decision. Revision has proceeded as follows:

1602 : vpon them
S-1 Sub. Rev. : vpon them
S-2 Rev. : ~~vpon them.~~

Turning again to the interlinear revision 'in at that' in Luke 2.38, it is likely that at the same time that the S-2 revision cancelled the Substitution 'vpon them', the interlinear S-2 revision 'in at that' was also added. Upon further review, only one of these S-2 revisions was approved, that being the cancellation of the prepositional phrase 'vpon them'. S-3 revision rejected, in part, the addition of the interlinear revision 'in at that', preferring instead to read 'in that'. Here, the stages of the work proceeded:

1602 : at the same
S-1 Rev. : [unrevised]
S-2 Rev. : in at that
S-3 Rev. : in that.

A fifth sort of deviation that indicates the presence of S-2 revision occurs whenever Greek letters used for recording annotations appear out of their normal alphabetical sequence. Luke 2.15 is an example (see Fig. 1). In the verse, pairs of alphas and betas occur between pis, used in Luke 2.14, and rhos, used in Luke 2.16.

prayers night and day.
38 And she comming at the same instant vpon them, gaue thankes likewise vnto the Lord,
and spake of him to all them that looked for redemption in Hierusalem.
39 And when they had performed all things
according to the law of the Lord, they returned
into Galilee, to their owne citie Nazareth.
40 And the childe grew, and waxed strong in
spirit, and was filled with wisedome, and the
grace of God was vpon him.
41 Now his parents went to Hierusalem e-
uery yere,* at the feast of the Passeouer.
42 And when he was twelue yeres old, they
ascended vp to Hierusalem, after the custome of
the feast day:
43 And when they had fulfilled the dayes, as
they returned home, the childe Iesus abode still
in Hierusalem, and Ioseph & his mother knewe
not of it.
44 But they supposing him to haue bene in
the company, came a dayes iourney, and sought
him among their kinsfolke and acquaintance.
45 And when they found him not, they turned backe againe to Hierusalem, seeking him.
46 And it came to passe, that after three dayes
they found him in the temple, sitting in the middest of the Doctors, hearing them, and posing
them.
47 And all that heard him, were astonied at
his vnderstanding and answeres.
48 And when they saw him, they were amazed: and his mother said vnto him, Sonne, why
hast thou thus dealt with vs? Beholde, thy father and I haue sought thee sorowing.
49 And he sayd vnto them, How is it that yee
sought me? Wist yee not that I must goe about
my fathers busnesse?
50 And they vnderstood not that saying which
he spake vnto them.
51 And hee went downe with them, and
came to Nazareth, and was obedient vnto
them: But his mother kept all these sayings in
her heart.
52 And Iesus increased in wisedome and stature, and in fauour with God and man.

Deut. 26.1.

The first Sunday after the Epiphanie.

The iij. Chapter.

3 The preaching of Iohn, 23 The age and genealo-
gie of Christ.

NOwe in the fifteenth yeere of the
reigne of Tiberius Cesar, Pontius
Pilate being lieutenant of Iurie,

Acts 4.6.

FIGURE 2.

The ML Scribe: Luke 2.38–3.1

Following the alphas in the margin, ML has written 'now goe', and following the betas, he has written 'made knowen'.

The question arises, do we view annotations here as evidence of S-2 revision or of S-1 Substitution revision, albeit out of order as the interruption of the Greek alphabet sequence reveals? One could argue that such a break in sequence is the result of oversight. Perhaps, while recording S-1 revisions in this column of the text, ML rechecked his work before going on to the second column and discovered that he had left out several Substitution revisions. He then quickly corrected the error in his normal manner, but using, of course, other Greek letters that interrupted the normal sequence in this chapter. Having made these corrections, ML went on with his work.

Such reasoning is plausible, but there are counter-arguments for viewing these instances as S-2 revision. First: Luke 2.15 does contain other S-1 revisions, those involving proposed Deletions—a second category of S-1 revision to be examined shortly. There are three such Deletions proposed: 'assoone', 'the men', and 'euen'. Two of these proposed Deletions were accepted, as the presence of strike-through lines indicates, and one—the adverb 'euen'—rejected, as the absence of a strike-through line indicates. Hence the question arises: would ML be careless enough, after having recorded three proposed Deletions, to overlook two needed Substitutions? One of these Substitutions precedes one of the proposed Deletions—the adverb 'euen'—which was later cancelled, probably at the same time that the S-2 revisions denoted by the use of alphas and betas were added. Secondly, such inserted pairs of Greek letters interrupting the normal sequence occur with enough frequency in ML's work—for example, a little farther on at 3.16—to argue against the 'oversight' hypothesis and for the presence of S-2 revision.

A sixth sort of deviation from S-1 Substitutions that reveals the presence of S-2 revision consequent to review involves some few verses, such as Luke 3.9, that ML has revised three times:

1602	:	Now also is the axe
S-1 Sub. Rev.	:	And now also the axe is
S-2 Rev. (1)	:	And now the axe is
S-2 Rev. (2)	:	And now also the axe is.

The 1602 text here of Luke 3.9 has been underlined once with a continuous line. (The adverb 'Now' bears a second short, slanting line beneath the letters 'ow'.) A pair of mus marks the revision: a superscript mu before the adverb 'Now', and another mu written opposite in the margin. After this latter mu, ML has written the S-1 Substitution revision cited above. A strike-through line crosses out the underlined 1602 text to signify approval of the Substitution. But this Substitution by the Oxford New Testament Company occasioned discord during the review process. A problem arose about the use of the adverb 'also'. Those reviewing the Company's work suggested that the adverb 'also' be cut. Receiving this suggestion, the Company agreed, for 'also' has been crossed out in the margin, resulting in S-2 revision (1). But further discussion ensued, the outcome of which was to restore the adverb 'also'. The adverb has been rewritten in the margin just above the point where it was crossed through, creating S-2 revision (2) which is identical to the S-1 Substitution revision first proposed.

One can infer that the problem involved style versus literal exactness and/or meaning. Perhaps, some of the translators thought that the adverb 'also' was superfluous, or stylistically, that the verse took too long in moving forward. Others may have argued that restoring the initial Substitution not only adhered more closely to the meaning of the Greek text—John the Baptist's emphasis here on conversion—but that such literalness in phrasing was also stylistically more effective.[14] There is a gain of emphasis from the heavier alliterative pattern: 'And . . . also . . . axe'. Moreover, some may have pointed out the slant rhyme between the final syllable of 'also' and 'now'. At any rate, the phrasing of the final S-2 revision was adequate. There was no S-3 revision here: the AV also reads 'And now also the axe is'.

The Substitution sequence is not the only way in which ML records S-1 revisions, nor do deviations from this sequence discussed above comprise the only sorts of S-2 revisions. ML employs two other methods to record S-1 revisions: Deletions and Additions. A Deletion requires ML to strike only through phrasing in a portion of verse. ML accomplishes a Deletion in the following manner: first, he twice underlines the phrasing to be deleted and writes a superscript dele in the text before the proposed Deletion; second, he writes another dele in the margin opposite the proposed Deletion; third, he draws a single strike-through line across the twice-underlined passage. Note in Luke 2.40 (see Fig. 2) the deletion of the phrase 'and was'.

As in Substitutions, here too in Deletions, ML uses the strike-through line as the final step in the revision sequence. Again, Luke 2.19 reveals this fact (compare Figs. 1 and 2). Here the conjunction 'and' has been underlined twice; a superscript dele has been written before the conjunction, and, opposite, a second dele has been written in the margin. Steps one and two of the Deletion process are complete. But step three is lacking: the conjunction 'and' has no strike-through line crossing it out. Instead, each dele has been cancelled with a short diagonal stroke. It is clear, then, that were the strike-through line any other than the third and final step of the Deletion process, it would be present in 2.19, just as it is present in the Deletion in Luke 2.40 and in other Deletions where the deles have not themselves been cancelled.

Other conclusions follow from the presence or absence of the strike-through line in Deletions, agreeing with those made for Substitutions that possess or lack the strike-through line. First, the presence of the strike-through line confirms that the Deletion is final—as far as the translators are concerned at this stage of the process. Before the strike-through line is drawn, it is possible to cancel the proposed Deletion. The conjunction 'and' in Luke 2.19 proves this point. Second, where there exist both a missing strike-through line and deles that have been cancelled, there is evidence of S-2 revision. Third, the decision to use, or not, the strike-through line in Deletions is one that the Oxford New Testament Company has made at a time after ML has recorded all his assigned work, and after that work has undergone the prescribed review. Such is also the case regarding ML's use of the strike-through line in Substitutions. With Substitutions, this deduction rests on ML's careful use of the Greek alphabet in structuring the Substitution sequence. In recording Deletions, ML does not use the Greek alphabet. But it is logical to view the use, or non-use, of the strike-through line in Deletions as occurring at the same time as its use in Substitutions. There is no evidence to the contrary.

Additions, the third subclass of S-1 revisions, require ML to insert only additional phrasing into a portion of verse. Luke 2.44 and 2.46 are typical examples (see Fig. 2). In Luke 2.44, ML inserts the pronoun 'they' before the verb 'sought'. He first writes a superscript phi before this verb and inserts a caret beneath the phi, at the base of the printed line. Second, he writes a matching phi in the margin opposite the text. After this phi, he writes the pronoun 'they' and follows it with a second caret. The proposed revision is clear: 'sought' is to be revised to 'they sought'. In the same way in Luke 2.46, the pair of chis signals the revision of the 1602 text from 'hearing' to 'both hearing'.

ML varies his recording sequence for one sort of Addition: marginal supplements, those proposed readings to be printed in the margin of the AV to elucidate the printed text. Luke 2.38 is illustrative (see Fig. 2). First, ML draws a small superscript flower (⚘) before the word in the text which the supplement is to elucidate. In Luke 2.38, the flower is before the noun 'Hierusalem'. Second, ML draws another flower in the margin opposite the text. After it, he writes the proposed supplement. At Luke 2.38, we read 'or, Israel'. Note that the conjunction 'or' precedes the supplement. This conjunction is important because sometimes its presence alone, without the flower sign, is all that indicates the occurrence of a marginal supplement. Then, logic determines the specific portion of text for which the marginal supplement is meant.

S-2 revision occurs, at times, in these supplements. Luke 2.19 (see Fig. 1) also demonstrates this. The example involves S-2 revision of both a marginal supplement and a Substitution in the phrase 'those sayings'. Stages of the revision move thus:

	1602	:	those sayings
	S-1 Sub. Rev.	:	theise ⚘ sayings
+	S-1 Marg. Suppl.	:	⚘ or things
	S-2 Rev.	:	theise things.

The flower sign is inserted in the text before the noun 'sayings'. A second flower appears in the margin, after which is written 'or things'. It is clear that the generic term 'things' is to be the proposed alternative reading for the 1602 noun 'sayings'.[15] Later, an S-2 revision has crossed out this supplement—'things'. But the noun 'things' has not been lost. Instead, a decision has been made to put this noun into the revised text. Thus, the 1602 noun 'sayings' has also been struck through at the same time that the supplement 'things' has been crossed out. After completing these actions, ML has written the noun 'things' just after the adjective 'theise' that he had recorded in the margin as his Substitution for the 1602 reading 'those'.

Being aware of ML's recording method, we can infer that ML recorded the supplement 'or things' and the Substitution 'theise' at the same time, and not that he made an error by proposing that the noun 'things' be used as a supplement directly after he had recorded 'things' as a part of the Substitution revision for 'those sayings'. He first recorded S-1 revisions—the Substitution and the marginal supplement—then later performed the S-2 revisions—cancellation of the supplement and the 1602 noun 'sayings', and the addition of the word 'things' after the already recorded adjective 'theise'.

One other aspect of ML's habits argues that we are observing an S-2 revision and not a mistake on ML's part at the S-1 stage. Here in Luke 2.19, ML draws a single line under each word in the phrase 'those sayings'. In S-1 Substitutions, ML's habit is to underline the entire phrase to be revised with one continuous line, not two discrete lines. It is evident, then, that at the S-1 phase only the pronoun 'those' was to be revised to 'theise'. Later, when the Oxford New Testament Company gathered to discuss the results of the review of its work, a decision was made, based on that review, to revise the noun 'sayings' to 'things'. At this point, 'sayings' was underlined separately; the use of the noun 'things' as a supplement was crossed out and rewritten after 'theise', thus creating an S-2 revision; and last, a single strike-through line was drawn across the 1602 phrasing 'those sayings'.

The LJ Scribe

In comparing the script and method of LJ—the Luke/John scribe—with that of ML, two points are evident: the difference in handwriting and the similarity in method. LJ has annotated Luke 19–24 and John 18–21. Clear, boldly delineated letters contrast to the small, closely written script of ML. Other notable differences between the scripts are the formation of minuscule 'r's' and 'a's'. LJ's 'r's' are often italic 'r's'. ML's 'r's' are typical Secretary 'r's'. LJ frequently attaches a small, curved ascender to the top of minuscule 'a's'. ML rarely does so. The method, however, that LJ uses to record revisions parallels closely that of ML's. In LJ's work we find the same categories of S-1 revision as in ML's work: Substitutions, Deletions, and Additions. LJ's work also reveals the same revision sequence: S-1 followed, at times, by S-2 and S-3 revision.

LJ makes Substitutions much like ML: he underlines once a portion of a verse; he flags it with a Greek letter written in superscript before the underlined portion; he records a matching letter in the margin opposite the underlined text, selecting letters according to the sequence of the Greek alphabet; and he writes the intended Substitution in the margin after the letter. See Luke 22.7 (Fig. 3) below.

In Luke 22.7, the adjective 'vnlevened' replaces 'sweet'. The one important difference between the methods of LJ and ML is that LJ does not use a strike-through line. Where ML, to complete a Substitution, crosses through the underlined text as the final step, LJ does not. Once LJ has recorded the Substitution in the margin, he is done. A minor difference between the methods of LJ and ML is that LJ, in marking Substitutions and Deletions, uses a short vertical or diagonal line drawn at one end, or both ends, of the underlining to identify further the passage to be revised. ML does not use this line.

Earlier, we noted that the absence of the strike-through line in ML's Substitutions and Deletions was important in determining the presence of S-2 revision. While LJ uses no such line, proof still exists that S-2 revision occurs amid LJ's S-1

Mat.26.17. mar.14.3. 7 *Then came the day of sweete bread, when
of necessitie the Passeouer must be killed.
8 And hee sent Peter and Iohn, saying,
Goe and prepare vs the Passeouer, that we may
eate.
9 They said vnto him, Where wilt thou that
we should prepare it?
10 And he said vnto them, Beholde, when ye
are entred into the citie, there shall a man meete
you, bearing a pitcher of water; him follow into the same house that he entreth in.
11 And ye shall say vnto the good man of the
house, The master saith vnto thee, Where is the
ghest chamber, where I shall eate the Passeouer
with my disciples?
12 And he shal shew you a great vpper chamber prepared, there make readie.
13 And they went, and found as hee had
said vnto them, and they made readie the Passeouer.
Mat.26.20. mar.14.18. 14 *And when the houre was come, he sate
downe, and the twelue Apostles with him.
15 And he said vnto them, With hearty desire,
I haue desired to eate this Passeouer with you
before that I suffer.
16 For I say vnto you, Hencefoorth I will
not in any wise eate of it any more, vntill it be
fulfilled in the kingdome of God.
17 And when he had taken the cup, and giuen thankes, he said, Take this, and diuide it a-
mong you.
18 For I say vnto you, I will not in any wise
drinke of the fruit of the vine, vntill the kingdom
of God shall come.
Mat.26.20. mar.14.22. 1.cor.11.24 19 *And when he had taken bread, and giuen
thanks, he brake it, and gaue vnto them, saying,
This is my body which is giuen for you, this do
in the remembrance of me.
20 Likewise also when he had supped, hee
tooke the cup, saying, This cup is the new Testament in my blood, which is shed for you.
Mat.26.21. mar.14.19. iohn 13.18. psal.40.11. 21 *Yet beholde, the hand of him that betrayeth me, is with me on the table.
22 And truely the sonne of man goeth as it is
appointed, but woe vnto that man by whom he
is betrayed.
23 And they began to enquire among themselues, which of them it was that should doe
this thing.
Mat.20.25. mar.10.42. 24 *And there was a strife among them,
which of them should seeme to be the greatest.

FIGURE 3.

The LJ Scribe: Luke 22.7–24

Substitutions consequent to review of the Oxford New Testament Company's work. John 20.23 is typical. This verse has revisions written in the margin that have been rejected.

1602	:	Whosoeuers sinnes ye remit, they are remitted vnto them, and whosoeuers sinnes ye retaine, they are retained.
S-1 Sub. Rev.	:	**If ye remit the sinnes of any,** they are remitted vnto them, and **if** ye retaine, **the sinnes of any,** they are retained.
S-2 Rev.	:	[as 1602]

I use three pairs of double asterisks in the Substitution to denote three recorded revisions, written one below the other in the margin opposite John 20.23, and marked with the letters chi, psi, and omega, respectively. A single large 'X' mark drawn over the annotations cancels the proposed S-1 revisions and creates S-2 revisions that return to the 1602 reading.

LJ's recording habits reveal that these S-2 revisions, and others present in his work, occurred at the same time as they occurred in ML's work—that is after he, too, had recorded all S-1 revisions into this portion of this copy of the New Testament. Recalling that LJ, like ML, selects letters following the sequence of the Greek alphabet, we can reason that if LJ had cancelled these revisions and accompanying letters for John 20.23 moments after having written them, he would have been able to use chi, psi, and omega as sigla in the following verses where he recorded revisions. But in the next verse demanding the use of Greek letters, John 20.25, LJ uses an alpha not a chi. And there are other places amid LJ's S-1 revisions where this same pattern occurs to support the logic used here at John 20.23 (for example, Luke 19.2, 19.44, and John 18.15). Finally, collation with the AV also reveals the presence of S-3 revision in John 20.23. For the AV reads here in both instances 'Whose soeuer' rather than 'Whosoeuers' (the AV uses a lower case 'w' in the second instance).

Other evidence of S-2 revision amid LJ's work is the presence of non-Greek signs. ML, we noted, uses astrological signs occasionally in recording Substitutions when, near the end of a chapter, he has completed the Greek alphabet and still has a few verses left to revise, but chooses not to restart the alphabet. But the non-Greek signs in LJ's work are non-astrological ones interspersed sporadically and unsystematically amid Substitutions, interrupting the sequence of LJ's alphabet and clearly indicating S-2 revisions. Luke 22.45 is typical (see Fig. 4). The noun 'heauinesse', is revised to 'sorrowe'. The non-Greek sign used to indicate the revision is a small half circle, drawn facing downwards. A short vertical line is drawn just beneath the half circle: ⫯. One sign is drawn in superscript before the noun 'heauinesse', and the other is drawn in the margin, with the proposed revision 'sorrowe' written after it. The sign interrupts use of the Greek letter sequence. There is a theta, above, in verse 44, and an iota, below, in verse 46. Although LJ's hand appears in some S-2 revisions, indicating that he took part in this later work, it appears that the word 'sorrowe' at Luke 22.45 may be the handwriting of ML, not LJ. This sign or other non-Greek signs occur at such places as Luke 20.18; 22.56, 64, 66; 23.34; and John 18.11, 15, 25. Here, they also interrupt the alphabet sequence, arguing for the presence of S-2 revision in LJ's work.

LJ's method of recording Deletions also resembles ML's. Looking again at Luke 22.7 (see Fig. 3), we note that the phrase '<u>of</u> <u>necessitie</u>' has been marked as a Deletion. As ML did, LJ first underlines twice the proposed Deletion. Then he records a superscript dele before the underlined text. Last, he records a matching dele in the margin opposite the twice-underlined text. The distinguishing trait between the methods of LJ and ML is again the use, or not, of a strike-through line crossing out the text to be deleted. LJ uses no strike-through line; ML does—as his final step. Although the use, or not, of this line in ML's Deletions is an aid in spotting S-2 revision, we can still spot such revision in LJ's Deletions, even without the line.

In Luke 23.26, LJ has marked the conjunction 'and' in the phrase 'and on him' as an S-1 Deletion: a superscript dele is written before the conjunction; two lines are drawn beneath the conjunction; and a second dele is written in the margin opposite

43 And there appeared an Angel vnto him
from heauen, comforting him.
44 And he was in an agonie, and he prayed
more earnestly, and his sweate was like droppes
of blood, trickling downe to the ground.
45 And when he rose vp from prayer, and was
come to his disciples, he found them sleeping for
heauinesse,
46 And said vnto them, Why sleepe ye? Rise,
and pray, least ye fall into temptation.
47 While hee yet spake, behold, there came a
company, and he that was called Iudas, one of
the twelue, went before them, and preassed nigh
vnto Iesus, to kisse him.
48 But Iesus said vnto him, Iudas, betrayest thou the sonne of man with a kisse?
49 When they which were about him, sawe
what would follow, they said vnto him, Lorde,
shall we smite with the sword?
50 And one of them smote the seruant of the
high Priest, and tooke away his right eare.

a He felt the horror of Gods wrath and iudgement against sinne.

Mat.26.47. mar.14.43. iohn 18,3.

FIGURE 4.

The LJ Scribe: Luke 22.43–50

the conjunction. The text is to be revised from 'and on him' to 'on him'. But consequent to review, S-2 revision occurs: the dele in the margin has been struck through,and the dele in the text and the two lines drawn beneath the conjunction 'and' have been partially erased. The 1602 reading 'and on him' has now been restored. The AV agrees with this S-2 revision, indicating that no S-3 revision occurred.

Lastly, turning to LJ's Additions: Here the methods of LJ and ML are identical. Just as ML did, LJ makes Additions by first recording a superscript Greek letter in the text where the Addition is to be made. He then adds a caret at the base of the line beneath the Greek letter. Last, he writes the same Greek letter in the margin, opposite the text where the first letter was recorded, and follows with the Addition plus a caret. Luke 22.9 and 22.24 are illustrative (see Fig. 3). In 22.9, the 1602 text 'They said' becomes 'And They said'. In 22.24, the 1602 phrasing 'a strife' becomes 'also a strife'. As ML did, LJ uses a flower sign to indicate marginal supplements. Luke 22.15 (see Fig. 3) contains a marginal supplement and a Deletion.

1602	:	With <u>hearty</u> desire
+ S-1 Del. Rev.	:	⚘ With desire
S-1 Marg. Suppl.	:	⚘ or I haue hartily desired.

After marking the adjective 'hearty' for deletion, LJ inserts a flower in the text before the preposition 'With'. In the margin appears the matching flower followed by the proposed supplement.

S-2 revision is also present in LJ's Additions. John 18.35 is typical. LJ revises the 1602 phrase 'and high Priests' by adding an article:

S-1 Add. Rev.	:	and the high Priests.

Later, S-2 revision occurs. In the margin, MT—the Matthew scribe—has written the adjective 'Chiefe' after LJ's recording of the article 'the' and its accompanying caret. MT has also underlined once the adjective 'high' in the 1602 text to indicate clearly that 'high' is to be replaced by 'Chiefe'. We know that this underlining occurs at the S-2 stage because LJ does not use underlining to record Additions. At the S-2 stage, John 18.35 now reads:

and the Chiefe Priests.

MT also revises the 1602 phrase 'high Priests' to 'Chiefe Priests' at other places, such as Luke 19.47, 22.52, and 22.66 (here the initial letter is written in lower case: 'chiefe'). But at Luke 22.54, the change does not occur.

Occasionally, MT records other S-2 revisions amid LJ's S-1 revisions. In John 18.8, we read: 'If ye seeke me therefore'. LJ has recorded no revisions for the phrase. But MT's hand is present. With a single strike-through line, MT has crossed out the adverb 'therefore' and written the letter pi over the pronoun 'ye'. Between the words 'If ye', he has inserted a caret. In the margin, he has written a second pi and, after it, the word 'therefore'. Thus, the revised text reads: 'If therefore ye seeke me'. Both this S-2 revision and the one involving the adjective 'Chiefe' at John 18.35 were accepted, passing into the AV without subsequent S-3 revision.

Before moving on to MT's work, a final aspect of LJ's work demands attention: those few verses wherein several layers of S-2 revision occur. Discussion of Luke 3.9 above noted this fact in ML's work. A particular phrase in Luke 19.44 presents an intriguing example in LJ's work.[16] The 1602 text reads:

> make thee euen with the ground.

This phrasing is underlined once. A superscript rho sign is written before the verb, and another rho sign is written in the margin, followed by this phrasing which produces an S-1 Substitution revision:

> shall lay thee, to the ground.

Later, after review, the handwritten revision in the margin has been revised: a strike-through line crosses out the verb 'lay', and the verb 'dashe' is written above it, producing the first S-2 revision:

> shall dashe thee, to the ground.

But this S-2 revision has been reworked. A single continuous strike-through line now crosses out the entire revision, although the verb 'dashe', previously written above the crossed out verb 'lay', has not been struck through. In the margin, beneath the crossed out revision, a second S-2 revision is written:

> shall beate thee, flatt to the ground.

LJ's hand has performed these S-2 revisions.[17] Collation with the AV reveals the presence of S-3 revision in addition to these S-1 and S-2 revisions. The AV, rejecting the variously proposed revisions, prefers a composite reading based upon the 1602 text and the S-1 Substitution:

> shall lay thee euen with the ground.

The MT Scribe

We encounter few difficulties studying the work of ML and LJ, but problems abound in the handwriting and method of MT, the Matthew scribe, who is responsible for the great majority of revisions recorded in Matthew, as well as those in John 17. MT's Secretary hand contrasts sharply with the small, neat script of ML and the bold, clear work of LJ. MT's hand is difficult to read because letters are poorly formed. A medial or terminal 'd' often looks like an 'l' because the ascender is not joined to the top of the semicircular base of the letter. Terminal 'r's' and 'e's' are also imprecisely formed. MT's script is undisciplined: one letter flows into another. It is hard to decipher annotations recorded interlinearly. At times, annotations recorded in this Gospel are the work of other hands. For example, annotations in the margin opposite 27.1–24 are most likely ML's. But the annotations in the margin opposite 6.26–34 raise doubts: some suggest a neater instance of MT's hand (see Fig. 5). Others suggest a different hand. The following remarks pertain, however, to the prevalent hand—MT's.

The work of MT, like that of ML and LJ, indicates three stages of revision: S-1, S-2, and S-3 revisions. But MT's method of recording S-1 revisions—Substitutions, Deletions, and Additions—differs, usually, from the methods of ML and LJ. To record Substitutions, MT will occasionally use ML's method: (1) underlining once the 1602 text to be replaced by a Substitution; (2) using matching Greek letters as signs—one before the 1602 text to be replaced, the other before the Substitution recorded in the margin; (3) writing the proposed Substitution in the margin after a Greek letter; (4) drawing a single strike-through line across the 1602 text to signify approval of a Substitution.

But there are two other methods of recording Substitutions more typical of MT, which may be termed the 'interlinear' and the 'varied signs' methods.

The interlinear method involves striking through a portion of verse with a single horizontal line and writing the revision immediately above the cancellation. In Matthew 6.22 (Fig. 5) the noun 'candle' is struck through, and the noun 'light' is substituted interlinearly for it. The letters 'wh' in the adverb 'wherefore' and the adverb 'if' are also struck through. Then the adverb 'If' is written interlinearly above and just before the adverb 'wherefore', and the letters 'th' are written interlinearly above the cancelled letters 'wh'. Finally, MT writes the letter 'X' in the margin to call attention to the various Substitutions. The S-1 Substitution revision reads:

> The light of the body is the eye:
> If therefore thine eye be single.

The varied signs method works thus: MT strikes through a portion of verse with a single horizontal line; he writes a superscript sign before the cancelled portion; he then duplicates the sign in the margin opposite the cancelled portion and follows with the intended Substitution. Differences between this method and the Greek sign method of ML are that MT uses no underlining and that MT uses many other signs in addition to Greek letters to mark the insertion of Substitutions. A sample of these signs includes ϒ, ||, =, ♀, ⟜, ⌒, ¢. Other differences include MT's use, at times, of both the interlinear and varied signs methods in the same verse (Matthew 7.11); MT's inconsistency, at times, in following the alphabet sequence when using Greek letters (the use of betas at Matthew 7.6 and 7.11, and then, when Greek letters are next used, the appearance of xis at 7.25); and MT's interlacing of the interlinear and varied signs methods throughout a series of verses according to no principle (Matthew 7.6–28; see Figs. 7, 8).

Unlike the consistent recording methods of ML and LJ, MT uses no single method, nor does he establish a pattern of use for those methods described. It is difficult, then, to determine whether the reworking of S-1 revisions occurring in Matthew are S-2 revisions performed after MT has completed recording all S-1 revisions, or changes made by MT as he is in the midst of recording S-1 revisions. Matthew 6.19b–20 (Fig. 5) illustrates this dilemma.

The verb 'breake', used in Matthew 6.19b and 6.20, is first revised interlinearly to read 'digge'. But these S-1 Substitutions have been lined out, and the strike-through line drawn across the verb 'breake' in 6.19 has been erased. Since the

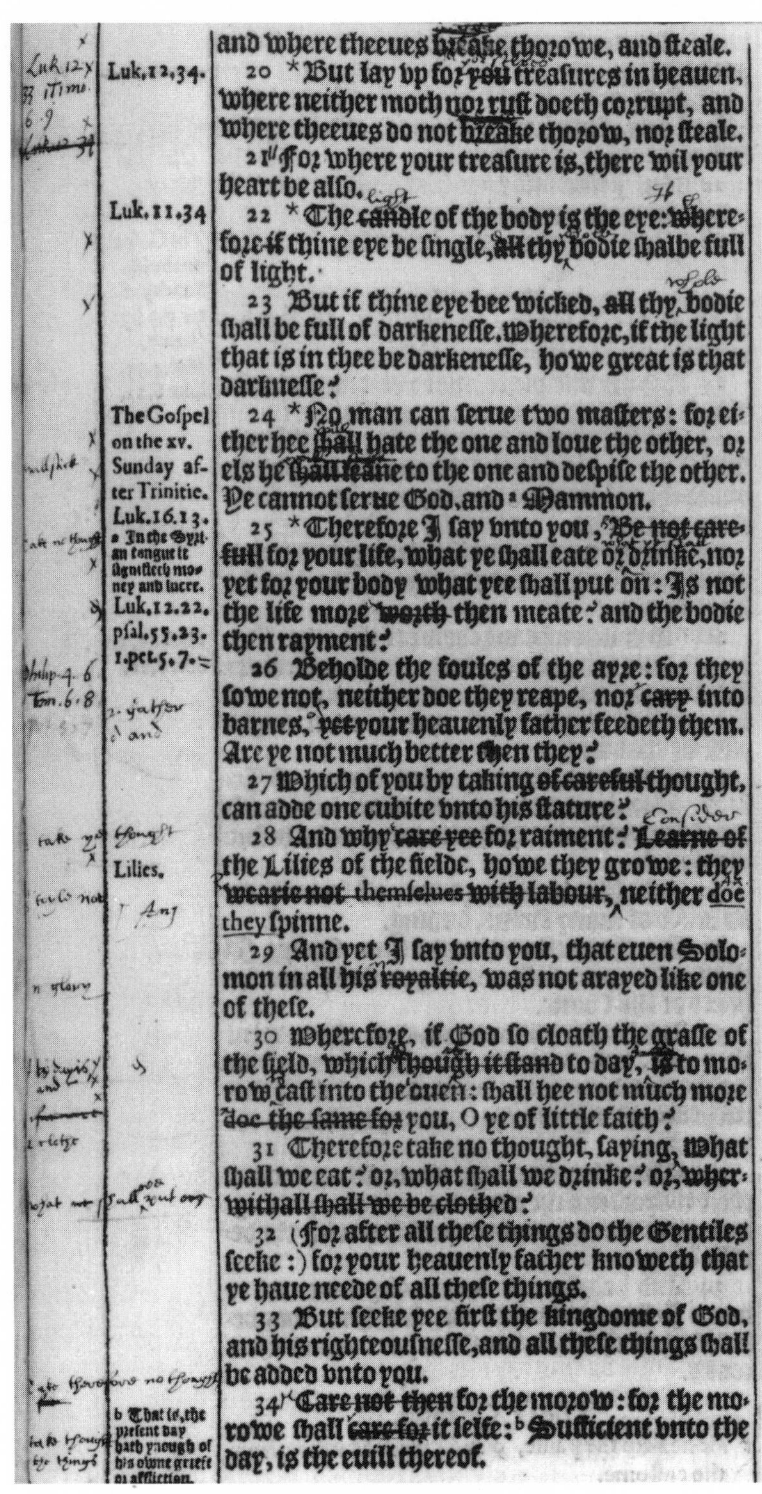
and where theeues breake thorowe, and steale.
Luk.12.34. 20 *But lay vp for you treasures in heauen,
where neither moth nor rust doeth corrupt, and
where theeues do not breake thorow, nor steale.
21 For where your treasure is, there wil your
heart be also.
Luk.11.34 22 *The candle of the body is the eye: wherefore if thine eye be single, all thy bodie shalbe full
of light.
23 But if thine eye bee wicked, all thy bodie
shall be full of darkenesse. Wherefore, if the light
that is in thee be darkenesse, howe great is that
darknesse?
The Gospel on the xv. Sunday after Trinitie. Luk.16.13.
24 *No man can serue two masters: for either hee shall hate the one and loue the other, or
els he shall leane to the one and despise the other.
Ye cannot serue God, and a Mammon.
a In the Syrian tongue it signifieth money and lucre. Luk.12.22. psal.55.23. 1.pet.5.7.
25 *Therefore I say vnto you, Be not care-
full for your life, what ye shall eate or drinke, nor
yet for your body what yee shall put on: Is not
the life more worth then meate? and the bodie
then rayment?
26 Beholde the foules of the ayre: for they
sowe not, neither doe they reape, nor cary into
barnes, yet your heauenly father feedeth them.
Are ye not much better then they?
27 Which of you by taking of carefull thought,
can adde one cubite vnto his stature?
28 And why care yee for raiment? Learne of
Lilies. the Lilies of the fielde, howe they growe: they
wearie not themselues with labour, neither doe
they spinne.
29 And yet I say vnto you, that euen Solomon in all his royaltie, was not arayed like one
of these.
30 Wherefore, if God so cloath the grasse of
the field, which though it stand to day, & to morowe cast into the ouen: shall hee not much more
doe the same for you, O ye of little faith?
31 Therefore take no thought, saying, What
shall we eat? or, what shall we drinke? or, wher-
withall shall we be clothed?
32 (For after all these things do the Gentiles
seeke:) for your heauenly father knoweth that
ye haue neede of all these things.
33 But seeke yee first the kingdome of God,
and his righteousnesse, and all these things shall
be added vnto you.
34 Care not then for the morow: for the morowe shall care for it selfe: b Sufficient vnto the
day, is the euill thereof.
b That is, the present day hath ynough of his owne griefe or affliction.

FIGURE 5.

The MT Scribe: Matthew 6.19–34

strike-through line used for the verb 'breake' in 6.20 was drawn across the base of the word, there apparently was no need to erase the line. Hence, even after the interlinear S-1 Substitution 'digge' has been lined out, it is perfectly clear that the 1602 verb 'breake' is meant to be restored to the text. This situation suggests that we are looking at two stages of revision—S-1 and S-2 revisions—but there is not enough proof based upon MT's recording methods to warrant any more than an assumption. However, in Matthew 7.4, the logic of the revisions argues more strongly for the presence of S-2 revision (see Fig. 6). S-1 revision of the 1602 text involves this Substitution:

1602	:	Suffer me, I will cast out a mote
S-1 Sub. Rev.	:	Suffer me, I will pul out the mote.

Such revision is evident, first, from the use of a caret inserted after the auxiliary 'will', pointing out the verb 'pul' written interlinearly above the verb 'cast'. Second, the verb 'cast' has been struck through with a single line drawn across the base of the word. Last, the article 'a' has been struck through and replaced by the article 'the' written interlinearly above it.

Next, we note that both the interlinearly written verb 'pul' and the 1602 phrasing 'Suffer me, I will cast' have been lined out. A pair of commas written above the capital 'S' calls attention to a revision written opposite in the margin: 'Let me pul'. Thus, a second revision of this passage now reads:

Let me pul out the mote.

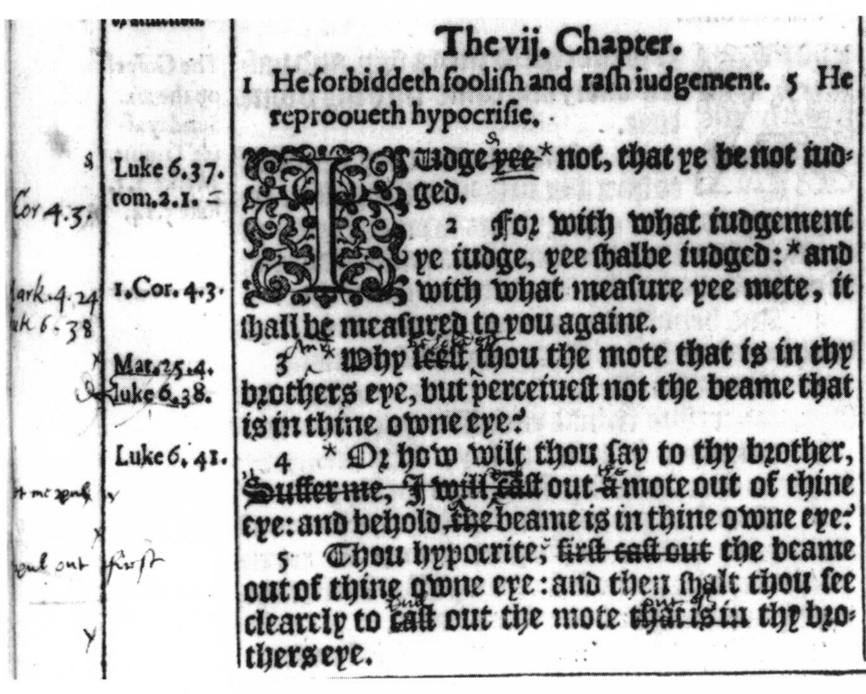

The vij. Chapter.

1 He forbiddeth foolish and rash iudgement. 5 He reprooueth hypocrisie.

Luke 6.37. rom.2.1. Iudge yee* not, that ye be not iudged.
1.Cor.4.3. 2 For with what iudgement ye iudge, yee shalbe iudged: *and with what measure yee mete, it shall be measured to you againe.
Mat.25.4. Luke 6.38. 3 *Why seest thou the mote that is in thy brothers eye, but perceiuest not the beame that is in thine owne eye?
Luke 6.41. 4 *Or how wilt thou say to thy brother, Suffer me, I will cast out a mote out of thine eye: and behold, the beame is in thine owne eye?
5 Thou hypocrite, first cast out the beame out of thine owne eye: and then shalt thou see clearely to cast out the mote that is in thy brothers eye.

FIGURE 6.

The MT Scribe: Matthew 7.1–5

Logic suggests that this second revision in the margin constitutes an S-2 revision. The interlinear recording of the verb 'pul' had to have been accomplished first, before the marginal revision 'Let me pul'. No other reasoning explains the interlinear recording of the verb 'pul', and then its lining out, as well as the lining out of the 1602 text 'Suffer me, I will cast'.

We cannot argue persuasively for the presence of an S-2 revision each time a Substitution recorded by MT has undergone additional revision, but collation with the AV nevertheless makes it clear that some of MT's Substitutions, like those of ML and LJ, have undergone S-3 revision. For example, in Matthew 6.26, the revision of the conjunctive adverb 'yet' to 'and' constitutes an S-1 revision (see Fig. 5). At the S-2 revision stage no change is made: the conjunction 'and' stands. But the AV reading 'yet' returns to the 1602 reading. It is clear, then, that in addition to the Second Oxford Company's incorporation of reviewers' (S-2) revisions into Matthew, further (S-3) revision occurred.

Turning next to Additions, we note that MT again uses his two basic recording methods: the interlinear and the varied signs methods. In Matthew 6.23, MT adds the adjective 'whole' interlinearly above the phrase 'thy bodie'. He calls attention to this revision by writing a caret below the adjective and by writing an 'X' sign in the margin. He repeats this pattern several times on this page—398 recto. In Matthew 6.25, 'what ye shall' is added interlinearly; likewise, in 7.3, 'And'; in 7.9, 'Or'; and in 7.11, 'how'. But at 7.24 and 7.26, MT uses his varied signs method. Here he enters the signs ⚲ and ϒ, respectively, in the verses and repeats the same signs in the margins opposite, followed by the Additions, 'of mine', and 'of mine', respectively (see Figs. 5–8). On occasion MT will also use Greek letters as signs: for example, in Matthew 1.22, 2.1, and 6.2. MT is just as unsystematic in using these methods for recording Additions as he is in using them for recording Substitutions. There is no apparent significance in the use of any one method at any given time. Furthermore, MT even varies his execution of the interlinear method, leaving out one part or another. For example, in Matthew 1.21, he fails to use the 'X' sign in the margin; in Matthew 2.15, he omits the use of the caret.

One final matter concerning MT's Additions is his method of recording marginal supplements. We recall that ML and LJ use a pair of flower signs, one drawn in the text, the other in the margin, to denote such Additions. The conjunction 'or' follows the flower sign in the margin, and then comes the proposed supplement. In the Gospel of Matthew, MT uses not only the flower sign but also other signs, such as ♀, ⚲, ||, and ⧺. Moreover, MT uses these signs, including the flower, to record other sorts of Additions, as well as Substitutions. At times, then, it is difficult to determine if such supplements are a part of S-1 or S-2 revision.

Some supplements, however, appear to be S-2 revisions, for they are recorded in other hands. At Matthew 5.21, a supplement reading 'or, by them of old tyme' appears in a hand that resembles ML's. For the supplement at Matthew 10.16, evidence involving strike-through lines and handwriting clearly reveals S-1 and S-2 revision. The final phrase of this verse reads: 'and harmelesse as the Doues'. MT has struck through the article 'the' with a single horizontal line, written a superscript dele before the cancelled article 'the', and a second dele in the margin opposite the first dele. Having completed this Deletion, MT then records a marginal supplement. He draws two short, vertical parallel lines in superscript before the 1602 adjective 'harmelesse', and then in the margin opposite this sign, he draws a matching sign and writes after it the phrase 'or, innocent as'. Thus far, the revision has proceeded:

	1602	:	and harmelesse as the Doues
+	S-1 Del. Rev.	:	and ‖ harmelesse as Doues
	S-1 Marg. Suppl.	:	‖ or, innocent as.

S-2 revision then enters. The S-1 revision of the text 'and harmelesse as Doues' remains unchanged, but the marginal supplement has been struck through with several horizontal lines, and beneath it, written in an Italic hand, is the phrasing 'or, simple'. S-2 revision has reworked this passage to read:

	1602	:	and harmelesse as the Doues
+	S-1 Del. Rev.	:	and ‖ harmelesse as Doues
	S-2 Marg. Suppl.	:	‖ or, simple.

In addition to revision of the adjective from 'innocent' to 'simple', the S-2 revision has also omitted the adverb 'as', it being already present in the 1602 text. No S-3 revision occurs later, for the AV agrees with the S-1 revision of this final clause of the 1602 text and with the S-2 revision of the marginal supplement intended for this clause.

Deletions, the last of MT's three major categories of S-1 revisions, are no trouble to detect, but again, MT's inconsistent recording method introduces difficulties. In Matthew 7.1, for example, MT uses the standard method that ML uses for Deletions: a 2+1 line sequence (see Fig. 6). MT underlines twice the pronoun 'yee', strikes through it with a single horizontal line, and writes deles, one in superscript before the pronoun, and the other in the margin opposite the pronoun. But this 2+1 sequence is only one of several sequences that MT uses to record Deletions. At Matthew 7.26, MT uses a 1+1 line sequence (see Fig. 8). The phrase 'of me' is underlined once and struck through once, along with its being marked with matching deles, one in superscript before the phrase, the other in the margin. At Matthew 7.6 (and also at 7.23–24) MT uses a 0+2 line sequence (see Figs. 7, 8). The participial ending 'ing' of 'turning' is struck through twice, but MT has not underlined it. Matching deles are again used in the same manner as previously described. A fourth pattern which MT uses is a 0+1 line sequence. In Matthew 7.6 the article in the phrase 'the swine' is struck through once, but not underlined. Matching deles are present (see Fig. 7). At times, verses will contain more than one of these different methods. Matthew 7.23 is a case in point: a 0+2 sequence deletes the connective 'That', and a 0+1 sequence deletes the adjective 'all' (see Fig. 8).

In ML's or LJ's work, we can identify a Deletion that is not an S-1 revision because both scribes use consistent recording methods. For ML, there is a 2+1 sequence (two lines to underline, one to strike through) plus matching deles. For LJ, there is a 2+0 sequence plus matching deles. Deviations from either method indicate the presence of S-2 revision. But in the case of MT, his use of various methods for recording Deletions makes it difficult to determine which, if any, are the product of S-2 revision. Occasionally, though, we can spot Deletions made by MT that have been recorded in such a way that the presence of S-2 revision is likely.

Matthew 6.5 and 6.16 are good examples. Both verses end with the same clause:

> 1602 : they haue their reward.

S-1 revision performed by MT deletes the possessive adjective 'their' in both verses. MT uses a 0+1 line sequence for each Deletion: that is, no underlining is used; a strike-through line is drawn across the adjective; no deles are used to identify the Deletion. Along with the Deletions, MT records Additions that are identical for both clauses. The past participle 'received' has been written in the margin opposite each clause. A Greek letter precedes each participle: an eta in the margin at verse 5; a zeta in the margin at verse 16. A matching eta and zeta appear in the text of verses 5 and 16, respectively, to indicate where the past participle 'received' is to go in each verse. Last, MT uses carets in revising verse 5, though not in verse 16, to clarify further where the participle 'received' is to be entered in the text. Hence, the S-1 revision for each verse reads identically:

> they haue received reward.

But in studying these revisions, we note that the S-1 revisions have been cancelled. In each verse, the strike-through line drawn across the adjective 'their'

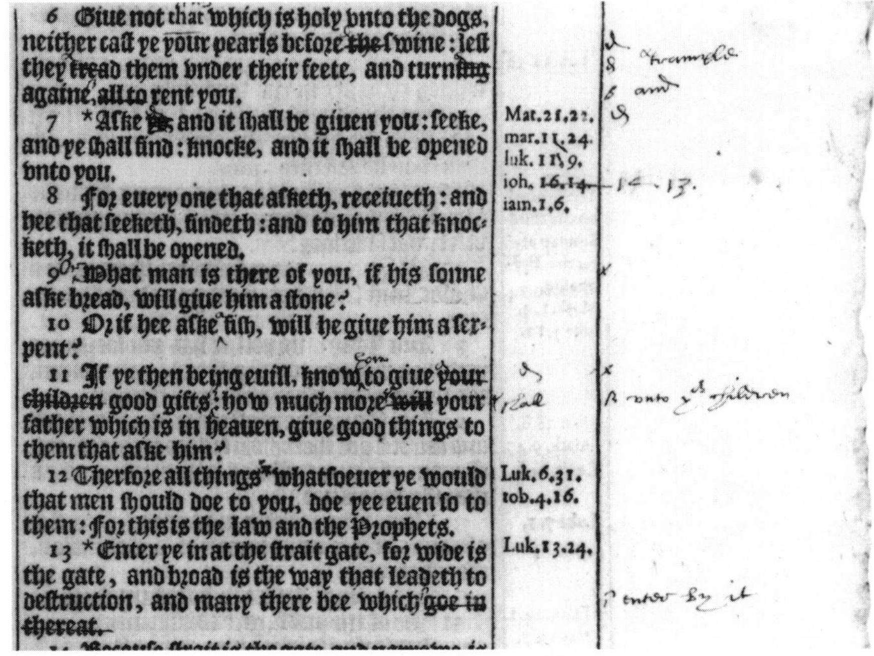
6 Giue not that which is holy vnto the dogs,
neither cast ye your pearls before the swine: lest
they tread them vnder their feete, and turning
againe, all to rent you.
7 *Aske ye, and it shall be giuen you: seeke, Mat.21.22.
and ye shall find: knocke, and it shall be opened mar.11.24.
vnto you. luk.11.9.
8 For euery one that asketh, receiueth: and ioh.16.14.
hee that seeketh, findeth: and to him that knoc- iam.1.6.
keth, it shall be opened.
9 What man is there of you, if his sonne
aske bread, will giue him a stone?
10 Or if hee aske fish, will he giue him a serpent?
11 If ye then being euill, know to giue your
children good gifts: how much more will your
father which is in heauen, giue good things to
them that aske him?
12 Therfore all things whatsoeuer ye would Luk.6.31.
that men should doe to you, doe yee euen so to tob.4.16.
them: For this is the law and the Prophets.
13 *Enter ye in at the strait gate, for wide is Luk.13.24.
the gate, and broad is the way that leadeth to
destruction, and many there bee which goe in
thereat.

FIGURE 7.

The MT Scribe: Matthew 7.6–13

has been partially erased. Cancellation of the Deletions restores, then, the 1602 adjective 'their', producing this reading for each verse:

> they haue received their reward.

Several points about the erasing of the strike-through lines suggest that we are witnessing S-2 revision rather than simply hurried changes made by MT while he is in the process of recording S-1 revisions. In verse 5, when MT records the Deletion of the adjective 'their' by use of a strike-through line, he also draws a caret beneath and between the letters 'ir' of 'their'. This caret points to the Greek letter eta written over the letter 'r' of the word. This eta matches the other eta written in the margin before the participle 'received'. The point to note is that MT is indicating where the new reading—the participle 'received' written in the margin—is to go in the revised text, after having deleted the adjective 'their'. But when the decision is made to restore this deleted adjective, so indicated by the partially erased strike-through line,

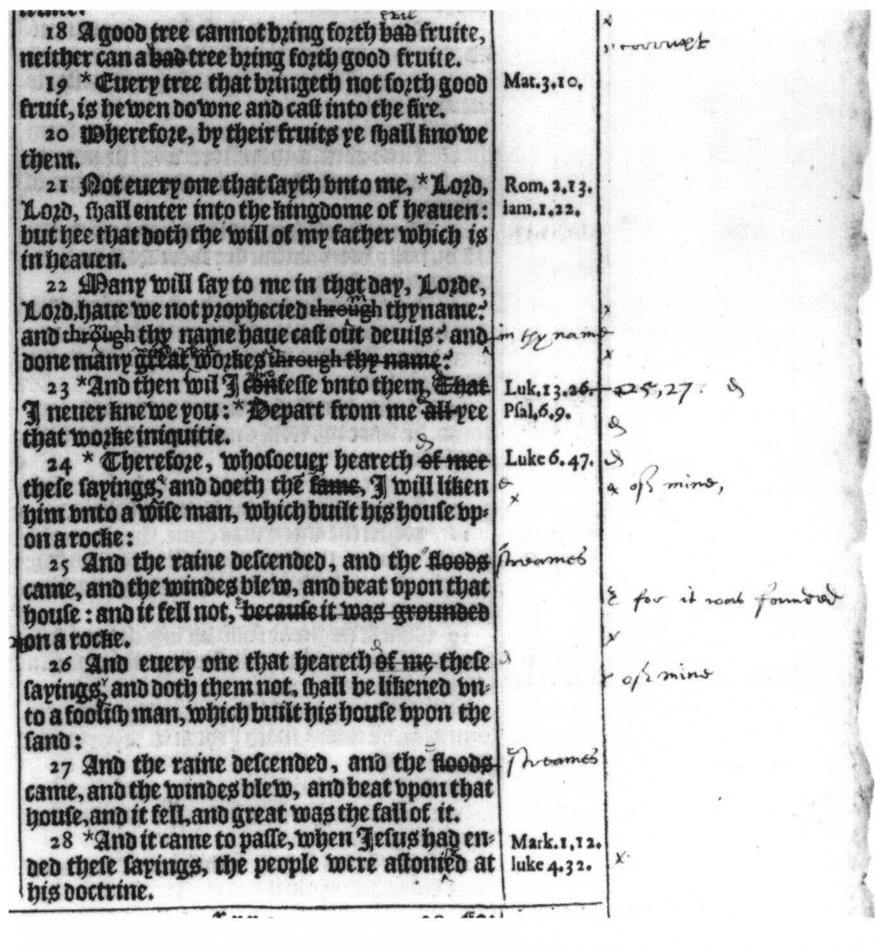

18 A good tree cannot bring forth bad fruite,
neither can a bad tree bring forth good fruite.
19 *Euery tree that bringeth not forth good Mat.3.10.
fruit, is hewen downe and cast into the fire.
20 Wherefore, by their fruits ye shall knowe
them.
21 Not euery one that sayth vnto me, *Lord, Rom.2.13.
Lord, shall enter into the kingdome of heauen: iam.1.22.
but hee that doth the will of my father which is
in heauen.
22 Many will say to me in that day, Lorde,
Lord, haue we not prophecied through thy name?
and through thy name haue cast out deuils? and
done many great workes through thy name?
23 *And then wil I confesse vnto them, That Luk.13.26.
I neuer knewe you: *Depart from me all yee Psal.6.9.
that worke iniquitie.
24 *Therefore, whosoeuer heareth of mee Luke 6.47.
these sayings, and doeth the same, I will liken
him vnto a wise man, which built his house vpon a rocke:
25 And the raine descended, and the floods
came, and the windes blew, and beat vpon that
house: and it fell not, because it was grounded
vpon a rocke.
26 And euery one that heareth of me these
sayings, and doth them not, shall be likened vnto a foolish man, which built his house vpon the
sand:
27 And the raine descended, and the floods
came, and the windes blew, and beat vpon that
house, and it fell, and great was the fall of it.
28 *And it came to passe, when Jesus had en- Mark.1.22.
ded these sayings, the people were astonied at luke 4.32.
his doctrine.

FIGURE 8.

The MT Scribe: Matthew 7.18–28

then the eta sign over the letter 'r' of the adjective 'their' becomes displaced. If the eta remains where it has first been put over the letter 'r', then the revised version reincorporating the now restored adjective 'their' will read:

> they haue their received reward.

To avoid such a possible reading, MT lines out the eta written above the letter 'r' of the adjective 'their' at the time that he partially erases the strike through-line that he has drawn earlier across the adjective. Then, having indicated the restoration of the adjective 'their', he writes another superscript eta in the text, but this time *before* the now restored adjective, and draws another caret beneath this newly written eta, both of which actions together are meant to signify that the participle 'received' written in the margin is to go before the adjective:

> they haue received their reward.

What argues further that all of the secondary revision described here in verse 5 is S-2 revision rather than immediate alteration during S-1 revision is the fact that nearly the same secondary revision process occurs again in the identical, final clause of verse 16. If MT, in verse 5, had made these secondary revisions to restore the adjective 'their' while recording S-1 revisions, then when he came to the identical clause in verse 16, he would not have recorded again the same initial annotations that he had recorded above in verse 5—'they haue received reward.' He would have glanced up to verse 5, noted his corrections, and recorded in verse 16 the revision: 'they haue received their reward'. But such is not the case. The final revised reading in verse 16—'they haue received their reward'.—is arrived at only through the same stages of revision described above for verse 5, save for the fact that no carets are used in verse 16. The conclusion seems patent: the identical secondary revision of the same clause in both verses has been done at some later time after a review of the S-1 revisions of the Oxford New Testament Company has been completed. The company translators have looked over the review suggestions sent back to them, and are in the process of incorporating those with which they agree into their own work. This later time is that which we have designated as S-2 revision.

These two verses also offer further proof that MT's Deletions have, on occasion, been subject to S-3 revision. Collating Matthew 6.5 and 6.16 with the AV reveals this reading:

> they haue their reward.

The AV rejects the use of present perfect tense 'haue received' in the S-2 revision and returns to the present tense 'haue' of the 1602 text.[18]

The evidence here has shown that three principal scribes recorded the annotations in the New Testament of 'Bibl. Eng. 1602 b.1' in the Bodleian Library. The work of each scribe is distinguishable through handwriting and annotating habits. The mediocre Secretary script of the Matthew scribe (MT) used in Matthew and John 17 is the most difficult hand to read. The small, neat Secretary hand of the Mark/Luke scribe (ML) used in Mark and Luke 1–18 is not difficult to read, with the exception of some problems of legibility in the inner margins, where annotations recorded on unbound sheets have been partly obscured in binding. The large bold script of the Luke/John scribe (LJ) found in Luke 19–24 and John 18–21 combines elements of both the Secretary and Italic hands and is admirably clear.

Admirably clear, too, are the annotating methods of the Mark/Luke scribe and the Luke/John scribe which differ from each other only in the absence of the strike-through line in the work of the Luke/John scribe. So methodical is each in recording Stage 1 revisions that one can also detect the presence of Stage 2 revisions in the text. These revise again Stage 1 revisions, or other portions of the Gospels not revised during Stage 1. In the work of the Matthew scribe, there is also evidence enough to argue for the presence of both Stage 1 and 2 revisions, but the unsystematic annotating methods of this scribe make it difficult to identify Stage 2 work.

Collation argues that Stage 1 revisions are a record of the work of the Second Oxford Company completed by late 1607/early 1608. Stage 2 revisions, recorded by the three scribes during late 1608/1609, represent the results of the review of 1608 that the Company accepted. At certain places, such as at Luke 3.9 and 19.44, these results occasioned differences among the translators. The revisions making up Stages 1 and 2 do not represent the complete text of the AV Gospels. The work recorded by the Matthew scribe represents about two-thirds of the AV text; that recorded by the Mark/Luke scribe, about three-fourths; and that recorded by the Luke/John scribe about five-sixths. It is clear, therefore, that additional (Stage 3) revision took place in order to arrive at that version which has long been familiar to us as the Authorized Version.

Those who study the collation that follows will no doubt discover, as we have, that the journey of the translators to the Authorized Version of 1611—a journey that began in 1604—was long, complex, and arduous. And the debts of the translators to earlier English Bibles were substantial. The translators, for example, in revising the text of the synoptic Gospels in the Bishops' Bible, owe about one-fourth of their revisions, each, to the Geneva and Rheims New Testaments. Another fourth of their work can be traced to the work of Tyndale and Coverdale. And the final fourth of their revisions is original to the translators themselves. The matter of these sources and the stages at which they originated are concerns for another work which I am anticipating.

NOTES

1. In addition to those works cited below in note 2, other important studies are J. G. Carleton, *The Part of Rheims in the Making of the English Bible* (Oxford, 1902); Gerald Hammond, *The Making of the English Bible* (New York: Philosophical Library, 1983); A. C. Partridge, *English Biblical Translation* (London: Andre Deutsch, 1973); A. W. Pollard, *Records of the English Bible* (Oxford, 1911); and W. F. Moulton, *The History of the English Bible,* 5th ed. (London, 1911).

2. B. F. Westcott, *A General View of the History of the English Bible,* rev. W. A. Wright, 3rd ed. (London, 1905); C. C. Butterworth, *The Literary Lineage of the King James Bible, 1340–1611* (1941; rpt. New York: Octagon Books, 1971); H. W. Robinson, ed., *The Bible in Its Ancient and*

English Versions (1940; rpt. Westport, Conn.: Greenwood Press, 1970); David Daiches, *The King James Version of the Bible* (1941; rpt. Archon Books, 1968).

3. Pollard, *Records of the English Bible,* 47–55.

4. Ward S. Allen, ed., *Translating the New Testament Epistles 1604–1611: A Manuscript from King James's Westminster Company* (Published for Vanderbilt University Press by University Microfilms International, 1977), xiv–xv.

5. Allen, *Translating the New Testament Epistles,* xii–xiii.

6. Allen, *Translating the New Testament Epistles,* xvi–xvii.

7. Paul Morgan, 'A King's Printer at Work: Two Documents of Robert Barker', *Bodleian Library Record,* 13, 5 (1990), 370–72.

8. Both works are by Ward S. Allen. Note 4 cites pertinent publication information for the latter. Vanderbilt University Press first published the former—*Translating for King James.*

9. W. D. Macray, *Annals of the Bodleian Library with a Notice of the Earlier Library of the University,* 2nd ed. (Oxford, 1890), 102.

10. Edward C. Jacobs, 'An Old Testament Copytext for the 1611 Bible', *The Papers of the Bibliographical Society of America,* 69 (1975), 1–15; and 'Two Stages of Old Testament Translation for the King James Bible', *The Library,* 6th ser., 2 (1980), 16–39. (A shorter version of the *PBSA* article without its extensive development appears as 'Old Testament Annotations in a Bishops' Bible, 1602', *Bodleian Library Record,* 9 [1974], 173–77.) Much of the present chapter appeared in *The Library,* 6th ser., 14 (1992), 100–126, as 'King James's Translators: The Bishops' Bible New Testament Revised', and permission for its use here is deeply appreciated.

11. Single annotations appear at Ephesians 4.8; II Thessalonians 2.15; I Corinthians 9.5; Galatians 3.13; and II Peter 1.10.

12. Pollard, *Records of the English Bible,* 53–54.

13. The Greek text, while clearly implying the presence of the pronoun 'them', does not contain it.

14. The Greek text supports the final reading.

15. The noun used in the Greek text allows for either English noun.

16. Allen looked briefly at this verse in *Translating the New Testament Epistles,* xxx.

17. LJ's first revision 'shall lay' is similar in tone and intent to the 1602 reading 'make . . . euen', which was first used by Tyndale. Both translations understate the Greek verb, which means 'to dash or raze to the ground'. This violent meaning comes out in later revisions of the passage and was no doubt suggested to the translators by the 1582 Rheims translation.

18. The Greek text employs the present tense and the possessive adjective in its phrasing.

How to Read This Collation

I. The Format

1. The word *company* refers in these instructions to members of the Oxford New Testament Company whose revisions are above the line of the Bishops' text. After the Oxford Company had completed the work recorded in the Bodleian Bishops' Bible, the translators made further revisions. In this collation these revisions are on the line below the Bishops' text. At Matthew 3.11, the members of the Oxford Company proposed three revisions, one of which the translators later rejected.

indeede with
*I baptize you †in† water unto repentance: but he that commeth

stronger
*after me, is †mightier† then I, whose shooes I am not worthy to beare, he shall
mightier

*baptize you with the holy Ghost and with fire.

The three proposed revisions are the addition of 'indeede', the revision of 'in' to 'with', and of 'mightier' to 'stronger'. The translators rejected 'stronger', the revision proposed for 'mightier'. The word *translators* refers in these instructions either to members of the Oxford Company, who revised their own work recorded in the Bodleian Bishops' Bible, or to members of the General Meeting, who adjudicated disputes between companies.

2. The main line of each verse in this collation reproduces the text of the Bishops' Bible (1602). An asterisk stands before the first word of each main line. At Matthew 4.5, the asterisk stands before 'Then' and 'pinacle'.

*Then the devill taketh him up into the holy Citie, and setteth him on a

*pinacle of the Temple,

Revisions proposed by members of the Oxford New Testament Company are above the Bishops' text. At Matthew 4.6, there are four revisions.

*And saith unto him, If thou be the Sonne of God, cast thy selfe downe: For

[Delete] concerning
*it is written, †that† he shall give his Angels charge †over† thee,

in beare
*and †with† their handes they shall †lift† thee up, lest at any time thou

*dash thy foote against a stone.

The company deleted 'that', and revised 'over' to 'concerning', 'with' to 'in', and 'lift' to 'beare'. The verse in the Authorized Version follows the Bishops' text as revised by the Oxford Company.

> And saith unto him, If thou bee the Sonne of God, cast thy selfe downe: For it is written, He shall give his Angels charge concerning thee, and in their hands they shall beare thee up, lest at any time thou dash thy foot against a stone. (1612)

At Matthew 4.10, the members of the Oxford Company proposed two revisions.

Avoyde
Get thee [Delete]
*Then sayeth Jesus unto him, †Get thee† hence †behinde mee,† Satan:

*for it is written, Thou shalt worship the Lord thy God, and him onely shalt thou

*serve.

They replaced the Bishops' 'Get thee' with 'Avoyde', the reading of Tyndale, the Great Bible, and the Geneva Bible. But rejecting this proposal, they returned to the Bishops' words. The verse in the Authorized Version follows this revision.

> Then saith Jesus unto him, Get thee hence, Satan: for it is written, Thou shalt worship the Lord thy God, and him onely shalt thou serve. (1612)

When there is more than one revision for a single passage in the Bishops' text, these revisions are set above the Bishops' text in order with the first revision at the top of the set and the final revision just above the Bishops' text. Thus, in Matthew 4.10, 'Avoyde' is at the top of the set and 'Get thee' is just above the Bishops' text.

3. To construct the text of the Authorized Version, take the Bishops' text except at those places enclosed in daggers or marked by a space. Daggers enclose a portion of the Bishops' text which has been revised; a space marks a place where there is an addition to the Bishops' text. A revision by the translators, which is below the main line, will always be the text of the Authorized Version. In revisions by the company, which are above the main line, the revision immediately above it will be the text of the Authorized Version, if there is no revision at this place below the main line. To put it more simply, the lowest line on the page, whether above or below the main line, is the phrase or word settled on for inclusion in the Authorized Version. Italic words and phrases in the Authorized Version are indicated by underlining.

    In the example below, Luke 19.44, those portions of the Bishops' text and the revisions by the company and translators which have become part of the Authorized Version are underlined.

shall lay thee, to the ground
shall dashe thee, to the ground
shall beate thee, flatt to the ground within
*And †make† †thee even with the ground,† and thy children †which are in†
shall lay thee even with the ground

even with the ground
even with the ground
[Delete]
*thee : and they shall not leave in thee one stone

*upon another, because thou †knowest† not the time of thy visitation.
knewest

4. Words and phrases written above the line of the Bishops' text reproduce all words and phrases written by the scribes for the Oxford Company, but do not reproduce in every case the manner of a scribe's revision.

EXAMPLE 1

Matthew 3.4

And the same John
And John him self   girdle of skyn
*†This John†   had his raiment of camels haire, and a †leatherne girdle†
And the same John   leatherne girdle

and
*about his loynes,   his meate was locusts and wilde hony.

THE SCRIBE'S MANNER OF REVISION

The scribe first cancelled 'This' in the Bishops' text and wrote in the space above the verse, 'And the same'. Thus the phrase in the collation, 'And the same John', does not reproduce the manner of the revision which combines the handwritten words, 'And the same', with the printed word, 'John'. Next the scribe extended the line which cancelled 'This' so that it also cancelled 'John'. He then wrote in the margin, 'And John him self'. The second proposed revision reproduces the manner of the revision. The line below the Bishops' text is from the Authorized Version. The translators rejected the second proposal and adopted the first.

The annotations were made on unbound leaves. The volume is now bound, and the binding obscures letters in certain places. Here 'him' is not visible. In these annotations, as in printed texts, 'him self' is sometimes written as two words, sometimes as one.

EXAMPLE 2

Luke 5.5

toyled all the
toyled all the
*And Simon answering, saide unto him, Master, wee have †laboured all†

word
*night, and have taken nothing: neverthelesse, at thy †commandement†

let downe
*I will †loose forth† the net.

THE SCRIBE'S MANNER OF REVISION

The scribe underlined 'laboured all' and wrote in the margin 'toyled all'. In the space above the text he wrote 'the' before 'night'. The company then cancelled 'toyled all' in the margin and 'the' above the text. Later they cancelled 'laboured all', and the scribe wrote a second time in the margin 'toyled all'. After the first 'toyled all' had been cancelled in the margin, a hand other than the scribe's put into the margin after the cancellation a caret and 'the'. It is possible, but not certain, that at some point the company proposed 'toyled all night'.

The scribe wrote in the margin, 'word I will let downe'. Convenience in tabulating sources accounts for the words—which form one phrase in the annotations—being separated in the collation. Tyndale is the source for 'word' and the Geneva Bible is the source for 'let downe'.

EXAMPLE 3

Matthew 3.10

And now even the axe is layd
And now also the axe is layd
*†Even now is the axe also put† unto the root of the trees: Therefore every tree

*which bringeth not foorth good fruit, is hewen downe, and cast into the fire.

THE SCRIBE'S MANNER OF REVISION

The scribe first cancelled in the Bishops' text 'Even now is' and wrote in the space above the printed text 'And now even'. He left untouched in the text 'the axe'. He cancelled the words of the text 'also put', and placed above them 'is layd'. The revision on the uppermost line above the Bishops' text represents this proposal. Then the scribe cancelled 'even', and wrote beside it 'also'. The line immediately above the Bishops' text represents this second proposal.

EXAMPLE 4

Matthew 1.6

And   and
*   Jesse begate David the King,   David the King begate Solomon,

and   that had bene   Urieas
*   of her †that was†   the wife of †Urie.†
[Delete]

THE SCRIBE'S MANNER OF REVISION

The scribe has cancelled in the text 'her that was' and has written in the margin 'her that had bene'. Although the collation does not follow this manner of the scribe's revision, the arrangement makes clear at a glance the exact words which the company revised.

5. Words and phrases under the line marked by an asterisk are from a 1612 quarto, 'Imprinted at London by Robert Barker'. These words and phrases from the 1612 quarto differ, by my enumeration, in 188 places from the standard 1611 folio in (a) spelling, (b) marks of punctuation, (c) abbreviations, (d) capital and lower case letters, and (e) typography.

A. SPELLING

Matthew 8.32

*And hee sayd unto them, Goe. †Then went they out, and departed†
And when they were come out, they went

[Delete]
*into the heard of †the† swine: and behold, the whole herd of †the†
[Delete]

violently from a steep place
*swine †rushed† †headlong† into the sea, and perished
ran violently downe a steepe place

*in the waters.

Quarto: ran   Folio: ranne

B. PUNCTUATION

Mark 4.21

a   brought   ♣bushell
*And hee saide unto them, Is †the† candle †lighted† to bee put under a bushell,
"bushel

a bed
*or under †the table?† and not to be †put† on a candlesticke?
set

♣the word in the originall signifyeth a less measure
"The word in the originall signifieth a lesse measure, as mat. 5.15

Folio: The word, in the originall, ...

C. Abbreviations

Matthew 26.27

hee tooke giving
*And †when hee had taken† the cup, & †given† thankes, †he† gave it them,
gave & to

*saying, Drinke ye all of it:

Folio: and gave it

D. Capital and Lower Case Letters

Matthew 26.30

sung an ♣hymne
*And when they had †praised God,† they went out †unto† the mount of Olives.
sung an "hymne into

♣Or, Psalme
"Or, Psalme

Folio: Or, psalme

E. Typography

Mark 7.11

*But ye say, If a man shal say to his father or mother,

that is, the offeringe whatsoever is from me by it thou mayst
that is the gift offered of me by it thou mayst
*†Corban† †(that is, by the gift) that is offered of me, thou shalt
It is Corban, that is to say, a gift, by whatsoever thou mightest bee

be benefited
be benefited
*be helped.†
profited by me: he shall be free

Folio: shalbe free

Luke 12.20

*But God said unto him, Thou foole, this night †do they require thy soule again from†
"thy soule shalbe required of

*thee: then whose shal those things be which thou hast provided?

"Gr. doe they require thy soule

Folio: shal be required

The quarto corrects errors in the folio, such as 'he began to wept' (Mark 14.72, margin). It introduces, in this collation, four wrong readings in Matthew, five in Mark, and three in Luke. These errors have been corrected in this collation to the text of the folio.

		Quarto	Folio
Matthew	7.23	prophesie	professe
	12.13	unto	to
	13.44	the field	a field
	19.16	inherit	have
Mark	2.9	unto	to
	4.36	was	were
	10.9	no	not
	10.35	came	come
	10.42	accounted	accompted
Luke	3.33	Nachor	Juda
	17.36	Or, this	This
	24.32	to	unto

The Bodleian Bishops' Bible supports the folio in these places. The members of the Oxford Company revised the Bishops' 'confesse' (Matthew 7.23) to 'professe' and 'the field' (13.44) to 'a field'. They let stand the Bishops' 'to' (12.13) and 'have' (19.16). They let stand the Bishops' 'to' (Mark 2.9), 'were' (4.36), 'come' (10.35). They revised the Bishops' 'no' (10.9) to 'not' and 'seeme' (10.42) to 'are accompted'. 'Nachor' (Luke 3.33) is a printer's error. The company's scribe wrote in the Bishops' Bible 'This', (17.36) not 'Or, this'. The company let stand the Bishops' 'unto' (24.32); modern editions of the King James Bible follow the quarto, 'to'.

6. Words and phrases under the line marked by an asterisk may (a) restore a passage in the Bishops' text, (b) revise a passage in the line, or lowest of several lines, above the Bishops' text, (c) introduce a fresh revision.
    a. Restores a passage in the Bishops' text.

EXAMPLE 1

Luke 19.31

*And if any man aske you, Why do ye loose him? Thus shall ye say unto him,

[Delete]
*†Because† the Lord hath neede of him.
Because

EXAMPLE 2

Luke 19.17

*And he said unto him, Well, thou good servant: because thou hast bene faithfull

the leaste
*in †a very litle thing,† have thou authoritie over ten cities.
a very little

The Oxford Company proposed a revision of the Bishops' 'a very litle thing' to 'the leaste'. The translators reworked this proposal. They restored the Bishops' 'a very litle' but followed the Oxford Company in omitting the word 'thing'.

    b. Revises lowest line above Bishops' text and the Bishops' text.

EXAMPLE 1

Luke 19.19

he said to him also
he said to him
he said to him also. And [Delete]
*And †to the same he said,† Be thou also †ruler† over
he said likewise to him

*five cities.

The Oxford Company's scribe cancelled the Bishops' 'to the same he said'. He then wrote in the margin 'he said to him also'. This first revision is on the top line of revisions above the Bishops' text. He next deleted 'also'. This second revision appears on the line immediately below the top line of revisions. The scribe did not cancel the entire phrase in the margin. He cancelled only 'also'. The words, 'he said to him', in the collation represent the phrase as it stood when the scribe had cancelled 'also'. The scribe then added to these words 'also. And'. The line immediately above the Bishops' text represents this revision. Although the phrase, 'he said to him', appears in the collation three times, it is written but once in the margin.

The line below the Bishops' text carries the phrase as it appears in the Authorized Version, 'he said likewise to him'. The translators have retained from the Oxford Company's proposal the Black Letter 'he' which replaces the Bishops' Roman 'he'. They have revised the Oxford Company's 'also' to 'likewise' and have changed the position of this adverb. This shift changes the position of the prepositional phrase, 'to him', but the translators have retained this phrase from the proposed revision.

EXAMPLE 2

Luke 19.7

[Delete]   all
*And when they †all†   saw it, they   murmured, saying, that he was gone

lodge
♣abide
abide
♣abide
*†in†   to †tary†   with a man that is a sinner.
[Delete]   bee guest

♣as a guest
♣as a guest

The scribe underlined 'tary' in the text and placed before it a superscript Greek letter, *kappa.* He then placed a *kappa* in the margin and wrote beside it 'lodge', which he cancelled. He then wrote 'abide' and placed beside it a symbol, ♣, to indicate a reading in the margin. Beneath that he repeated the symbol and wrote beside it 'as a guest'. Since he did not include the notation 'Or', it is uncertain whether the company meant for this to be an alternative translation or a supplemental phrase, 'abide as a guest'. The scribe then drew a line through 'as a guest' but let stand 'abide'. Next beneath the cancelled 'as a guest' he wrote for a second time 'as a guest'. Thus the Oxford Company let the revision stand. But the translators rejected that reading and put in the text 'bee guest'.

c. Introduces a fresh revision.

Example 1

Luke 19.37

of Olives
*And when he was †nowe come nigh to the going downe† of the mount †Olivet,†
come nigh, even now at the descent

to rejoyce and
*the whole multitude of the disciples beganne †rejoycing to† praise God with a

mighty workes
*loud voice, for al the †miracles† that they had seene,

Example 2

Luke 14.1

*And it came to passe, as he went into the house of one of the chiefe Pharisees

watched
*to eate bread on the Sabboth day, they †were watching† him.
that

On the lower line in Example 1 the text of the Authorized Version differs from the reading of the Bishops' Bible. The Bishops' words which have been revised are in daggers. In Example 2 the translators have supplied a word for which there is no equivalent in the Bishops' text. There is a space in the Bishops' text.

7. Words in each line of this collation reproduce the spelling of words copied. But long ʃ has been rendered as s, and u, v, i, and j have been conformed to modern usage.

8. Casual differences of spelling between the Bishops' Bible and the Authorized Version are not shown in this collation.

Mark 2.17

it are strong
*When Jesus heard †that,† hee sayeth unto them, They that †be whole,†
are whole

*have no neede of the Physition, but they that are sicke: I came not to call the

*righteous, but sinners to repentance.

Authorized Version (1611): no need of the Physition.
Authorized Version (1612): no neede of the Physician.

9. Where the spelling of a proper name in the Bishops' text differs from the spelling in the Authorized Version that difference does not appear in the collation unless the scribe has altered the spelling of the Bishops' text.

Example 1

Matthew 1.2

and and
*Abraham begate Isahac, Isahac begate Jacob, Jacob begate Judas &

*his brethren.

The Bishops' 'Isahac' is in the Authorized Version 'Isaac'. The variation is not shown in this collation.

Example 2

Matthew 1.6

And and
* Jesse begate David the King, David the King begate Solomon,

and that had bene Urieas
* of her †that was† the wife of †Urie.†
[Delete]

The scribe has added '-as' to the ending of the Bishops' word 'Urie'. The Authorized Version carries the scribe's '-as', but has respelled the scribe's 'Urieas' to 'Urias'. This respelling does not appear in the collation.

Example 3

Matthew 1.9

And & & Ezekias
* Ozias begat Joatham, Joatham begate Achas, Achas begate †Ezecias.†

The scribe's 'Ezekias' is thus spelled in the Authorized Version. Where the scribe has used an ampersand in this verse, the Authorized Version spells out 'and'. Casual differences between the scribe and the Authorized Version in typography, spelling, and other accidentals do not appear in this collation.

10. The only revisions of punctuation shown are those made by the Oxford Company, or those which occur in extended passages from the Authorized Version.

Revision of punctuation appears in the Authorized Version.

Luke 19.22

And Out
*†Then† he saieth unto him, Of thine owne mouth will I judge thee, thou

wicked Thou knewest was a severe
*†evill† servant: †Knewest thou† that I †am† †a straite† man, taking up that I layd
an austere

.
*not downe, and reaping that I did not sow †?†

Revision of punctuation does not appear in the Authorized Version.

Luke 4.18

for which cause
*The Spirit of the Lord upon me, †because† he hath anointed me,
is because

.
*to preach the Gospel to the poore †:† he hath sent me, to heale the broken hearted,
,

captives
*to preach deliverance to the †captive,† and recovering of sight to the blinde,

[Delete]
*†freely† to set at libertie them that are bruised,

Punctuation in extended passage from the Authorized Version.

Matthew 10.42

unto one of these little ones a cup of cold water
unto one of these little ones a cup of cold water
*And whosoever shall give †unto one of these little ones to drinke a cup of
to drinke unto one of these little ones, a cup of

to drinke only
only to drinke
*cold water only,† in the name of a disciple, verily I say unto you, he shall in
cold water onely

*no wise lose his reward.

11. The Bishops' Bible and the Authorized Version have in their margins (a) references to Biblical passages which parallel the subject of a verse, (b) alternate readings for words and phrases, and (c) explanatory notes, such as explanations of weights and measures.

(a) References to parallel verses do not appear in this collation. (b) Alternate meanings for words and phrases are designated in the Bishops' Bible by parallel vertical lines, as they are in the Authorized Version. Only where an alternate meaning in the margin of the Bishops' Bible has influenced a revision in the Authorized Version does that meaning appear in this collation. (c) The designation in the Bishops' Bible for explanatory notes is a letter in lower case type. Only where an explanatory note has influenced the revision of the Authorized Version does that note appear in this collation.

All alternate meanings for words and phrases which are in the margins of the Authorized Version appear in this collation. The explanatory notes in the margins of the Authorized

Version which have some relation to the annotations in the Bodleian Bishops' Bible appear in this collation. All other explanatory notes in the Authorized Version have been omitted.

The scribes used various symbols to signal a marginal reading proposed by the Oxford Company. One of these symbols, ♣, signals in this collation all marginal readings proposed by the Oxford Company. *Or,* with a capital *O,* to introduce a variant reading, stands in place of *or* with a lower case *o,* the scribe's usual form. Words and notes in the Bishops' Bible and the Authorized Version are closed with a full stop. All end punctuation of notes in the Bishops' Bible, the Authorized Version, and proposals by the Oxford Company has been omitted in this collation.

Words from the Margin of the Bishops' Bible Which Have Influenced the King's Translators

Example 1

Luke 10.2

truely
*Therefore sayd hee unto them, The harvest is great, but the labourers

that he would thrust forth
*are few: pray ye therefore the Lord of the harvest, †to† †send "forth†
send foorth

*labourers into his harvest.

"Or, thrust forth

Example 2

Luke 5.21

reason Whoe
*And the Scribes and the Pharsees began to †"thinke,† saying, †what fellow†

alone
*is this which speaketh blasphemies? Who can forgive sinnes, but God †onely?†

"Or, reason

EXAMPLE 3

Luke 4.29

[Delete]
*And rose up, and thrust him out of the city, and led him †even† unto

brow
*the †"top† of the hil (whereon their city was built) that they might cast him
"brow

*downe headlong.

"The Greek readeth, brow of the hill
"Or, edge

EXPLANATORY NOTES FROM THE MARGIN OF THE BISHOPS' BIBLE WHICH HAVE INFLUENCED THE KING'S TRANSLATORS

EXAMPLE 1

Luke 16.9

to your selves unjust ♣Mammon
*And I say unto you, Make †you† friends of the †[c]unrighteous Mammon,†
"Mammon of unrighteousnes

fayle [Delete]
*that when yee †shall have neede,† they may receive you into †the†

*everlasting habitations.

♣Or, riches
[c]Not that riches are evill of themselves, but that for the most part they be occasions of evill
"Or, riches

EXAMPLE 2

Luke 17.20, 21

And
* When he was demanded of the Pharisees when the kingdom of God

should come he answered them and
*†commeth, he answering them,† said, The kingdome of God commeth not

♣observation
*with observation.
"observation

♣Or, with outward shew
"Or, with outward shew

or
*Neither shall they say, Lo here, lo there: for behold, the kingdome of God

*is [d]within you.
"within you

[d]It cannot be discerned by any outward shew
"Or, among you

12. Miscellaneous notes.
   (a) Contractions, such as 'y^e' for 'the' and 'w^{ch}' for 'which', have been expanded. The ampersand has been retained wherever it occurs in the Bishops' text, the annotations, or the Authorized text.
   (b) Typographical errors in the Bishops' text, uncorrected by the scribe, are reproduced in this collation.

Matthew 26.68

Thou
*Saying, Prophecie unto us, †O† Christ, who is he †thae† smote thee?
that

   (c) Where the scribe has written a revision and failed to delete a word in the text, that error is not shown.

Matthew 25.25

[Delete] I was
*And †therefore† †was I† afraid, and went and hid thy talent in the earth:

is thine
*loe, there thou hast that †thine is.†

The scribe has written 'I' so that it is the subject of 'was' as it appears in the Authorized Version. But he failed to delete the 'I' in the Bishops' text.

   (d) Where the scribe has made an error and has corrected that error, error and correction are shown.

Mark 5.40

when he he
when he
*And they laughed him to scorne: but †hee, after that he† had put them all out,

hee
* taketh the father and the mother of the Damosell, and them that were with him:

was laying
was lying
*and entreth in where the Damosel †lay.†

The scribe wrote in the margin 'when he' and did not delete 'he' in the text. He then deleted 'he' in the margin.

II. Words

The King's translators spent six years in their work. One imagines their reforming sentences and giving shape to series of sentences. But the six years went largely to revising words, and those scattered. A study of those words will push aside the notion that the work was light. The translators were masters of Greek words, and they had an astonishing command of the full range of meaning for English words. Even more surprising is their sense for the current status of English words. They revised words that were passing out of use, and they availed themselves of words which had recently come into use. When need arose they coined words.

The five exercises which follow suggest the thought and imagination which the translators brought to bear on words. *Austere,* in the first exercise, illustrates the attention the translators gave to matching the range of meaning in Greek and English words. In the second example, *lodge* matches the image in the literal meaning of a Greek word, and *shoot out* is the translator's invention to translate a pedestrian Greek word. Gerald Hammond has written that the 'Renaissance Bible translator saw half of his task as reshaping English so that it could adapt itself' to Biblical languages.[1] The translators have done that overtly with *shoot out.* In the third example, the translators have designed for the margin words which supply an image and ambiguous senses as a comment on the abstract sense in the text. The translators were taught as schoolboys to recognize and use the fanciful and indirect ways of thought mapped out by figures of speech. As men they kept poetry and its ways at the forefront of their minds. They quoted poetry from memory at the General Meeting. Horace is in their preface to illustrate the point that the word is the word even though the translation may have blemishes. The translators' lifelong use of poetry has left its mark on the King's Bible. 'The modern English translations', writes Stephen Prickett, 'seem to be quite unanimous in *rejecting* any ambiguity or oddity perceived in the original'.[2] Modern translators are likely to be 'scholars and exegetes', writes Gerald Hammond, 'whose instincts are to replace dangerous ambiguities of poetry with the safer specificities of prose'.[3] In the fourth example, the translators have devised an image, 'the bright shining of a candle' to join a victorious life to eternal brightness. In the fifth example, the revised diction heightens the pathos of Mark's expression in the account of Peter's denying Jesus.

These revisions are typical. To the eye they appear easy and quick work. But the work was, as the translators say in the preface, 'labour'. Such labour, they said, was 'to bee speeded with maturitie'. And such, dear reader, is the labour required of those who in this collation retrace the footsteps of the King's translators.

Lexicons are at hand for retracing those footsteps. Definitions of Greek words in these exercises come from Liddell and Scott's *A Greek English Lexicon* (9th edition, 1948) and from Arndt, Gingrich, and Danker's *A Greek-English Lexicon of the New Testament and Other Early Christian Literature* (2nd edition, 1979), a translation and adaptation of Walter Bauer's lexicon. Cross references to Greek and English words are from Ethelbert W. Bullinger's *A Critical Lexicon and Concordance to the English and Greek New Testament* (rpt. 1975). All references to English words are from the *Oxford English Dictionary* (1st edition).

Luke 19.21

a severe
*For I feared thee, because thou art †a strait† man: thou takest up that
an austere

*thou laiedst not down, and reapest that thou diddest not sow.

Tyndale, Coverdale, the Genevans, and the Bishops had translated *αὐστηρός* by 'strait'. The Greek word means literally *'making the tongue dry and rough, harsh, rough, bitter',* and hence metaphorically, *'austere, harsh'.* It means also *'exacting, strict'.* The King's translators used *strait* to describe a narrow passage, a sense which is still current. But the use of *strait* as an attribute of a person or agent was, in 1611, slipping from the language. The last example cited in the *Oxford English Dictionary* for its use as an attribute of a person is dated 1612. This is but one of many revisions which attest to the remarkable grasp which these translators had on the status of living speech.[4]

The members of the Oxford Company replaced 'strait' with 'severe', 'Rigorous in one's treatment of, or attitude towards, offenders'. But the translators rejected 'severe' and put in its place 'austere', which Gregory Martin had chosen for the Rheims New Testament.

There is a reason for this choice. The Greek word occurs in this and the next verse and nowhere else in the New Testament. While the Greek word conveys the sense that the man is exacting, it also delineates the wicked servant's view of his lord's character. The servant sees his lord as harsh, bitter, severe in self-discipline, stern in manner, and judicially severe. *Austere* is 'harsh in flavour, rough to the taste . . . stern in manner . . . rigorous, judiciously severe' (*Oxford English Dictionary*). With this word the translators caught those very connotations of the Greek word which reveal the wicked servant's attitude.

Mark 4.31–32

[Delete]
*†It is† like a graine of mustard seed: which when it is sowen in the
It is

*earth, is lesse then all seedes that be in the earth:
the

becommeth
*†And† when it is sowen, it groweth up, and †is† greater then all herbes,
But

shooteth out
*and †beareth† great branches, so that the fowles of the aire may

lodge
*†make their nestes† under the shadow of it.

In deleting 'It is' in verse 31, the company conformed its text to the Rheims New Testament. In restoring the phrase the translators followed Tyndale and other Protestant versions. In supplying 'the' before 'seeds', they followed the Rheims New Testament. In revising 'And' to 'But', in verse 32, they followed Tyndale and the Genevans. In revising 'is' to 'becommeth', the company followed the Rheims New Testament. The revisions of 'beareth' to 'shooteth out' and 'make their nestes' to 'lodge' are their very own.

Each of their own revisions is extraordinary. *Shoot out* stands for the Greek word ποιέω, a common word in the New Testament for which two common English words, *make* and *do,* generally suffice. In the Authorized Version, ποιέω is rendered by *do* in 357 places, by *make* in 115 places, and by *bear* in four places. This is the only use of *shoot out* in the New Testament. The single use of *shoot out* in the Old Testament is in Psalm 144. God casts forth lightning and shoots out arrows. 'Lodge', which stands for κατασκηνόω, 'to pitch a tent' or 'to settle', is also a singular word. Bucks, beavers, and otters occupy a lodge, but not birds. This Greek word occurs in the three accounts of this parable and in one other place in the New Testament, Acts 2.26, where the Authorized Version renders Peter's words, 'my flesh shall rest in hope'.

This parable describes a natural process. The seed is sown, grows, becomes great, and 'bears' branches. So Tyndale, the Great Bible, the Geneva Bible, and the Bishops' Bible have it. The seed 'maketh great boughes' in the Rheims New Testament. Although modern translators have introduced new terms for the growth of the branches, *puts forth, puts out, forms,* these terms, like the Renaissance terms, suggest the slow growth of branches. *Shoots out* suggests swift, forceful movement, which defies the natural process as one sees it under the aspect of time. But the Kingdom of God is not subject to time or place. At one moment there is a seed. And, lo, at the next the energy in the seed has shot out great branches. To use the terms of the natural process lulls a reader into shifting the subject of these verbs from a seed to an herb, bush, shrub, or tree. 'Shooteth out' jolts a reader into recovering the subject of the verse, the seed. The energy of the seed brings to mind God's inexplicable energies. King James's translators had at hand *shoots forth,* first used in 1526 to describe the growth of branches (s.v. *Shoot,* 19, *Oxford English Dictionary*). In Tyndale, trees 'shute forth their buddes', as they do in the Authorized Version (Luke 21.30). To gain the effect of a seed exploding into great branches, the translators reshaped *shoot forth* to *shoot out.* The *Oxford English Dictionary* offers *shoots out* at Mark 4.32 as the first example of this phrase used to describe the growth of branches.

The Greek verb κατασκηνόω has two directions of meaning in classical usage. One is to pitch a tent or encamp. The other is to settle or to rest. The English verb *lodge* fits the Greek verb hand in glove. Examples in the *Oxford English Dictionary* for the transitive sense of *lodge,* 'To place in tents or other temporary shelter; to encamp, to station (an army)', date from 1225 to 1598. Examples for its intransitive use, 'to encamp', date from the fourteenth century to 1603. The English word also carries the Greek sense of 'to settle'. Both Renaissance and modern translators have adjusted the Greek image to what birds literally do, make nests, build, dwell, perch, nest, roost, and shelter. With such adjustments they have abandoned suggestions which rise from the image in the Greek word. Exegetes do not agree on the meaning of this parable. But whatever the meaning may be, the images of an encamped army or a settled household apply. The birds are encamped, settled, or at rest in the shadow. Yet like an encamped army they hold the potential for warfare. In this they reflect the essential qualities of the seed.

Luke 12.22–29

This call to the carefree life is by and large Tyndale's translation. The Bishops made a few changes in Tyndale's version and the King's translators made a few changes in the Bishops' version.

sayd
*And he †spake† unto his disciples, Therefore I say unto you, Take no thought for

*your life what ye shall eate, neither for the body what yee shall put on.

*The life is more then meate, and the body is more then raiment.

*Consider the ravens, for they neither sowe nor reape, which neither have

[Delete]
*storehouse nor barne, & †notwithstanding† God feedeth them: How much more

*are ye better then the foules?

And
* Which of you with taking thought can adde to his stature one cubite?

*If yee then bee not able to doe that thing which is least, why take ye thought

rest
*for the †remnant?†

toyle
*Consider the Lilies how they growe, they †labour† not, they spinne not: and

glory arayed
*yet I say unto you, that Solomon in all his †royalty,† was not †clothed†

*like one of these.

then
*If God so clothe the grasse, which is to day in the field, and to morow

oven
*is cast into the †fornace:† how much more will he clothe you, O ye of little faith?

seeke
*And †aske† not ye what ye shall eate, or what ye shal drinke, neither be
"neither bee

*ye of doubtfull mind.
ye of doubtfull mind

"Or, live not in carefull suspence

The Bishops revised Tyndale's 'youre body' to 'the body' (verse 22), Coverdale's revision in the Great Bible. They changed Tyndale's 'yet' to *'notwithstanding'* and added 'more' (verse 24). They changed Tyndale's 'lyke to one' to 'like one' (verse 27), Coverdale's version. They revised Tyndale's syntax, 'Yf the grasse which is to daye in the felde, and to morowe shalbe cast into the fornace, God so clothe' (1534) to 'If God so clothe the grasse, which is to day in the field, and to morow is cast into the fornace' (verse 28), Coverdale's syntax and Tyndale's (1526). They changed Tyndale's 'endued with' to 'of' (verse 28), and Tyndale's 'axe not' to 'aske not ye' (verse 29), both Coverdale's revisions. Their revision of Tyndale's 'nether clyme ye up an hye' to 'neither be ye of doubtfull mind' (verse 29) was their own.

The King's translators deleted the Bishops' *'notwithstanding'* (verse 24). In supplying 'And' (verse 25) and 'then' (verse 28) and in revising 'fornace' to 'oven' (verse 28), they followed the Geneva Bible. They followed the Rheims New

Testament with 'sayd' (verse 22), 'rest' (verse 26), 'glory' and 'arayed' (verse 27), and 'seeke' (verse 29). Their own revisions are 'toyle' (verse 27) and 'Or, *live not in carefull suspence*' (verse 29). *Suspense* reproduces the literal sense of Luke's μετεωρίζεσθε, which means to be raised to a height. The Greek also carries the metaphorical senses found in *suspense:* false hope, anxiety, worry, and an unsettled state of mind. Coverdale followed Tyndale's 'nether clyme ye up an hye'. The Genevans put in their text 'nether stand in doute' and in the margin 'Or, *make discourses in the ayre*'. The Bishops rendered the Greek by 'neither be ye of doubtfull mind', which the translators kept in their text. Gregory Martin rendered the Greek by 'be not lifted up on high'. The versions by Tyndale and Gregory Martin fit ambition as well as doubt. The Genevans' *'discourses'* probably means, 'onward courses' a sense which disappeared from English in 1612. The Genevans' note is vague. Splicing *careful* from the margin of Laurence Tomson's revised Geneva Bible and *suspense* from Tomson's text, the translators contrived a bountiful image. *Care* is, on the one hand, worry, anxiety, and doubt. On the other hand, it is caution. *Suspense* carries by way of its etymology the sense of height. *Careful* emphasizes the mental states which rise from suspense, both worry and wariness.

Luke 11.33–36

hidden place
vaulte
cave
*No man when he hath lighted a candle, putteth it in a †privie place,†
secret place

*neither under a bushell: but on a candlesticke, that they which come in, may

*see the light.

light
*The †[a]candle† of the body is the eye: therefore when thine eye is single,

[Delete]
thy whole full of when is wicked
*†all thy† body also is †full of† light, but †if† thine eye †be evill,†
is evill

[Delete]
[Delete] full of
*†all† thy body also is †full of† darkenesse.

[a]That is, the light

*Take heede therefore, that the light which is in thee, be not darkenesse.

light
thy whole full of light
*If †all thy† bodie therefore bee †cleere,† having no part darke:

[Delete]
all
the whole shall full of [Delete]
*†then shall it all† be †full of† light, †even† as when

a light lightneth thee with shining
*†a candle doth light thee with brightnesse.†
the bright shining of a candle doeth give thee light

Images sharpen and expand the lines of thought in this parable. The candle leads to an eye, the eye to a moral quality, and the moral quality to a bright shining which comes from a candle. While thought which moves by images stays within the bounds of a theme, within those bounds thought is elastic. A translator must attend to images.

The revision of two images, central to the theme of this parable, was long in coming. In revising 'privie place', the company tried and rejected two versions before it settled on a third. The translators rejected that revision, too, and settled finally on a fourth rendering. The translators rejected also the company's revision of the Bishops' 'a candle doth light thee with brightnesse', but in preparing the final version of this simile, they did draw from the company's work, 'a light lightneth thee with shining', the word 'shining'.

The 'secret place', the translators' final revision of 'privie place', comes to represent in this parable a body full of darkness, which itself represents the enormity of spiritual evil. The opening sentence introduces the literal terms and situation of the parable, a candle, a secret place, a bushel, and a candlestick. The word *privy* was ancient when Tyndale introduced it into this parable. The first citation for its use in the sense 'withdrawn from public sight' is dated in the *Oxford English Dictionary* as 1290. By long use it had gained connotations which were useful in Tyndale's context. But its days were numbered. It faded from use in 1613, after which it became archaic, used now and then in the eighteenth and nineteenth centuries. The King's translators, alert to words on the wing, rejected the Bishops' 'privie place'. The company replaced 'privie' with 'hidden'. Whereas *privy* had gathered connotations from centuries of use, *hidden* was a newcomer. The first example cited in the *Oxford English Dictionary* is from a poem by Surrey, in which the poet hopes to find a 'hidden place'. The company rejected 'hidden place' for 'vaulte', a word which has many noxious associations; crypts, burial chambers, cellars, drains, sewers, privies, caverns, and caves. Here the company found images aplenty to specify the enormity of evil. But the word also denotes interior spaces, some fine and public. This is wrong for the context, because this private place stands in contrast to a place where people 'which come in, may see the light'. The company replaced 'vaulte' with 'cave', a dark place and secluded where dangers lurk. But the translators rejected 'cave' and put in its place 'secret place'. This phrase denotes a secluded place and suggests seclusion and wickedness, such as actions done to conceal wickedness, disguised feelings and thought, doors designed to conceal assignations, and drawers designed to protect private papers. With this phrase the translators denoted the idea of a secluded place and joined to that the suggestions of the evil which that place represents in this parable, a place where paradoxically light is darkness.

In the opening sentence the image for the good life is a candle on a candlestick. It lights the room, so that all who enter may see the light. The lighted room reappears in the final sentence. The candle in that sentence casts a remarkable light. It is in Greek a candle 'with lightning'. The Bishops followed Tyndale, Coverdale, and the Genevans in translating the Greek word as 'brightnesse'. They followed also the syntax of the Greek, 'with brightnesse'. The members of the Oxford Company replaced 'brightnesse' with 'shining'. The translators revised both diction and syntax. They chose 'bright shining' to carry the sense of the Greek 'lightning' and made 'shining' the subject of the sentence.

The Greek word *ἀστραπή* occurs in the New Testament nine times. The translators rendered it as 'lightning' eight times and as 'bright shining' once. Lightning is used in Matthew and Luke as a simile to describe the second coming. Matthew uses it to describe the countenance of the angel who sat at the tomb. Luke quotes Jesus's description of Satan's falling like lightning. Had the translators chosen to substitute 'lightning' for the Bishops' 'brightnesse', they would have joined the candle light to extraordinary events. But they chose another way.

They chose with 'bright shining' a phrase which is, like lightning, distinguished. Both 'bright' and 'shining' are uncommon words in the King's version, and both words describe things which elevate their use in the parable of the candle. There are three other uses of *bright* in the New Testament. A bright cloud overshadows Peter, James, and John at the transfiguration. From it a voice speaks. Cornelius explains that as he prayed a man in bright clothing appeared. An angel reports that Jesus is 'the bright and morning star'. The use of *shining* as a noun in the parable of the candle is singular. But *shining* occurs four times in the King's New Testament as a participle. At the transfiguration Jesus's raiment became 'shining'; the two men at the tomb wore 'shining' garments; Jesus says that John was 'a burning and shining light'; and Paul describes to King Agrippa a light from heaven, shining at midday 'above the brightness of the sun'. The phrase 'bright shining' is natural in describing the flame of a candle. And the image gains from the contexts of the two words in other passages of the New Testament ideas which transfigure the flame of the candle by association with events which are 'full of light'.

By revising the syntax, the translators emphasized 'bright shining' and, in addition, brought the parable to a close with the strong word 'light'. Sentence and clause end with a phrase which echoes in diction and rhythm the concluding phrase of the first sentence, 'may see the light'. Thus, 'doeth give thee light' recalls candle, secret place, bushel, and candlestick, literal objects in the first sentence, but now transfigured. The span of life is brief. 'Out, out brief candle'. Yet 'bright' and 'shining' join this brief light to that which is eternally bright, eternally shining.

Mark 14.72

called to minde
*And the second time the cocke crew: and Peter †remembred† the word

*that Jesus sayd unto him, Before the cocke crow twise, thou shalt deny me

thrice he fell a weeping
*†three times:† And †he began to weepe.†
when he thought thereon, "he wept

"Or, he wept abundantly, or he began to weepe

In this handsome sentence syntax, sound, rhythm, and diction give life to the thought which surges through Peter's mind and the action which erupts from this thought.

The first clause opens with an adverbial phrase of time and ends abruptly with subject and predicate. The second clause opens with subject and predicate and moves to a direct object. This forms an interlocking chiastic pattern. The third clause opens with an adverbial subordinate clause of time and ends abruptly with a subject and predicate. The first and third clauses describe actions, 'the cocke crew' and 'he wept'. The second clause reproduces the strange ways of thought in a human mind.

The transition of the first to the second clause rides on alliteration, consonance, and assonance. Alliteration joins 'cocke crew' to 'called to minde'. Consonance joins 'second' to 'minde' and 'time' to 'Peter'. Assonance joins 'time' to 'minde'. The cock calls to Peter's mind 'the word'. With that phrase one enters Peter's mind. With 'he wept', one moves from mind to action. *Word* and *wept* alliterate.

The opening of the second clause introduces a rhythmical pattern which underlies the thought that dominates Peter's mind,

x / x / x / x / x / x /
'And Peter called to minde / the word that Jesus sayd'.

Then 'unto him' interrupts the pattern. With Jesus's words the pattern becomes clamorous and forms a rhymed couplet,

x / x / / / / / x / x /
'Before the cocke crow twise, thou shalt deny me thrice'.

This reproduces a common experience. A line of poetry or a snatch of a song repeats itself over and over in the mind. Try as one will to drive the rhythm out, it persists. The words haunt Peter with a couplet which mocks an effort at thought. The third clause opens with a subordinate clause which repeats the rhythm of the couplet,

x / x / x /
'And when he thought thereon'.

But sound and words are at discord with the couplet. Alliteration joins 'thought thereon' to the mocking 'thrice'. The subject, 'he', is an important fulcrum. A man by an act of will drives a haunting rhythm from his mind by way of 'thought', which is the single strong word in this adverbial clause. With 'he wept' there is an abrupt end to the rhythmical pattern which reproduces the movement of thought through Peter's mind. Abrupt rhythm corresponds to abrupt action. But the action is not spontaneous, 'he thought . . . he wept'.

The revision of diction does double duty. It establishes patterns and sharpens the focus of thought. The English 'called to minde' is an accurate translation, as is 'remembred', but 'called to minde' is more specific than 'remembred'. To *call to mind* describes an act of will and specifies the mind as the faculty which receives the words. On the other hand, 'remembred' may describe a voluntary or involuntary act and may carry the sense of 'bear in mind'. The Bishops' 'three times' is satisfactory, but the translators' 'thrice' specifies 'in succession'. The succession lays an emphasis on the lapse of time in which Peter passes unrepentant from one state to another. The Greek participle, translated by the Bishops as 'began', may be translated with equal accuracy as 'when he thought thereon'. The meaning of the participle, such an authority as Walter Bauer has noted, is in doubt. The King's translators were conscientious. They put into the margin the possible meanings, 'he began to weepe' and 'he wept abundantly'. The members of the Oxford Company devised an appealing rendering, 'he fell a weeping', which forms a variation on the ideas found in most modern versions, 'he broke down and wept' and 'he burst into tears'. But the company's version, brilliant and appealing as it is, brings the sentence to a flat end. The Geneva Bible had supplied the translators with the idea of their striking ending, 'and waying that with him self, he wept'. In reworking this to 'when he thought thereon', the translators prepared a clause which fit their pattern of underlying rhythm and introduced the word 'thought' which completes 'called to minde' and intensifies Peter's act of will in having called to mind the word that Jesus said to him.

So moving forward word by word, the King's translators, 'building upon their foundation that went before us, and being holpen by their labours',[5] brought to pass a work which quickens even to this day mind and heart.

NOTES

1. Gerald Hammond, *The Making of the English Bible* (Manchester, 1982), 2.
2. Stephen Prickett, *Words and* The Word (Cambridge, 1986; rpt. 1988), 7.
3. Hammond, 2.
4. For other specimens, see Ward S. Allen, 'King James's Translators and Words on the Wing', in *Miscellanea Moreana Essays for Germain Marc'hadour,* ed. Clare M. Murphy, Henri Gibaud, and Mario A. Di Cesare (Binghamton, NY: 1989), 27–38.
5. From the preface to the Authorized Version, 'The Translators to the Reader', (1611, A6[r]).

The Collation

Bishops' Bible

The Gospel by S. Matthew

Annotation

The Gospel according to S. Matthew

Authorized Version

The Gospel according to S. Matthew

The first Chapter.

[Delete]
1 *†This is† the booke of the generation of Jesus Christ the sonne of
*David, the sonne of Abraham.

and and
2 *Abraham begate Isahac, Isahac begate Jacob, Jacob begate Judas &
*his brethren.

And & &
3 * Judas begate Phares and Zara of Thamar, Phares begat Esrom, Esrom
*begat Aram.

And & &
4 * Aram begate Aminadab, Aminadab begate Naasson, Naasson begate Salmon.

And and &
5 * Salmon begate Boos of Rachab, Boos begate Obed of Ruth, Obed begate Jesse.

And and
6 * Jesse begate David the King, David the King begate Solomon,

and that had bene Urieas
* of her †that was† the wife of †Urie.†
[Delete]

And & &
7 * Solomon begate Roboam, Roboam begate Abia, Abia begate Asa.

And & &
8 * Asa begate Josaphat, Josaphat begat Joram, Joram begate Ozias.

And & & Ezekias
9 * Ozias begat Joatham, Joatham begate Achas, Achas begate †Ezecias.†

And Ezekias & &
10 * †Ezecias† begate Manasses, Manasses begate Amon, Amon begate Josias.

And ♣Josias
11 * "Josias begate Jechonias and his brethren, about the time they were caried
"Josias

*away to Babylon.

♣Some read Josias begat Jacim & Jacim begate Jechonias
"Some read Josias begat Jacim, Jacim begate Jechonias
"Some read, Josias begate Jakim, and Jakim begate Jechonias

&
12 *And after they were brought to Babylon, Jechonias begate Salathiel, Salathiel

*begate Zorobabel.

And And And
13 * Zorobabel begate Abiud, Abiud begate Eliacim, Eliacim

*begate Azor.

And & Achim & Achim
14 * Azor begate Sadoc, Sadoc begate †Achen,† †Achen† begate Eliud.

And & &
15 * Eliud begate Eleazar, Eleazar begate Matthan, Matthan begate Jacob.

And
16 * Jacob begate Joseph the husband of Marie, of whom was borne Jesus,

whoe
*†that† is called Christ.

[Delete]
17 *†And† so all the generations from Abraham to David, are fourteene
*generations: and from David untill the carying away into Babylon, are foureteene
*generations: and from the carying away into Babylon unto Christ, are foureteene
*generations.

Now
18 * The birth of Jesus Christ was on this wise. When as his mother Mary was
*†betrothed† to Joseph (before they came together) shee was found with childe of the
espoused
*holy Ghost.

just
19 *Then Joseph her husband being a †righteous† man, and not willing to make
*her a publique example, was minded †privily† to put her †way.†
[Delete] away privily

20 *But while hee thought these things, beholde, the Angel of the Lord appeared
on
*unto him in a dreame, saying, Joseph thou sonne of David, feare not to
unto thee
*take †unto thee† Mary thy wife, for that which is conceived in her, is of the
*holy Ghost.

And
21 * She shall bring foorth a sonne, and thou shalt call his Name Jesus:
*for hee shall save his people from their sinnes.

Now
22 *(All this was done, that it might be fulfilled, which was spoken of the
*Lord by the Prophet, saying,

23 *Behold, a Virgin shalbe with childe, and shall bring foorth a sonne,
beeing translated, is
♣they beeing interpreted, is
*and they shall call his Name Emmanuel, which †is by interpretation,†
"they
*God with us.)

♣Or, thou shalt call Etc
"Or, his Name shall be called

24 *Then Joseph, being raised from sleepe, did as the Angel of the Lord had

tooke unto him
*bidden him, and †he tooke† his wife:

25 *And knewe her not, till shee had brought foorth her first borne sonne,

*and called his Name Jesus.
he

The ii. Chapter.

Now [Delete]
1 * When Jesus was borne in Bethlehem, †a citie† of †Jurie,† in the dayes
Judea

*of Herode the King: beholde, there came wise men from the East to Hierusalem,

2 *Saying, Where is hee that is borne King of the Jewes? For wee have seene

*his Starre in the East, and are come to worship him.

[Delete] these things
3 *When Herode the King †had† heard †these things,† he was troubled,
had

[Delete]
*and all †the citie of† Hierusalem with him.

4 *And when hee had gathered all the chiefe Priests & Scribes of the people

*together, hee demaunded of them where Christ should be borne.

In of
5 *And they said unto him, †At† Bethlehem †in† †Jurie:† For thus it is written by
Judea

*the Prophet,

[Delete]
6 *And thou Bethlehem †in the† land of Juda, art not the least among the
in the

[Delete] Governour
*Princes of Juda: For out of thee shall †there† come a †captaine,†

rule
*that shall †governe† my people Israel.
"rule

"Or, feed

7 *Then Herode, when he had privily called the wise men, enquired of them diligently

*what time the Starre appeared:

8 *And he sent them to Bethlehem, and said, Goe, and search diligently for the yong

*childe, and when ye have found him, bring me word againe, that I may come and worship

*him also.

9 *When they had heard the King, they departed, and lo, the Starre which they saw in

[Delete]
*the East, went before them, till it came and stood over †the place†

where
*†wherein† the yong childe was.

10 *When they saw the Starre, they rejoyced †exceedingly with† great joy,
with exceeding

♣found
11 *And †went† into the house, †and† they †sawe† the yong
when they were come [Delete] saw

*childe with Mary his mother, and fell downe, and worshipped him: and when they

offered
*had opened their treasures, †presented† unto him gifts, golde, and
they "presented

*frankincense, and myrrhe.

♣Or, sawe
"Or, offered

being
12 *And †after they were† warned of God in a dreame that they should not returne

*to Herode, they departed into their owne countrey another way.

13 * When they were departed, behold, the Angel of the Lord †appeared† to Joseph
And appeareth

*in a dreame, saying, Arise, and take the yong childe, and his mother, and flee

untill [Delete]
*into Egypt, & be thou there †till† I bring thee word: for †it will come

will
*to passe, that† Herod †shall† seeke the yong childe, to destroy him.

14 *When hee arose, hee tooke the yong childe and his mother by night, and
*departed into Egypt:

untill
15 *And was there †unto† the death of Herode, that it might bee fulfilled which
*was spoken of the Lord by the Prophet, saying, Out of Egypt have I called
*my sonne.

16 *Then Herode, when hee saw that he was mocked of the wise men, was exceeding wroth,
*and sent foorth, and slewe all the children that were in Bethlehem, and in all the
from
*coastes thereof, †as many as were† two yeres old and under, according to the time,
*which hee had diligently †searched out† of the wise men.
enquired

17 *Then was fulfilled that which was spoken by Jeremie the Prophet, saying,

18 *In Rama was there a voyce heard, lamentation, weeping, and great mourning, Rachel
and

are
*weeping for her children, and would not be comforted, because they †were† not.

19 *But when Herode was dead, beholde, an Angel of the Lord appeareth in a dreame
*to Joseph in Egypt,

20 *Saying, Arise, and take the yong childe and his mother, and goe into the land
*of Israel: For they are dead, which sought the yong childs life.

21 *And hee arose, and tooke the yong childe and his mother, and came into the lande
*of Israel.

22 *But when hee heard that Archelaus did reigne in †Jury† in the roome of his father
Judea

being
*Herod, he was afraid to goe thither: notwithstanding, †after he was† warned of God
*in a dreame, he turned aside into the parts of Galilee:

he came and [Delete]
23 *And †when he was come thither, he† dwelt in a city, †which is† called
*Nazareth, that it might be fulfilled which was spoken by the Prophets, He shall
*be called a †Nazarite.†
Nazarene

The iii. Chapter.

1 *In those dayes came John the Baptist, preaching in the wildernesse of †Jury,†
Judea

2 *And saying, Repent ye: for the kingdom of heaven is at hand.

3 *For this is hee that was spoken of by the Prophet Esaias, saying, The voyce of one
*crying in the wildernes, Prepare ye the way of the Lord, make his paths straight.

And the same John
And John him self girdle of skyn
4 *†This John† had his raiment of camels haire, and a †leatherne girdle†
And the same John leatherne girdle

and
*about his loynes, his meate was locusts and wilde hony.

5 *Then went out to him Hierusalem, and all †Jury,† and all the region rounde
Judea
*about Jordane,

6 *And were baptized of him in Jordane, confessing their sinnes.

7 *But when he saw many of the Pharisees and Sadducees come to his Baptisme, he saide
generations wrath
*unto them, O †generation† of vipers, who hath warned you to flee from the †anger†
generation
*to come?

♣worthy
8 *Bring foorth therefore fruits †meete for† repentance.
"meete for

♣Or, answearable to amendment of life
"Or, answerable to amendement of life

seeme not to
9 *And †be not of such minde, that ye would† say within your selves, We have
thinke not to

*Abraham to our father: For I say unto you, that God is able of these stones to

*raise up children unto Abraham.

And now even the axe is layd
And now also the axe is layd
10 *†Even now is the axe also put† unto the root of the trees: Therefore every tree

*which bringeth not foorth good fruit, is hewen downe, and cast into the fire.

indeede with
11 *I baptize you †in† water unto repentance: but he that commeth

stronger
*after me, is †mightier† then I, whose shooes I am not worthy to beare, he shall
mightier

*baptize you with the holy Ghost and with fire.

his
12 *Whose fanne is in his hand, and he will throughly purge †the† floore, & gather

the he will burne fire unquenchable
*his wheate into †his† garner: but †will burne up† the chaffe with †unquenchable fire.†
will burne up unquenchable fire

13 *Then commeth Jesus from Galilee to Jordane, unto John, to be baptized of him:

14 *But John forbade him, saying, I have neede to be baptized of thee, and commest

*thou to me?

[Delete]
And it to be so
15 * Jesus answering, said unto him, Suffer †it to be so† now: for thus it

*becommeth us to fulfill all righteousnesse. Then he suffered him.

came
16 *And Jesus, when he was baptized, †went† up straight way out of the water:
went

hee
*and loe, the heavens were opened unto him, and †John† saw the Spirit of God

*descending like a dove, and lighting upon him.

17 *And loe, †there came† a voyce from †the heavens,† saying, This is
[Delete] heaven

[Delete]
*my †dearly† beloved sonne, in whom I am well pleased.

The iiii. Chapter.

away the
1 *Then was Jesus led †up† of the Spirit into wildernesse, to be tempted
up

*of the devil.

2 *And when he had fasted fourtie dayes and fourtie nights, hee was afterward

*an hungred.

3 *And when the tempter came to him, hee said, If thou be the Sonne of God,

*commaund that these stones be made bread.

alone
4 *But hee answered, and saide, It is written, Man shall not live by bread †onely,†

*but by every word that proceedeth out of the mouth of God.

5 *Then the devill taketh him up into the holy Citie, and setteth him on a

*pinacle of the Temple,

6 *And saith unto him, If thou be the Sonne of God, cast thy selfe downe: For

[Delete] concerning
*it is written, †that† he shall give his Angels charge †over† thee,

in beare
*and †with† their handes they shall †lift† thee up, lest at any time thou

*dash thy foote against a stone.

7 *Jesus said unto him, It is written againe, Thou shalt not tempt the

*Lord thy God.

8 *Againe the devill taketh him up into an exceeding high mountaine, & sheweth

*him all the kingdoms of the world, & the glory of them:

9 *And sayth unto him, All these things will I give thee, if thou wilt fall

*downe and worhip mee.

Avoyde
Get thee [Delete]
10 *Then sayeth Jesus unto him, †Get thee† hence †behinde mee,† Satan:

*for it is written, Thou shalt worship the Lord thy God, and him onely shalt thou serve.

[Delete]
11 *Then the devill leaveth him, and beholde, †the† angels came and ministred

*unto him.

Now
12 * When Jesus had heard that John was "delivered up, he departed into Galilee,
"cast into prison

"That is, cast in prison
"Or, delivered up

13 *And †when he had left† Nazareth, he †went† and dwelt in Capernaum, which
leaving came

[Delete]
*is †a citie† upon the Sea coast, in the borders of Zabulon and Nephthali:

14 *That it might be fulfilled which was spoken by Esaias the Prophet, saying,

15 *The lande of Zabulon, and the lande of Nephthali, †by† the way of the Sea
by

*beyond Jordane, Galilee of the Gentiles.

16 *The people which sate in darkenesse, sawe great light: and to them which sate

*in the region and shadow of death, light is sprung up.

17 *From that time Jesus began to preach, and to say, Repent, for the kingdome of

*heaven is at hand.

[Delete]
18 *And Jesus walking by the Sea of Galilee, sawe two brethren, Simon, †which was†

*called Peter, and Andrew his brother, casting a net into the sea (for they

*were fishers)

Come ye after me
19 *And he sayth unto them, †Follow me:† and I will make you fishers of men.
Follow me

20 *And they straightway left their nets, and followed him.

21 *And †when he was gone forth† from thence, he saw other two brethren, James
going on

*the sonne of Zebedee, and John his brother, in †the† ship with Zebedee their father,
a

*mending their nets: and he called them.

22 *And they immediatly left the ship and their father, and followed him.

23 *And Jesus went about all Galilee, teaching in their Synagogues, and preaching

*the Gospel of the kingdome, and healing all maner of sicknesse, and all maner

*of disease among the people.

24 *And his fame †spread abroad† thorowout all Syria: and they brought unto him all
went

torments
*sicke people that were taken with divers diseases, and †gripings,† and those

*which were possessed with devils, & those which were lunatike, and those that

*had the palsie, and he healed them.

25 *And there followed him great multitudes of people, from Galilee, and from

[Delete]
*Decapolis, and from Hierusalem, and from †Jury,† and from †the regions that lye†
Judea

*beyond Jordane.

The v. Chapter.

And seeing multitudes
1 *†When hee sawe† the †multitude,† hee went up into a mountaine: and when hee was

*set, his disciples came unto him.

he and
2 *And †when he had† opened his mouth, †he† taught them, saying,

3 *Blessed are the poore in spirit: for theirs is the kingdome of heaven.

4 *Blessed are they that mourne: for they shall be comforted.

5 *Blessed are the meeke: for they shall inherite the earth.

6 *Blessed are they which doe hunger and thirst †after† righteousnesse:
after

filled
*for they shall be †satisfied.†

7 *Blessed are the mercifull: for they shall obtaine mercie.

8 *Blessed are the pure in heart: for they shal see God.

9 *Blessed are the peacemakers: for they shall be called the children of God.

10 *Blessed are they which †have beene† persecuted for righteousnesse sake:
are

*for theirs is the kingdome of heaven.

11 *Blessed are ye, when †men† shall revile you, and persecute you, and †lying,†
men you [Delete]

*shall say all maner of evill †saying† against you, for my sake.
[Delete] "falsely

"Gr. lying

[Delete] exceeding
12 *Rejoyce †ye† and be glad: for great is your reward in heaven.

*For so persecuted they the Prophets which were before you.

become savourlesse wherewith
13 *Yee are the salt of the earth: But if the salt †become unsavory,† †wherein†
have lost his savour

*shal it be salted? It is thenceforth good for nothing, but to be cast out, and

*to be troden under foot of men.

14 *Ye are the light of the world. A citie that is set on an hill, cannot be hid.

15 *Neither doe men light a candle, and put it under a bushell: but on a

*candlesticke, and it giveth light unto all that are in the house.

16 *Let your light so shine before men, that they may see your good works, and

*glorifie your father which is in heaven.

17 *Thinke not that I am come to destroy the law or the Prophets. I am not come

*to destroy, but to fulfill.

For verily
For verily
18 *†For truely† I say unto you, Till heaven and earth passe, one iote

[Delete] in no wise passe
*or †one† title †of the lawe† shall †not scape,†
one [Delete] from the Law

*till all be fulfilled.

19 *Whosoever therefore shall breake one of these least commandements, and shall

*teach men so, hee shall be called the least in the kingdome of heaven: but

[Delete]
*whosoever shall doe and teach †so,† the same shall be called great in the
them

*kingdome of heaven.

20 *For I say unto you, Except your righteousnesse shall exceede the righteousnesse
That

*of the Scribes and Pharises, ye shall in no case enter into the kingdome of

*heaven.

♣to and
21 *Ye have heard, that it was sayd to them of old time, Thou shalt not kill:
"by

shall kille liable to
*whosoever †killeth,† shalbe †in danger of† judgement.
in danger of the

♣Or, by them of old tyme
"Or, to them

22 *But I say unto you, That whosoever is angry with his brother †unadvisedly,†
without a cause

liable to
*shall be †in danger of† judgement: And whosoever shall say †unto†
in danger of the to

liable to
*his brother, †Racha,† shall be †in daunger of† †a† counsell: but whosoever shall
Racha in danger of the

liable to
*say, Thou foole, shalbe †in danger of† hell fire.
in danger of

offerest at
23 *Therefore if thou †bring† thy gift †to† the altar, and there remembrest
bring to

*that thy brother hath ought against thee:

24 *Leave there thy gift before the altar, and goe thy way, first be reconciled

*to thy brother, and then come and offer thy gift.

25 *Agree with thine adversary quickely, whiles thou art in the way with him:

*least at any time the adversary deliver thee to the judge, and the judge deliver

officer [Delete]
*thee to the †minister,† and †then† thou be cast into prison.

26 *Verely I say unto thee, thou shalt by no meanes come out thence, till thou

*hast payd the uttermost farthing.

27 *Ye have heard that it was said †unto† them of olde time, Thou shalt not
by

*commit adulterie.

28 *But I say unto you, That whosoever looketh on a woman to lust after her, hath

*committed adultery with her already in his heart.

And ♣offend
29 * If thy right eye offend thee, pluck it out, and cast it from thee: For
"offend

*it is profitable for thee that one of thy members should perish, and not

*that thy whole body should be cast into hell.

♣Or, Doe cause the to offende
"Or, do cause thee to offend

30 *And if thy right hand offend thee, cut it off, and cast it from thee: For

*it is profitable for thee that one of thy members should perish, and

thy whole
*not that †all thy† body should be cast into hell.

shall
31 *It hath beene sayd, Whosoever †will† put away his wife, let him give her

*a writing of divorcement.

shall saving for the cause of
32 *But I say unto you, That whosoever †doth† put away his wife, †except it be for†

shall marie
*fornication, causeth her to commit adultery: and whosoever †marieth†

*her that is divorced, committeth adultery.

33 *Againe, ye have heard that it hath beene sayd †unto† them of old time, Thou
by

*shalt not forsweare thy selfe, but shalt performe unto the Lord thine othes.

34 *But I say unto you, Sweare not all, neither by heaven, for it is
at

throne
*Gods †seate:†

35 *Nor by the earth, for it is his footestoole: neither by Hierusalem, for it

*is the citie of the great king.

36 *Neither shalt thou sweare by thy head, because thou canst not make one

*haire white or blacke.

37 *But let your communication be Yea, yea: Nay, nay: For whatsoever is more then these,

*commeth of evill.

38 *Ye have heard that it hath bene sayd, An eye for an eye, and a tooth for

*a tooth.

shall smite thee
39 *But I say unto you, that ye resist not evil: but whosoever †will give thee a blowe†

*on thy right cheeke, turne to him the other also.

40 *And if any man will sue thee at the lawe, and take away thy coat, let him have
*thy cloake also.

shall
41 *And whosoever †will† compell thee to goe a mile, goe with him twaine.
42 *Give to him that asketh thee: and from him that would borowe of thee, turne
*not thou away.
43 *Yee have heard that it hath beene sayde, Thou shalt love thy neighbour, and hate
*thine enemie:
44 *But I say unto you, Love your enemies, blesse them that curse you, doe good to

dispitefully use
*them that hate you, pray for them which †hurt† you,
and

*and persecute you:
45 *That ye may be the children of your father which is in heaven: for hee maketh
*his sunne to rise on the evill and on the good, and sendeth raine on the just and on
*the unjust.

even
46 *For if yee love them which love you, what reward have ye? Doe not the

doe [Delete]
*Publicanes †even† the same?
[Delete]

♣brethren
47 *And if yee salute your brethren onely, what †singular thing doe yee?†
doe you more <u>then</u> <u>others</u>

even doe so
*Doe not †also† the Publicanes †likewise?†
[Delete]

♣Or, <u>frendes</u>

48 *†Ye shall therefore be† perfect, even as your father which is in heaven
Be ye therefore

*is perfect.

The vi. Chapter.

[Delete]
1 *Take heede that yee doe not your almes before men, to †the intent that ye would†

*be seene of them, †or els† ye have no reward of your father which is in heaven.
otherwise "of

♣Or, give not your almes [Cancelled]
"Or, with

sounde
2 *Therfore, when thou doest thine almes, doe not †blowe† a trumpet before thee,
"doe

the
*as hypocrites doe, in the Synagogues, & in the streetes, that they

may have glory received
*†might be esteemed† of men. Verely, I say unto you, they have
[Delete]

*their reward.

"Or, cause not a trumpet to be sounded

3 *But when thou doest almes, let not thy left hand know, what thy right doeth:

4 *That thine almes may be in secret: And thy father which seeth in secret,

repay
*himselfe shall †reward† thee openly.
reward

5 *And when thou prayest, thou shalt not be as the hypocrites are: for they

stand and pray
*love to †pray standing† in the Synagogues, and in the corners of the streets,
pray standing

received
*that they may be seene of men. Verely I say unto you, they have
[Delete]

[Delete]
their
*†their† reward.

thou
6 *But when thou prayest, enter into thy closet, and when thou hast

*shut thy doore, pray to thy father which is in secret, and thy father which

repay
*seeth in secret, shall †reward† thee openly.
reward

use not vaine repetitions
7 *But when yee pray, †babble not much,† as the heathen doe.

*For they thinke that they shall be heard, for their much †babblings sake.†
speaking

8 *Be not yee therefore like unto them: For your father knoweth what things

*ye have need of, before ye aske †of† him.
[Delete]

[Delete]
9 *After this manner therefore pray ye: †O† our father which art in heaven,

*hallowed be thy name.

as in heaven, so also in
[Delete] in earth, as it is in
10 *†Let† thy kingdome come, Thy wil be done, †as well in earth, as it is in

earth
heaven
*heaven.†

11 *Give us this day our daily bread.

12 *And forgive us our debts, as wee forgive our debters.

13 *And lead us not into temptation, but deliver us from evill: for thine is the

*kingdome, and the power and the glory, for ever, Amen.

will
14 *For, if yee forgive men their trespasses, your heavenly father †shall†

*also forgive you.

neither will
15 *But, if yee forgive not men their trespasses: †no more shall† your

[Delete]
*father forgive †you† your trespasses.

as the hypocrites of a sad countenaunce
16 *Moreover, when ye fast, be not †of an heavie countenance, as the hypocrites are:†

may
*for they disfigure their faces, that they †might† appeare unto men to fast:

[Delete]
received their
*Verely I say unto you, they have †their† reward.
[Delete]

17 *But thou, when thou fastest, anoint thine head, and wash thy face:

18 *That thou appeare not unto men to fast, but unto thy father which is in secrete:

repay
*and thy father which seeth in secret, shall †reward† thee openly.
reward

Lay
19 *†Hoard† not up for your selves treasures upon earth, where moth and rust doth

digge
breake
*corrupt, and where theeves †breake† thorowe, and steale.

yourselves
20 *But lay up for †you† treasures in heaven, where neither moth nor rust

digge
breake
*doeth corrupt, and where theeves do not †breake† thorow, nor steale.

21 *For where your treasure is, there wil your heart be also.

light If therefore
22 *The †candle† of the body is the eye: †wherefore if† thine eye be single,

thy whole
*†all thy† bodie shalbe full of light.

thy whole
23 *But if thine eye bee †wicked,† †all thy† bodie shall be full of darkenesse.
evil

*†Wherefore, if† the light that is in thee be darkenesse, howe great is that
If therefore

*darknesse?

will
24 *No man can serve two masters: for either hee †shall† hate the one and love

will stick
will stick
*the other, or els he †shall leane† to the one and despise the other. Ye
will hold

*cannot serve God, and Mammon.

Take no thought
25 *Therefore I say unto you, †Be not carefull† for your life, what ye shall eate

what ye shall
*or drinke, nor yet for your body what yee shall put on: Is

[Delete]
*not the life more †worth† then meate? and the bodie then rayment?

26 *Beholde the foules of the ayre: for they sowe not, neither doe they reape,

gather and
*nor †cary† into barnes, †yet† your heavenly father feedeth them. Are ye
yet

*not much better then they?

[Delete]
27 *Which of you by taking †of carefull† thought, can adde one cubite unto

*his stature?

take ye thought Consider
28 *And why †care yee† for raiment? †Learne of† the Lilies of the fielde, howe

toyle not doe they
*they growe: they †wearie not themselves with labour,† neither †doe they† spinne.

glory
29 *And yet I say unto you, that even Solomon in all his †royaltie,† was not

*arayed like one of these.

is to day, and to morrow
to day is, and to morrow
30 *Wherefore, if God so cloath the grasse of the field, which †though it stand to day,

is furnace
is oven clothe
*is to morrow† cast into the †oven:† shall hee not much more †doe the same for†

*you, O ye of little faith?

31 *Therefore take no thought, saying, What shall we eat? or, what shall we drinke?

what we shall put on
what shall we put on
*or, †wherwithall shall we be clothed?†
wherewithall shall we be clothed

32 *(For after all these things do the Gentiles seeke:) for your heavenly father

*knoweth that ye have neede of all these things.

33 *But seeke yee first the kingdome of God, and his righteousnesse, and all these

*things shall be added unto you.

Take therefore no thought for
Take therefore no thought
34 *†Care not then† for the morow: for the morowe shall

take thought for the things of
*†care for† it selfe: Sufficient unto the day, is the evill

*thereof.

The vii. Chapter.

[Delete]
1 *Judge †yee† not, that ye be not judged.

2 *For with what judgement ye judge, yee shalbe judged: and with what measure yee

*mete, it shall be measured to you againe.

And beholdest
3 * Why †seest† thou the mote that is in thy brothers eye, but †perceivest†
considerest

*not the beame that is in thine owne eye?

Suffer me, I will pul out the
Let me pul out the
4 *Or how wilt thou say to thy brother, †Suffer me, I will cast out a† mote

a
*out of thine eye: and behold, †the† beame is in thine owne eye?

pul out first
5 *Thou hypocrite, †first cast out† the beame out of thine owne eye: and then shalt
first cast out

pull out of
*thou see clearely to †cast† out the mote †that is in† thy brothers eye.
cast

that
6 *Give not †that† which is holy unto the dogs, neither cast ye your pearls

[Delete] trample
*before †the† swine: lest they †tread† them under their feete,

turn and [Delete]
*and †turning† againe, †all to† rent you.

[Delete]
7 *Aske †ye,† and it shall be given you: seeke, and ye shall find:

*knocke, and it shall be opened unto you.

8 *For every one that asketh, receiveth: and hee that seeketh, findeth: and to him

*that knocketh, it shall be opened.

Or
9 * What man is there of you, if his sonne aske bread, will give
whom hee

*him a stone?

a
10 *Or if hee aske fish, will he give him a serpent?

how to give good gifts unto your children
11 *If ye then being evill, know †to give your children good gifts:†

shall
*how much more †will† your father which is in heaven, give good things

*to them that aske him?

12 *Therfore all things whatsoever ye would that men should doe to you, doe yee

*even so to them: For this is the law and the Prophets.

13 *Enter ye in at the strait gate, for wide is the gate, and broad is the way that

enter by it
*leadeth to destruction, and many there bee which †goe in thereat.†
goe in thereat

14 *Because strait is the gate, and narrowe is the way which leadeth unto life,
"Because

*and fewe there be that find it.

"Or, how

[Delete]
15 *Beware of †the† false prophets which come to you in sheepes cloathing,

*but inwardly they are ravening wolves.

16 *Ye shall know them by their fruits: Doe men gather grapes of thorns? or figs of

*thistles?

17 *Even so, every good tree bringeth foorth good fruit: but a corrupt tree

*bringeth forth evil fruite.

evil corrupt
18 *A good tree cannot bring forth †bad† fruite, neither can a †bad† tree

*bring forth good fruite.

19 *Every tree that bringeth not forth good fruit, is hewen downe and cast

*into the fire.

20 *Wherefore, by their fruits ye shall knowe them.

21 *Not every one that sayth unto me, Lord, Lord, shall enter into the

*kingdome of heaven: but hee that doth the will of my father which is in

*heaven.

in
22 *Many will say to me in that day, Lorde, Lord, have we not prophecied †through†

in
*thy name? and †through† thy name have cast out devils? and

in thy name done many wonderfull workes
*†done many great workes through thy name?†

professe [Delete]
23 *And then wil I †confesse† unto them, †That† I never knewe you: Depart

[Delete]
*from me †all† yee that worke iniquitie.

these sayings of mine them
24 *Therefore, whosoever heareth †of mee these sayings,† and doeth †the same,†

*I will liken him unto a wise man, which built his house upon a rocke:

streames
25 *And the raine descended, and the †floods† came, and the windes blew, and beat
floods

for it was founded upon
*upon that house: and it fell not, †because it was grounded† †on† a rocke.

these sayings of mine
26 *And every one that heareth †of me these sayings,† and doth them not, shall be

*likened unto a foolish man, which built his house upon the sand:

streames
27 *And the raine descended, and the †floods† came, and the windes blew, and beat
floods

*upon that house, and it fell, and great was the fall of it.

28 *And it came to passe, when Jesus had ended these sayings, the people

astonished
*were †astonied† at his doctrine.

authoritye
29 *For he taught them as one having †power,† and not as the Scribes.

The viii. Chapter.

1 *When he was come downe from the mountaine, great multitudes followed him.

2 *And beholde, there came a leper, and worshipped him, saying, Lord, If thou

*wilt, thou canst make me cleane.

[Delete] and
3 *And Jesus, †when hee had† put foorth his hand, touched him,

*saying, I wil, be thou clean. And immediatly his leprosie was cleansed.

thy way
4 *And Jesus sayth unto him, See thou tell no man, but goe , shewe

*thy selfe to the priest, and offer the gift that Moses commaunded, for

testimonye
*a †witnesse† unto them.

5 *And when Jesus was entred into Capernaum, there came unto him a Centurion,

*beseeching him,

6 *And saying, Lorde, my servant lyeth at home sicke of the palsie,

tormented
*grievously †pained.†

unto I will come, and
7 *And Jesus sayth †to† him, †When I come, I will† heale him.

8 *The Centurion answered, and said, Lord, I am not worthy that thou shouldest

*come under my roofe: but speake the word only, and my servant shall be healed.

[Delete] [Delete]
9 *For I †also† †my selfe† am a man †set† under authority,
[Delete]

*having souldiers under me: and I say to this man, Goe, and he goeth: and to

*another, Come, and he commeth: and to my servant, Do this, and he doeth it.

it
10 *When Jesus heard †these things,† he marveiled, and sayd to them that followed,

*Verely, I say unto you, I have not found so great faith, no not in Israel.

But
11 * I say unto you, that many shal come from the East and West, and
And

be sett
*shall †rest† with Abraham, and Isahac, and Jacob, in the kingdome of heaven:
sit downe

outer
12 *But the children of the kingdome shalbe cast out into †utter† darknesse:

*there shall be weeping and gnashing of teeth.

13 *And Jesus sayd unto the Centurion, Goe thy way, and as thou hast beleeved,

*so be it done unto thee. And his servant was healed in the selfe same houre.

14 *And when Jesus was come into Peters house, he sawe his wives mother layd, and

*sicke of a fever:

15 *And he touched her hand, and the fever left her: and she arose, and ministred

*unto them.

16 *When the Even was come, they brought unto him many that were possessed with
*devils: and he cast out the spirits with †a† word, and healed all that were sicke,
his
17 *That it might be fulfilled which was spoken by Esaias the Prophet, saying,
[Delete]
*†He† tooke †on him† our infirmities, and bare our sicknesses.
Himselfe
18 * When Jesus sawe great multitudes about him, he †commanded them†
Now gave commandement
*to depart unto the other side.
19 *And a certaine Scribe came, and sayd unto him, Master, I will follow thee
*whithersoever thou goest.
20 *And Jesus sayeth unto him, The Foxes have holes, and the birds of the ayre have
lie
lay
*nests: but the sonne of man hath not where to †rest† his head.
21 *And another of his disciples sayde unto him, Lorde, suffer me first to goe,
*and bury my father.
22 *But Jesus said unto him, Follow me, and let the dead bury their dead.
was
23 *And when he entred into a ship, his disciples followed him.
24 *And behold, there arose a great tempest in the Sea, in so much that the shippe
*was covered with the waves: but he was asleepe.
25 *And his disciples came to him, and awoke him, saying, Lord, save us: we perish.
26 *And he sayth unto them, Why are ye fearefull, O yee of little faith? Then
was
*he arose, and rebuked the windes and the sea, and there †followed† a great calme.
27 *But the men marveiled, saying, What maner of man is this, that

[Delete]
the
*†both† †the† winds and the sea obey him?
even

28 *And when he was come to the other side, into the countrey of the Gergesenes, there

tombes exceeding
*met him two possessed with devils, comming out of the †graves, very† fierce,

*†so† that no man might passe by that way.
so

29 *And behold, they cryed out, saying, †O Jesu, thou sonne of God, what have
What have we to doe with thee, Jesus

*we to do with thee?† Art thou come hither to torment us before the time?
thou Sonne of God

30 *And there was a good way off from them, an heard of many swine, feeding.

31 *So the devils besought him, saying, If thou cast us out, suffer us to goe

[Delete]
*away into the heard of †the† swine.

32 *And hee sayd unto them, Goe. †Then went they out, and departed†
And when they were come out, they went

[Delete]
*into the heard of †the† swine: and behold, the whole herd of †the†
[Delete]

violently from a steep place
*swine †rushed† †headlong† into the sea, and perished
ran violently downe a steepe place

*in the waters.

And fed
33 *†Then† they that †kept† them, fled, and went their wayes into the city, and
kept

befallen to of
*told every thing, and what was †done of† the possessed †with† the devils.

34 *And beholde, the whole city came out to meete Jesus: and when they saw him,

*they besought him that hee would depart out of their coasts.

The ix. Chapter.

1 *And he entred into a ship, and passed over, and came into his owne citie.

2 *And behold, they brought to him a man sicke of the palsie, lying †in† a bed:
on

*and †when Jesus sawe the faith of them, he† said unto the sicke of the palsie, Sonne,
Jesus seeing their faith

*be of good cheere, thy sinnes be forgiven thee.

3 *And behold, certaine of the Scribes sayd within themselves, This man blasphemeth.

4 *And †when Jesus saw† their thoughts, †he† sayd, Wherefore thinke ye
Jesus knowing [Delete]

*evill in your hearts?

For it
5 * Whether is easier to say, Thy sinnes be forgiven thee: or to
[Delete]

*say, Arise, and walke?

on earth to forgive
6 *But that yee may know that the sonne of man hath power †to forgive sinnes

sinnes sayth
*in earth† (Then †sayd† he to the sick of the palsie) Arise, take up thy bed, and

*goe unto thine house.

7 *And he arose, and departed to his house.

8 *But when the multitudes saw †it,† they marveiled and glorified God, which had
it

*given such power unto men.

9 *And as Jesus passed foorth from thence, he saw a man named Matthew, sitting

*at the receite of custome: and hee sayth unto him, Follow me. And he arose and

*followed him.

the
10 *And it came to passe, as Jesus sate at meat in †his† house, behold, many

[Delete]
*publicanes †also† and sinners came and sate downe with †Jesus†
him

*and his disciples.

11 *And when the Pharises saw it, they sayd unto his disciples, Why eateth your

*master with publicanes and sinners?

strong
12 *But when Jesus heard that, he sayd unto them, They that be †whole,†
whole

*neede not a Physicion, but they that are sicke.

But
13 * Goe ye and learne what that meaneth, I will mercie, and not
have

*sacrifice: for I am not come to call the righteous, but sinners to repentance.

to him the disciples of John
14 *Then came †the disciples of John unto him,† saying, Why doe we and the Pharises

*fast oft, but thy disciples fast not?

15 *And Jesus sayd unto them, Can the children of the bride chamber mourne, as

*long as the bridegrome is with them? But the dayes will come when the bridegrome

*shall be taken from them, and then shall they fast.

♣new cloth on
16 *No man putteth a piece of "new cloth †in† an old garment, for
"new cloth unto

that which should fill it up [Delete]
*†then the piece† taketh †away† †some thing† from
that which is put in to fill it up [Delete]

*the garment, and the rent is made worse.

♣Or, rawe cloth, or unwrought
"Or, rawe cloth
"Or, raw or unwrought cloth

17 *Neither doe men put new wine into olde bottels: els the bottels breake, and

*the wine runneth out, and the bottels †will† perish: but they put new
[Delete]

[Delete]
*wine into new bottels, and both are preserved †together.†

18 *While he spake these things unto them, behold, there came a certaine ruler

[Delete]
*†of the synagogue† and worshipped him saying, My daughter is even now dead:

*but come, and lay thy hand upon her and she shall live.

19 *And Jesus arose, and followed him, and so did his disciples.

20 *(And beholde, a woman which was diseased with an issue of blood twelve yeeres,

garment
*came behinde him, and touched the hemme of his †vesture.†

garment
21 *For shee sayd within her selfe, If I may †touch but even† his †vesture†
but touch

whole
*†onely,† I shall bee †safe.†
[Delete]

[Delete] when he
22 *But Jesus †when hee had† turned him about, and saw her,

he whole
* sayd, Daughter, bee of good comfort, thy faith hath made thee †safe.†

[Delete]
*And the woman was made whole from that †same† houre.

[Delete]
23 *And when Jesus came into the rulers house †of the synagogue,† and sawe

*the minstrels and the people making a noise,

Get you hence
24 *Hee sayd unto them, †Give place,† for the maide is not dead, but sleepeth.
Give place

*And they laughed him to scorne.

25 *But when the people were put foorth, he went in, & tooke her by the hand: and

*the maide arose.

this fame
26 *And †the fame of this† went abroad into all that land.
"the fame hereof

"Or, this fame

27 *And when Jesus departed thence, two blinde men followed him, crying, and

[Delete]
*saying, †O† thou sonne of David, have mercie on us.

28 *And when hee was come into the house, the blind men came to him: and Jesus sayth

*unto them, Beleeve ye that I am able to doe this? They sayd unto him, Yea, Lord.

29 *Then touched he their eyes, saying, According to your faith be it unto you.

30 *And their eyes were opened: and Jesus straightly charged them, saying, See

*that no man know †it.†
it

fame
31 *But they, when they were departed, spred abroad his †name† in all

*that †land.†
countrey

32 *As they went out, behold, they brought to him a dumbe man possessed with

*a devill.

33 *And when the devill was cast out, the dumbe spake, and the multitudes

*marveiled, saying, It was never so seene in Israel.

34 *But the Pharisees sayd, He casteth out the devils through the prince of the

*devils.

35 *And Jesus went about all the cities and villages, teaching in their Synagogues,

*and preaching the Gospell of the kingdome, and healing every sicknesse, and every

*disease among the people.

36 *But when hee saw the multitudes, hee was moved with compassion on them,

were faynt
*because they †were destitute,† and scattered abroade, as sheepe having no
"fainted were

*shepheard.

"Or, were tyred and lay downne

37 *Then sayth hee unto his disciples, The harvest truely is plenteous, but the

*labourers are fewe.

38 *Pray yee therefore the Lorde of the harvest, that he will †thrust† forth
send

*labourers into his harvest.

The x. Chapter.

unto him
1 *And when hee had called his twelve disciples, hee gave them

over
*power †against† uncleane spirits, to cast them out, and to heale all
"against

*maner of sickenesse, and all maner of disease.

"Or, over

Now whoe
2 * The names of the twelve Apostles are these: The first, Simon, †which†

the sonne
*is called Peter, and Andrew his brother, James †the sonne† of Zebedee, and

*John his brother:

the
3 *Philip, and Bartholomew, Thomas, and Matthew, †which had bene a† Publicane,

the sonne
*James †the sonne† of Alphee, & Lebbeus, whose surname was Taddeus:

the who
4 *Simon †the† Chanaanite, and Judas Iscariot, †which† also betrayed him.

these twelve Jesus sent foorth &
5 *†Jesus sent foorth these twelve, when hee had† commanded them, saying, Goe

any
*not into the way of the Gentiles, and into †the† citie of the Samaritanes enter ye

*not:

rather
6 *But goe †gather† to the lost sheepe of the house of Israel.

And
7 * As ye go, preach, saying, The kingdome of heaven is at hand.

8 *Heale the sicke, cleanse the lepers, raise the dead, cast out devils:

*freely ye have received, freely give.

Provide neither monye
9 *†Possesse not† gold, nor silver, nor brasse
"Provide neither [Delete]

to put into gird
for purses
*†in† your †purses:†
in

"Or, get

for
10 *Nor scrip †towards† your journey, neither two coates, neither shooes, nor

staves
*yet †a staffe:† (For the workeman is worthy of his meate.)

And into enter
11 *†But† †to† whatsoever citie or towne yee shall †come,† enquire who

in it is worthy
*†is worthy in it:† and there abide till ye goe thence.

12 *And when ye come into an house, salute †the same.†
it

13 *And if the house be worthy, let your peace come upon it: but if it be not

[Delete]
*worthy, let your peace returne to you †againe.†

[Delete] words
14 *And whosoever shall not receive you, nor †will† heare your †preaching:†

[Delete]
*when ye depart out of that house, or †that† citie, shake off the dust of

*your feete.

more tolerable
15 *Verily I say unto you, it shall be †easier† for the land

Sodom Gomorrha
*of †the Sodomites† and †Gomorrheans† in the day of judgement, then for that citie.

16 *Behold, I send you forth as sheepe in the midst of Woolves: be yee therefore

[Delete] ♣harmelesse [Delete]
*wise as †the† serpents, and harmelesse as †the† Doves.
"harmelesse

♣Or, innocent as [Cancelled]
♣Or, simple
"Or, simple

will
17 *But beware of men: for they †shall† deliver you up to the councels, and

they will
*†shall† scourge you in their Synagogues,

before governours
18 *And ye shall be brought †to the head rulers† and kings for my sake,

for a testimonye against [Delete]
*†in witnesse to† them, and †to† the Gentiles.

19 *But when they deliver you up, take †ye† no thought, how or what yee shall
[Delete]

*speake: for it shall be given you in that same houre what yee shall speake.

20 *For it is not yee that speake, but the spirit of your father,

[Delete]
[Delete] which
*†hee it is† †which† speaketh in you.

And
21 * The brother shall deliver up the brother to death, and the father the

childe child up parents, & cause them to
*†sonne:† the †children† shal rise against their †fathers and mothers,
and children

be put to death
*and shall put them to death.†

22 *And yee shall bee hated of all men for my names sake: but he that endureth

*to the ende, shall be saved.

one
23 *But when they persecute you in †this† city, flee ye into another: for verily
this

pass thorough fully
have gone over
*I say unto you, ye shall not †ende all† the cities of Israel,
"have gone over

*till the sonne of man be come.

"Or, end or finish

24 *The disciple is not above his master, nor the servant above his lord.

[Delete]
that he [Delete]
25 *It is enough for the disciple †that he† be as his master †is,†

[Delete] [Delete]
*and †that† the servant †be† as his lord †is.†
[Delete]

master
*If they have called the †the† †Lord† of the house Beelzebub, how much more
[Delete]

*shall they call them of his houshold?

covered
26 *Feare them not therefore: for there is nothing †close,† that shall not be

revealed
*†opened,† and †nothing† hid, that shall not be knowen.
[Delete]

27 *What I tell you in darkenesse, †that† speake ye in light: and what ye heare
that

upon
*in the eare, that preach ye †on† the †houses.†
house tops

[Delete]
28 *And feare †ye† not them which kill the bodie, but are not able to

soule and body
*kill the soule, But rather feare him which is able to destroy both †bodie and soule†

*in hell.

[Delete]
29 *Are not two †little† Sparrowes solde for a farthing? And one of them

fall
*shall not †light† on the ground without your father.

But the very all
30 *†Yea,† †even all the† haires of your head are numbred.

31 *Feare ye not therefore, ye are of more value then many Sparrowes.

Whosoever [Delete]
32 *†Every one† therefore †that† shall confesse me before men, him will

heaven
*I confesse also before my father, which is in †heavens.†

33 *But whosoever shall deny me before men, him will I also denie before my

heaven
*father, which is in †heavens.†

on
34 *Thinke not that I am come to send peace †into the† earth: I came not to send

*peace, but a sword.

35 *For I am come to set a man at variance against his father, and the

*daughter against her mother, and the daughter in law against her mother

*in law.

36 *And a mans foes shall be they of his owne houshold.

37 *Hee that loveth father or mother more then me, is not worthy of me: and he

*that loveth sonne or daughter more then me, is not worthy of mee.

after
38 *And hee that taketh not his crosse, and followeth me, is not

*worthy of me.

39 *Hee that findeth his life, shall lose it: and hee that loseth his life for my

*sake, shall finde it.

40 *He that receiveth you, receiveth me: and he that receiveth mee, receiveth him

*that sent mee.

41 *He that receiveth a Prophet in the name of a Prophet, shall receive a
*Prophets reward: and hee that receiveth a righteous man, in the name of a
*righteous man, shall receive a righteous mans reward.

unto one of these little ones a cup of cold water
unto one of these little ones a cup of cold water
42 *And whosoever shall give †unto one of these little ones to drinke a cup of
to drinke unto one of these little ones, a cup of

to drinke only
only to drinke
*cold water only,† in the name of a disciple, verily I say unto you, he shall in
cold water onely

*no wise lose his reward.

The xi. Chapter.

[Delete]
1 *And it came to passe, †that† when Jesus had made an end of commaunding
*his twelve disciples, he departed thence to teach and to preach in their cities.

Now
2 * When John had heard in the prison the workes of Christ, hee sent two
*of his disciples,

3 *And sayd unto him, Art thou hee that should come? Or doe we looke for another?

4 *Jesus answered, and sayd unto them, Goe and shew John againe those things
*which yee doe heare and see:

& the lame
5 *The blinde receive their sight, †the halt do† walke, the lepers are cleansed,
*& the deafe heare, the dead are raised up, and the poore have the Gospell preached
*to them.

blessed
6 *And †happie† is he, whosoever shal not be offended in me.

multitudes
7 *And as they departed, Jesus began to say unto the †multitude† concerning John,
*What went ye out into the wildernesse to see? a reede shaken with the winde?

But
8 *†Or† what went ye out for to see? A man clothed in soft raiment? Behold,

clothing
*they that weare soft †clothing,† are in kings houses.

9 *But what went ye out for to see? A Prophet? yea, I say unto you, and more

*then a prophet.

10 *For this is he of whom it is written, Behold, I send my messenger before

*thy face, which shall prepare thy way before thee.

11 *Verily I say unto you, Among them that are borne of women, there hath not

*risen a greater then John the Baptist: notwithstanding, he that is

least
*†lesse† in the kindgome of heaven, is greater then he.

And
12 * From the dayes of John the Baptist, untill nowe, the kingdome of heaven

take it by force
*suffereth violence, and the violent †plucke it unto them.†
"suffereth

"Or, is gotten by force, and they that thrust men

[Delete] untill
13 *For all the Prophets, and the law †it selfe,† prophecied †unto† John.

14 *And if yee will receive †it,† this is Elias which was for to come.
it

15 *Hee that hath eares to heare, let him heare.

[Delete]
16 *But whereunto shall I liken this generation? It is like unto †little†

*children, sitting in the markets, and calling unto their fellowes,

17 *And saying, We have piped unto you, and ye have not daunced: we have mourned

lamented
*unto you, and ye have not †sorrowed.†

18 *For John came neither eating nor drinking, and they say, He hath a devill.

19 *The sonne of man came eating and drinking, and they say, Behold, a man

[Delete] of
*gluttonous, and a wine bibber, †and† a friend †unto† publicanes and sinners:

is
*†and† wisedome †was† justified of her children.
but

20 *Then beganne he to upbraid the cities, wherein most of his mighty workes were

*done, because they repented not.

21 *Woe unto thee Chorazin, woe unto thee Bethsaida: for if the mightie workes

*which were done in you, had beene done in Tyre and Sidon, they would have repented

*long agoe in sackecloth and ashes.

more tolerable in
22 *But I say unto you, It shall be †easier† for Tyre and Sidon †at†
at

*the day of judgement, then for you.

23 *And thou Capernaum, which †hast beene lifted up into† heaven, shalt be brought
art exalted unto

*downe to hell: For if the mighty workes which have bene done in thee, had bene

in
*done †among them of† Sodome, †they† would have remained untill this day.
it

more tolerable
24 *But I say unto you, that it shall be †easier† for the land of Sodom,

*in the day of judgement, then for thee.

25 *At that time Jesus answered, and sayde, I thanke thee, O Father, Lorde of

*heaven and earth, because thou hast hid these things from the wise and prudent,

reveiled
*and hast †shewed† them unto babes.

[Delete] it seemed good in thy sight
26 *Even so, †O† Father, for so †was it thy good pleasure.†

27 *All things are †given† unto mee of my father: and no man knoweth the sonne,
delivered

*but the father: neither knoweth any man the father, save the sonne, and hee to

reveale him
*whomesoever the sonne will †open him.†

[Delete]
28 *Come unto me all ye that labour †sore,† and are laden, and
heavy

give you rest
*I will †ease you.†

29 *Take my yoke upon you, and learne of me, for I am meeke and lowly in heart:

*and yee shall find rest unto your soules.

30 *For my yoke is easie, and my burden is light.

The xii. Chapter.

1 *At that time, Jesus went on the Sabboth †dayes† thorow the corne, and his
day

*disciples were an hungred, and beganne to plucke the eares of corne, and to

*eate.

it
2 *But when the Pharises sawe †them,† they sayde unto him, Beholde, thy disciples

*doe that which is not lawfull to doe upon the Sabboth day.

3 *But he sayd unto them, Have ye not read what David did when hee was an

him self
[Delete]
*hungred , and they that were with him,

4 *How he entred into the house of God, and did eate the shewe bread, which was

*not lawfull for him to eat, neither for them which were with him, but only for

*the priests?

5 *Or have yee not read in the law, howe that on the Sabboth dayes the Priestes

*in the Temple profane the Sabboth, and are blamelesse?

6 *But I say unto you, that in this place is one greater then the temple.

7 *But if ye had known what this meaneth, I will mercie, and not sacrifice,
have

*yee would not have condemned the guiltlesse.

even
8 *For the sonne of man is Lord of the Sabboth day.

9 *And when he was departed thence, hee went into their Synagogue.

[Delete]
which had withered
10 *And behold, there was a man †which had† his hand †dryed up,† and

*they asked him, saying, Is it lawfull to heale on the Sabboth dayes? that

*they might accuse him.

shall there be among you
11 *And he sayd unto them, What man †of you will there be† that shall have

*one sheepe: and if it fall into a pit on the Sabboth day, will hee

lay on
*not †take† hold †of† it, and lift it out?

12 *How much †more† then is a man better then a sheepe? Wherefore it is
[Delete]

*lawfull to doe well on the Sabboth dayes.

13 *Then sayth he to the man, Stretch forth thine hand: and he stretched it

*forth, and it was restored whole, like as the other.

14 *Then the Pharises went out, and held a counsell against him, howe they might
"held a counsell

*destroy him.

"Or, tooke counsell

withdrew him self from
15 *But when Jesus knewe †it,† hee †departed† thence: and great
it

*multitudes followed him, and he healed them all,

16 *And charged them that they should not make him knowen:

17 *That it might be fulfilled which was spoken by Esaias the Prophet, saying,

servant
18 *Behold my †child† whome I have chosen, my beloved, in whom my soule

is well pleased
*†well delighteth:† I will put my spirit upon him, and he shall shew
*judgement to the Gentiles.
19 *Hee shall not strive, nor cry, neither shall any man heare his voyce
*in the streets.
20 *A bruised reede shall hee not breake, and smoking flaxe shall hee not quench,
*till hee send forth judgement unto victory.
21 *And in his name shall the Gentiles trust.
22 *Then was brought unto him one possessed with a devill, blind, and dumbe:
*and he healed him, in so much that the blinde and dumbe both spake and saw.
the
23 *And all the people were amazed, and said, Is †not† this †that†
[Delete]
*sonne of David?
24 *But when the Pharisees heard †it,† they sayd, This fellowe doth not cast
it
[Delete]
*out †these† devils, but by Beelzebub the prince of the devils.
And &
25 *†But when† Jesus knew their thoughts, †he† sayd unto them, Every kingdome divided
*against it selfe, is brought to desolation: and everie citie or house divided
*against it selfe, shall not stand.
26 *And if Satan cast out Satan, †then were he† divided against himselfe, how shall
he is
stand
*then his kingdome †endure?†
And
27 *†Also† if I by Beelzebub cast out devils, by whom doe your children cast them
*out? Therefore they shall be your Judges.

[Delete] no doubt
28 *But if I cast out †the† devils by the spirit of God, †then is†
then

is
*the kingdome of God come †upon† you.
unto

spoile his stuffe
rifle his stuffe
29 *Or else, howe can one enter into a strong mans house, and †spoile his goods,†
spoile his goods

he rifle
*except he first binde the strong man, and then will †spoile† his house?
spoile

30 *He that is not with me, is against me: and hee that gathereth not with mee,

*scattereth abroade.

31 *Wherefore I say unto you, All maner of sinne and blasphemie shalbe forgiven

Ghost
*unto men: but the blasphemie against the holy †spirit,† shall not be forgiven

*unto men.

32 *And whosoever speaketh a word against the sonne of man, it shall bee forgiven

*him: but whosoever speaketh against the holy Ghost, it shall not be forgiven him,

*neither in this world, neither in the world to come.

corrupt
33 *Either make the tree good, and his fruit good: Or else make the tree †evil,†

corrupt
*and his fruit †evill:† For the tree is knowen by his fruit.

being evill
34 *O †generations† of vipers, howe can yee speake good things,
generation

[Delete]
*†when ye your selves are evill?† For out of the abundance of the heart

*the mouth speaketh.

35 *A good man out of the good treasure of the heart, bringeth forth good things:

*and an evill man out of the evill treasure, bringeth forth evill things.

[Delete]
36 *But I say unto you, That †of† every idle word that men shall speake,

*they shall give account thereof in the day of judgement.

by by
37 *For †of† thy words thou shalt bee justified, and †of† thy words thou shalt

*be condemned.

[Delete]
38 *Then certaine of the Scribes, and of the Pharises, answered †him,†

would from
*saying, Master, we †will† see a signe †of† thee.

39 *But he answered, and sayd to them, An evill and adulterous generation seeketh

after
* a signe, and there shall no signe be given to it, but the signe of the

*Prophet Jonas.

40 *For as Jonas was three dayes and three nights in the Whales belly: so shall

*the sonne of man be three daies and three nights in the heart of the earth.

up [Delete]
41 *The men of Nineve shall rise in †the† judgement with this
[Delete]

generation shall
*†nation,† and condemne it, because they repented at the preaching

more then Jonas is here
*of Jonas, and behold, †here is one greater then Jonas.†
a greater then Jonas is here

up [Delete]
42 *The Queene of the South shall rise in †the† judgement with this
the

*generation, and shall condemne it: for she came from the uttermost parts of the

more then Solomon is
*earth to heare the wisedome of Solomon, and behold, †in this place is one
a greater then Solomon is

here
*greater then Solomon.†
here

it thorow
43 *When the uncleane spirit is gone out of a man, †he† walketh †thorowout†
hee

*drie places seeking rest, and findeth none.

it
44 *Then †he† sayth, I will returne into my house from whence I came out. And when
he

*hee is come, he findeth it empty, swept and garnished.

more wicked
45 *Then goeth he, and taketh with himselfe seven other spirits †worse†

*then himself, and they enter in, and dwell there: And the last state of

wicked
*that man is worse then the first. Even so shall it be also unto this †froward†

*generation.

46 *While he yet talked to the people, behold, his mother and his brethren stood

*without, desiring to speake with him.

47 *Then one sayd unto him, Beholde, thy mother & thy brethren stand without,

*desiring to speake with thee.

And
48 *But he answered, and sayd unto him that told him, Who is my mother? †Or†

*who are my brethren?

he and
49 *And †when he had† stretched forth his hand toward his disciples, †he†

*sayd, Beholde, my mother and my brethren.

50 *For whosoever shall doe the will of my father which is in heaven, the same is

*my brother, and sister, and mother.

The xiii. Chapter.

[Delete]
went Jesus out and
1 *The same day †when Jesus was gone† †out† of the house, †he† sate by the sea side.

2 *And great multitudes were gathered together unto him, so that he went into

a
*†the† ship, and sate, and the whole multitude stoode on the shore.

a
3 *And he spake many things †to† them in parables, saying, Behold, †the†
unto

*sower went foorth to sowe.

4 *And when hee sowed, some †seedes† fell by the wayes side: and the foules came,
seedes

*and devoured them up.

forthwith
5 *Some fell upon stony places, where they had not much earth: and †anon†

*they sprung up, because they had no deepenesse of earth.

were parched
were scorched
6 *And when the sunne was up, they †caught heate:† and because they had not roote,

*they withered away.

And
7 *†Againe,† some fell among thornes: and the thornes sprung up, and choked them.

other
8 *But †some† fell into good ground, and brought forth fruit, some an hundred fold,

*some sixty fold, some thirty fold.

9 *Who hath eares to heare, let him heare.

in
10 *And the disciples came, and sayd unto him, Why speakest thou unto them †by†

*parables?

11 *Hee answered and sayd unto them, Because it is given unto you to know

*the †secrets† of the kingdome of heaven, but to them it is not given.
mysteries

12 *For whosoever hath, to him shall be given, and hee shall have more abundance:

*but whosoever hath not, from him shall be taken away, even that he hath.

13 *Therefore speake I to them in parables: because they seeing, see not: and

*hearing they heare not, neither do they understand.

By hearing
14 *And in them is fulfilled the prophesie of Esaias, which sayth, †With the eare†

*ye shal heare, and shall not understand: and seeing, ye shal see, and shall not

*perceive.

15 *For this peoples heart is waxed grosse, and their eares are dull of hearing,

they have
*and their eyes †have they† closed: lest at any time they should see with their

*eyes, and heare with their eares, and should understand with their heart, and

And I should
and I should
*should †convert,† †that I might† heale them.
be converted

But
16 * Blessed are your eyes, for they see: and your eares, for they heare.

For
17 * Verily I say unto you, that many Prophets and righteous men have desired to

them
*see those things which ye see, and have not seene : and to heare those things

them
*which ye heare, and have not heard

parable
18 *Heare ye therefore the †similitude† of the Sower.

any
19 *When †one† heareth the word of the kingdome, and understandeth it not, then
any one

the wicked one
*commeth †that Evill,† and catcheth away that which was sowen in his heart:

was sowen
*this is he which †received seede† by the way side.
received seede

was sowen
20 *But he that †received the seede† into stonie places, the same is he that heareth
received the seede

*the word, and anon with joy receiveth it:

tyme
21 *Yet hath he not roote in himselfe, but dureth for a †season:† for when
while

*tribulation or persecution ariseth because of the word, by and by he is

*offended.

And he that was sowen among
22 *†He also that received seed into the† thornes, is he that heareth the word,
Hee also that received seede among the

carefull thought
care
*and the †care† of this world, and the deceitfulnesse of riches

[Delete] it becometh
*choke †up† the word, and †so is he made† unfruitfull.
hee becometh

was sowen upon
was sowen on
23 *But he that †received seede into the† good ground, is he that heareth the word,
received seede into the

*and understandeth it, which also beareth fruit, and bringeth foorth, some an

[Delete] [Delete]
*hundred fold, some sixty †fold,† some thirty †fold.†

24 *Another parable put hee foorth unto them, saying, The kingdome of heaven is

*likened unto a man which sowed good seede in his field.

25 *But while men slept, his enemie came and sowed tares among the wheate, and went

*his way.

26 *But when the blade was sprung up, and †had† brought foorth fruit, then appeared
[Delete]

*the tares also.

27 *So, the servants of the housholder came, and said unto him, Sir, diddest not

*thou sowe good seede in thy field, from whence then hath it tares?

28 *He sayd unto them, † The malicious man† hath done this. The servants saide unto
An enemie

*him, Wilt thou then that we goe and gather them up?

29 *But he saide, Nay: least while yee gather up the tares, ye root up also the

*wheat with them.

the
30 *Let both grow together untill the harvest: and in time of harvest, I

*will say to the reapers, Gather ye together first the tares, and bind them

gather ye
*in bundles to burne them: but †carie† the wheate into my barne.
gather

31 *Another parable put he foorth unto them, saying, The kingdome of heaven is

*like to a graine of mustard seede, which a man tooke and sowed in his field.

32 *Which indeede is the least of all seedes: but when it is growen, it is the

becommeth so
*greatest among hearbs, and †is† a tree: †so† that the birdes of the aire

lodge
*come and †make their nests† in the branches thereof.

[Delete]
33 *Another parable spake he unto them, †saying,† The kingdome of heaven is

*like unto leaven, which a woman tooke, and hid in three †peckes† of meale,
measures

the whole was
*till †all were† leavened.

multitude
34 *All these things spake Jesus unto the †people† in parables, and without

*a parable spake he not unto them:

35 *That it might bee fulfilled which was spoken by the Prophet, saying, I will open

utter
*my mouth in parables, I will †speake foorth† things which have bene kept secret
*from the foundation of the world.

sent [Delete]
sent multitud and went
36 *Then Jesus, †when he had sent† the †people† away , †went† into the
*house: And his disciples came unto him, saying, Declare unto us the parable of the
*tares of the field.

And
[Delete]
37 * He answered, and said unto them, He that soweth the good seed, is
*the sonne of man.

[Delete]
38 *The field, is the world. The good seede, †these† are the children of the
one
*kingdome. But the tares, are the children of the wicked .

[Delete]
39 *And the enemie that sowed them, is the devill. The harvest, is the end
And are
*of the world. The reapers, †be† the Angels.

As therefore the tares
40 *†Even as the tares therefore† are gathered and burnt in the fire: so shall it
this
*be in the end of †the† world.

they
41 *The sonne of man shall send foorth his Angels, and †they† shall gather out of
*his kingdome all things that offend, and them which do iniquity:
"things

"Or, scandals

42 *And shall cast them into a furnace of fire: there shall be wayling and gnashing
*of teeth.

forth
43 *Then shall the righteous shine as the sunne in the kingdom of their father.

*Who hath eares to heare, let him heare.

a
44 *Againe, the kingdome of heaven is like unto treasure hid in †the† field:

he departeth
*the which, when a man hath found, hideth, and for joy thereof †goeth†
goeth

*and selleth all that he hath, and buyeth that field.

45 *Againe, the kingdom of heaven is like unto a marchant man, seeking goodly

*pearles:

of greate price he
Whoe pearle of greate price he
46 *†Which† when hee had found one †precious pearle,† went and sold all

*that he had, and bought it.

47 *Againe, the kingdom of heaven is like unto a net that was cast into the sea,

every
*and gathered of †all† kind,

shore
48 *Which, when it was full, †the Fishers† drew to †land,† and sate downe,
they

*and gathered the good into vessels, but cast the bad away.

49 *So shall it be at the end of the world: the angels shall come foorth, and

wicked
*sever the †bad† from among the just,

50 *And shall cast them into †a† furnace of fire: there shalbe wayling and
the

*gnashing of teeth.

51 *Jesus sayth unto them, Have ye understood all these things? They say unto him,

*Yea, Lord.

instructed unto
52 *Then sayd he unto them, Therefore every Scribe which is †taught in†

[Delete]
*the kingdome of heaven, is like unto a †man that is an† housholder,
man that is an

*which bringeth foorth out of his treasure things new and old.

53 *And it came to passe, that when Jesus had finished these parables, he

*departed thence.

was come
54 *And when he †came† into his owne countrey, he taught them in their

astonished
*Synagogue, insomuch that they were †astonied,† and said, Whence †commeth†
hath this man

*this wisedome, and †mighty workes unto him?†
these mighty workes

55 *Is not this the Carpenters sonne? Is not his mother called Marie? and his

*brethren, James, and Joses, and Simon, and Judas?

his sisters are they not all
56 *And †are not all his sisters† with us? whence †hath he then†
then hath this man

*all these things?

57 *And they were offended in him. But Jesus said unto them, A Prophet is not

*without honour, save in his owne countrey, and in his owne house.

58 *And hee did not many mightie workes there, because of their unbeliefe.

The xiiii. Chapter.

1 *At that time Herod the Tetrarch heard of the fame of Jesu,

2
†4† *And said unto his servants, This is John the Baptist, he is risen from

*the dead, and therefore †great† workes do shew forth themselves in him.
mighty "do shew forth

"Or, are wrought by him

had layd hold on John, and
3 *For Herode, †when he had taken John, he† bound him, and put him in prison for

*Herodias sake, his brother Philips wife.

4 *For John said unto him, It is not lawfull for thee to have her.

multitude
5 *And when he would have put him to death, he feared the †people:†

*because they counted him as a Prophet.

6 *But when Herodes birth day was kept, the daughter of Herodias daunced

*before them, and pleased Herode.

Whereupon promised
7 *†Wherefore† he †promiseth† with an oath, to give her whatsoever she would aske.

8 *And she, being before instructed of her mother, said, Give me here John Baptists

charger
*head in a †platter.†

9 *And the king was sorie: neverthelesse, for the othes sake, and them which

with him at meate
*sate †also at the table,† he commanded it to be given her:

hee [Delete]
10 *And sent †a tormentor,† and beheaded John in the prison.

charger she
11 *And his head was brought in a †platter,† and given to the damsell: and †she†

*brought it to her mother.

the
12 *And his disciples came, and tooke up †his† bodie, and buried it: and went and

*told Jesus.

by into
13 *When Jesus heard of it, hee departed thence †in a† ship, †unto† a desert

apart
*place †out of the way:† and when the people had heard thereof, they followed him

*on foote out of the cities.

[Delete] and a greate multitude
14 *And †when† Jesus went forth, †he† saw †much people,† and was

compassion
*mooved with †mercie† towarde them, and he healed their sicke.

15 *And when it was evening, his disciples came to him, saying, This is a desert

send the multitude away
*place, and the †houre† is now past: †let the people depart,† that they may goe into
time

them themselves
*the villages, and buy †them† victuals.
themselves

16 *But Jesus said unto them, They †have no neede to goe away:† give ye
neede not depart

*them to eate.

And [Delete]
17 * They say unto him, We have †not† here but five loaves, and

*two fishes.

18 *He said, Bring them hither to me.

he multitude
19 *And †when he had† commanded the †people† to sit downe on the grasse, and

tooke looking up
*†had taken† the five loaves, and the two fishes, and †lifted up his eies†

to brake and
*†toward† heaven, he blessed: and †when he had broken them, he† gave the loaves to his

the multitude
*disciples: and †his† disciples to the †people.†

filled
20 *And they did all eate, and were †sufficed:† and they tooke up

(the overplus of the broken pieces)
*(†of the fragments that remained†) twelve baskets full.
of the fragments that remained

21 *And they that had eaten, were about five thousand men, beside women and

*children.

22 *And straightway Jesus constrayned his disciples to get †up† into a ship, & to
[Delete]

multitude
*go before him unto the other side, while he sent the †people† away.
multitudes

multitude
23 *And when he had sent the †people† away, he went up into a mountaine
multitudes

apart the evening [Delete]
*†alone† to pray: and when †night† was come, he was there †himselfe†

*alone:

tossed
24 *But the ship was now in the middest of the sea, †and was tost† with

[Delete]
*†the† waves: for †it was a contrary winde.†
the wind was contrary

25 *And in the fourth watch of the night, Jesus went unto them, walking on the

*sea.

26 *And when the disciples saw him walking on the sea, they were troubled, saying,

[Delete]
*†That† it is a spirit: and they cryed out for feare.

27 *But straightway Jesus spake unto them, saying, Be of good cheare: it is I,

*be not afraid.

And
28 * Peter answered him, and said, Lord, if it be thou, bid me come unto thee

*on the water.

29 *And he said, Come. And when Peter was come downe out of the ship, he walked on

*the water, to goe to Jesus.

beginning to
beginning
30 *But when he saw †a mightie winde,† hee was afraid: and †when he began† to sinke,
the wind “boistrous

*he cryed, saying, Lord save me.

“Or, strong

[Delete] and
31 *And immediatly Jesus, †when he had† stretched foorth his hand,
*caught him, and said unto him, O thou of little faith, wherefore diddest
*thou doubt?

up
32 *And when they were come into the ship, the winde ceased.
[Delete]

33 *Then they that were in the ship, came and worshipped him, saying, Of a trueth
*thou art the sonne of God.

34 *And when they were gone over, they came into the land of Genezaret.

35 *And when the men of that place had knowledge of him, they sent out into all
*that countrey round about, and brought unto him all that were †sicke,†
diseased

onely
36 *And besought him that they might touch the hemme of his
it
[Delete] [Delete]
*garment †onely:† and as many as touched , were made perfectly
*whole.

The xv. Chapter.

of
1 *Then came to Jesus Scribes and Pharises, which were †come from†
*Hierusalem, saying,

2 *Why do thy Disciples transgresse the tradition of the elders? for they wash
*not their handes when they eate bread.

3 *But he answered, and saide unto them, Why doe you also transgresse the
*commaundement of God by your tradition?

[Delete]
4 *For God commanded, saying, Honour thy father and †thy† mother: And
*he that curseth father or mother, let him die the death.

by it thou mayst be benefitted
[Delete] thou mayst be benefitted
5 *But ye say, Whosoever shall say to his father or his mother,
*†By the gift †that <u>is</u>† <u>offered</u> of me,† †thou shalt be helped:†
It is a gift by whatsoever thou mightest be profited by me

6 *And †so shall he not honour his father or his mother.†
honour not his father or his mother, <u>he</u> <u>shall</u> <u>be</u> <u>free</u>

[Delete]
[Delete] thus
*†And† †thus† have yee made the commandement of God of none effect

*by your tradition.

[Delete]
7 *Ye hypocrites, †full† well did Esaias prophecie of you, saying,

8 *This people draweth nigh unto mee with their mouth, and honoureth mee with

But
but
*their lippes: †howbeit,† their heart is farre from me.

the commandments
9 *But in vaine they do worship me, teaching doctrines, †precepts†
for

*of men.

he multitude and
10 *And †when he had† called the †people to him, he† said unto them, Heare

*and understand.

Not [Delete] a
11 * That which goeth into the mouth, defileth †not† †the† man:

this a
*but that which commeth out of the mouth, defileth †the† man.

doest thou perceave
12 *Then came his disciples, and saide unto him, †Knowest thou not† that the
Knowest thou

*Pharisees were offended after they heard this saying?

13 *But he answered, and said, †All manner planting† which my heavenly father
Every plant

*hath not planted, shalbe rooted up.

And
14 *Let them alone: they be blind leaders of the blind. If the blind lead the
*blind, both shall fall into the ditch.

15 *Then answered Peter & said unto him, Declare unto us this parable.

And
16 * Jesus said, Are ye also yet without understanding?

17 *Doe not ye yet understand, that whatsoever entreth in at the mouth, goeth into
♣draught
*the belly, and is cast out into the draught?

♣the naturall passage. Suidas

18 *But those things which proceed out of the mouth, come forth from the heart,
*and they defile the man.

fornications
19 *For out of the heart proceed evil thoghts, murders, adulteries, †whoredomes,†
*thefts, false witnesse, blasphemies.

20 *These are the things which defile a man: But to eate with unwashen hands,
*defileth not a man.

[Delete] and
21 *†And† Jesus, †when he† went thence , departed into the coasts of
Then
*Tyre and Sidon.

Chanaan [Delete]
22 *And behold, a woman of †the Chanaanites,† †which† came out of the same
and
*coasts, cryed unto him, saying, Have mercie on me, O Lord, thou sonne of
*David, my daughter is grievously vexed with a devill.

her
23 *But he answered not a word. And his disciples came, and besought him,
*saying, Send her away for she cryeth after us.

24 *But he answered, and said, I am not sent but unto the lost sheepe of the house

*of Israel.

25 *Then came she, and worshipped him, saying, Lord, helpe me.

26 *But he answered, and said, It is not meet to take the childrens bread, and to

*cast it to †little† [Delete] dogges.

27 *And she said, †Yes,† Trueth Lord: †for† yet the †litle† [Delete] dogs †also† [Delete]

*eate of the crummes which fall from their masters table.

28 *Then Jesus answered, and said unto her, O woman, great is thy faith:

*be it †done† [Delete] unto thee even as thou wilt. And her daughter was made

*whole †even† [Delete] from that †same† [Delete] very houre.

29 *And Jesus, †when he was† [Delete] departed from thence, and came nigh unto

*the sea of Galilee, and †when he was gone† went up into a mountaine, †he† and

*sate downe there.

30 *†Then† And great multitudes came unto him, having with them †those that were† [Delete] those that were

*lame, blinde, dumbe, maymed, and †other many,† many others and cast them downe at Jesus

*feete, and he healed them:

31 *In so much that the †people† multitude wondered, when they saw the dumbe to speake,

*the maymed to be whole, the lame to walke, and the blind to see: and they

*glorified the God of Israel.

32 *Then Jesus called his disciples unto him, and sayde, I have compassion

*on the †people,† multitude because they continue with me now three dayes, and

send them away
*have nothing to eate: & I will not †let them depart† fasting, lest they

*faint in the way.

should we get
33 *And his disciples say unto him, Whence †should we get† so much bread in the
should wee have

fill
*wildernesse, as to †suffice† so great a multitude?

34 *And Jesus saieth unto them, How many loaves have ye? And they said, Seven,

*and a few litle fishes.

multitude
35 *And he commanded the †people† to sit downe on the ground.

he tooke gave
36 *And †when he had taken† the seven loaves and the fishes, and †had given†

and [Delete]
*thankes, †he† brake †them,† and gave to his disciples: and the
them

[Delete] multitude
*disciples †gave them† to the †people.†

filled
37 *And they did all eate, and were †sufficed:† and they tooke up

the overplus of the broken pieces
*†of the broken meate that was left,† seven baskets full.
of the broken meat that was left

[Delete]
38 *And †yet† they that did eat, were foure thousand men, beside women and

*children.

he multitude and
39 *And †when he had† sent away the †people,† †he† tooke ship, and came into the

coasts
*†partes† of Magdala.

The xvi. Chapter.

1 *The Pharisees also, with the Sadducees, came, and tempting, desired him that

*he would shewe them a signe from heaven.

2 *He answered, and said unto them, When it is evening, ye say, It will be

*faire weather: for the skie is red.

3 *And in the morning, It will be foule weather to day: for the skie

red and lowring face
*is †lowring red.† O yee hypocrites, ye can discerne the †outward appearance†

*of the skie: but can yee not discerne the signes of the times?

wicked generation seeketh after
4 *A †froward† and adulterous †nation requireth† a signe, and there

*shall no signe be given unto it, but the signe of the Prophet Jonas.

*And he left them, and departed.

his disciples came
his disciples goeing [Delete]
5 *And †when his disciples were come† to the other side †of the water,†
when his disciples were come

[Delete] [Delete]
*†they† had forgotten to take bread †with them.†
they

6 *Then Jesus said unto them, Take heede and beware of the leaven of the

*Pharisees, and of the Sadducees.

reasoned among because
7 *And they †thought in† themselves, saying, †For† we have taken
It is

[Delete]
*no bread †with us.†

Which perceived
8 *†Which† when Jesus †understood,† he said unto them, O ye of litle faith,

reason among
*why †think† †you† †within† your selves, because ye have brought no bread?
yee

the
9 *Do ye not yet †perceive,† neither remember †those† five loaves of the five
understand

ye tooke
*thousand, and how many baskets †tooke ye† up?

10 *Neither the seven loaves of the foure thousand, and how many

ye tooke
*baskets †tooke ye† up?

spake
11 *How is it that ye doe not understand that I †speake† it not †unto† you
to

*concerning bread, that ye should beware of the leaven of the Pharisees, and of

*the Sadducees?

them not
12 *Then understoode they how that he bad †not them† beware of the leaven

[Delete]
*of †the† bread: but of the doctrine of the Pharisees and of the

*Saducees.

[Delete]
13 *When Jesus came into the coastes of Cesarea, †which is called†

*Philippi, he asked his disciples, saying, Whom doe men say that I the sonne

*of man am?

the
And say [Delete]
14 * They said, Some †say† that thou art John Baptist, some
the

& others
*Elias, †some† Jeremias, or one of the Prophets.

15 *He saith unto them, But whom say ye that I am?

And
16 * Simon Peter answered, and said, Thou art Christ, the sonne of the

*living God.

Blessed
17 *And Jesus answered, and said unto him, †Happie† art thou Simon Bar Jona:

reveiled it
*for flesh and blood hath not †opened that† unto thee, but my father which is in
reveiled it

*heaven.

I will
18 *And I say also unto thee, that thou art Peter, and upon this rocke †will I†

church
*build my †congregation:† and the gates of hel shal not prevaile against it.

19 *And I will give unto thee the keyes of the kingdome of heaven: and whatsoever

on
*thou shalt binde †in† earth, shall be bound in heaven, †and† whatsoever thou
[Delete]

on
*shalt loose †in† earth, shal be loosed in heaven.

20 *Then charged he his disciples that they should tell no man that he was

the
*Jesus Christ.

21 *From that time forth began Jesus to shew unto his disciples, how that he must

*go unto Hierusalem, and suffer many things of the Elders and †high† Priests
chiefe

[Delete]
*and Scribes, and †must† be killed, and be raised againe the third day.

Then Peter tooke him &
22 *†And when Peter had taken him aside, he† began to rebuke him, saying,

*†Lord, favour thy selfe,† this shall not be unto thee.
Bee it farre from thee Lord

[Delete]
23 *But he turned †him about,† and sayd unto Peter, †Goe after me,†
Get thee behind me

*Satan, thou art an offence unto me: for thou savourest not the things that be

*of God, but those that be of men.

come
24 *Then said Jesus unto his disciples, If any man will †goe† after me,

denye
*let him †forsake† himselfe, and take up his crosse, and follow me.

And
25 *For whosoever will save his life, shal lose it: †againe,† whosoever

*will lose his life for my sake, shall find it.

gaine
26 *For what is a man profited if he shal †win† the whole world,

And suffer the losse of his owne
And suffer the losse of owne
*†and lose† his owne soule? Or what
and loose

exchange shall a man give for his owne soule
exchange shall a man give for his soul
*†shall a man give for the ransome of his soule?†
shall a man give in exchange for his soule

27 *For the sonne of man shall come in the glorie of his father with his angels:

*and then †shall hee† rewarde every man according to his workes.
hee shall

28 *Verely I say unto you, There be some standing here, which shall †in no wise†
not

*taste of death till they see the sonne of man comming in his kingdome.

The xvii. Chapter.

1 *And after sixe dayes, Jesus taketh Peter, James, and John his brother, and bringeth

apart
*them up into an high mountaine, †out of the way,†

2 *And was transfigured before them, and his face did shine as the Sunne,

raiment was
*and his †clothes were as† white as the light.

3 *And beholde, there appeared unto them Moses, and Elias talking with him.

4 *Then answered Peter, and sayde unto Jesus, Lord, it is good for us to be here.

*If thou wilt, let us make here three tabernacles: one for thee, and one for Moses, and
*one for Elias.
5 *While hee yet spake, beholde, a bright cloud overshadowed them: and
[Delete]
*behold, †there came† a voyce out of the cloud, which said, This
*is my beloved sonne, in whom I am well pleased, heare ye him.
it
6 *And when the disciples heard †these things,† they fell on their face, and were
*sore afraid.
[Delete]
7 *And Jesus came and touched them, and said, Arise †ye,† and
*be not afraid.
8 *And when they had lift up their eyes, they saw no man, save Jesus only.
as
9 *And †when† they came downe from the mountaine, Jesus charged them, saying,
*†Shew† the vision to no man, untill the sonne of man be risen againe from the
Tel
*dead.
10 *And his disciples asked him, saying, Why then say the Scribes that Elias must
*first come?
And
11 * Jesus answered, and said unto them, Elias truely shall first come, and
*restore all things:
12 *But I say unto you, that Elias is come alreadie, and they knew him not, but
listed
*have done unto him whatsoever they †lusted:† Likewise shal also the sonne of man
*suffer of them.
the
13 *Then the disciples understood that hee spake unto them of John Baptist.

multitude

14 *And when they were come to the †people,† there came to him a certaine man,

*kneeling downe to him, and saying,

15 *Lord, have mercie on my sonne, for he is lunatike, and sore vexed: for oft

*times he falleth into the fire, and oft into the water.

16 *And I brought him to thy disciples, and they could not †heale† him.

cure

Then generation

17 * Jesus answered, and saide, O faithlesse and perverse †nation,† how long

indure

*shall I be with you? how long shall I †suffer† you? bring him hither to me.

suffer

it

devill it

18 *And Jesus rebuked the †devill,† and †he† departed out of him: and the

he

from that very hour

*child was †healed† †even that same time.†

cured

to apart

19 *Then came the disciples †of† Jesus †secretly,† and said, Why could

it

*not we cast †him† out?

him

And

20 * Jesus said unto them, Because of your unbeliefe: for verily I say unto you,

As much faith as is

*If ye have †faith “as† a graine of mustard seede, ye shall say unto this

faith as

& nothing shall

*mountaine, Remove hence to yonder place: and it shal remove, †neither shal any thing†

*be unpossible unto you.

“Or, <u>As</u> <u>much</u>

21 *Howbeit, this kind goeth not out, but by prayer and fasting.

And abode
22 * While they †were conversant† in Galilee, Jesus said unto them,

[Delete]
*†It will come to passe, that† the sonne of man shall be betraied into the

*hands of men:

hee shall be raysed
23 *And they shall kill him, and the thirde day †shall hee rise† againe.

*And they were exceeding sorie.

24 *And when they were come to Capernaum, they that received tribute money, came

*to Peter, and said, Doeth not your master pay tribute?

25 *He saith, Yes. And when he was come into the house, Jesus prevented him,

*saying, What thinkest thou, Simon? of whom doe the kings of the earth

custome or tribute [Delete]
*take †tribute or toll?† of their owne children, or of †the† strangers?

[Delete]
26 *Peter sayeth unto him, Of †the† strangers. Jesus saith unto him, Then

*are the children free.

27 *Notwithstanding, lest wee should offend them, goe thou to the sea, and cast

*an hooke, and take up the fish that first commeth up: and when thou hast opened

♣stater
*his mouth, thou shalt finde a †piece of twentie pence:† that take, and give
"piece of money

*unto them for me, and thee.

♣a piece of silver weighing half an ounce
"Or, a stater. It is halfe an ounce of silver, in value two shillings
sixe pence, after five shillings the ounce

The xviii. Chapter.

1 *At the same time came the disciples unto Jesus, saying, Who is the greatest

*in the kingdome of heaven?

And [Delete]
2 * Jesus called a †litle† child unto him, and set him in the middes
little

*of them,

3 *And said, Verily I say unto you, Except ye †turne† and become
be converted

[Delete]
*as †litle† children, ye shal not enter into the kingdome of heaven.
little

[Delete]
4 *Whosoever therefore shal humble himself as this †litle† child,
litle

[Delete]
*the same is †the† greatest in the kingdome of heaven.

one [Delete]
5 *And who so shall receive such †a litle† childe in my name,
litle

*receiveth me.

6 *But who so shall offend one of these litle ones which beleeve in me, it were
*better for him that a milstone were hanged about his necke, and that hee were
*drowned in the depth of the sea.

for
7 *Woe unto the world because of offences, it must needes be that offences
*come: but woe to that man by whom the offence commeth.

Wherefore if them
8 *†If then† thy hand or thy foote offend thee, cut them off, and cast †them†

rather
*from thee: it is better for thee to enter into life halt or maimed, †rather†

[Delete] to
*then †thou shouldest,† having two hands or two feete, be cast into †the†
[Delete]

*everlasting fire.

9 *And if thine eye offend thee, plucke it out, and cast †it† from thee: it is
it

rather
*better for thee to enter into life with one eye, †rather† then having two eyes,
*to be cast into hell fire.
10 *Take heede that ye despise not one of these litle ones: for I say unto you,
*that in heaven their angels doe alwayes behold the face of my father which is in
*heaven.
11 *For the sonne of man is come to save that which was lost.
12 *How thinke ye? if a man have an hundred sheepe, and one of them be gone astray,
the
*doth he not leave †those† ninetie and nine, and goeth into the mountaines,
is gone
*and seeketh that which †went† astray?
13 *And if so be that he find it, verily I say unto you, he rejoyceth more of that
*sheepe, then of the ninetie and nine which went not astray.
14 *Even so it is not the will of your father which is in heaven, that one of these
*litle ones should perish.
15 *Moreover, if thy brother shall trespasse against thee, go and tell him his fault
gained
*betweene thee and him alone: if he shall heare thee, thou hast †wonne† thy
*brother.
[Delete] more
16 *But if he will not heare thee, then take †yet† with thee one or two :
established
*that in the mouth of two or three witnesses, every word may be †stablished.†
But If shall neglect to
17 *If he †will not† heare them, tell it unto the Church: †if†
And if But if
neglect to
neglect to heare
*he †will not heare† the Church, let him be unto thee as an Heathen man and a
*Publicane.

18 *Verely I say unto you, Whatsoever ye shall binde on earth, shall be bound in

*heaven: and whatsoever ye shall loose on earth, shall be loosed in heaven.

verily I say on
19 *Againe, †truely I say† unto you, that if two of you shal agree †in† earth
I say

shall
*as touching any thing that they †shall† aske, it shal be done for them of my

*father which is in heaven.

20 *For where two or three are gathered together in my name, there am I in the

*midst of them.

21 *Then came Peter to him, and sayd, Lord, how oft shall my brother sinne against

*me, and I forgive him? till seven times?

thee
22 *Jesus saith unto him, I say not unto †you,† untill seven times: but untill

*seventie times seven.

23 *Therefore is the kingdome of heaven likened unto a certain †man that was a†
[Delete]

*king, which would take account of his servants.

24 *And when he had begun to reckon, one was brought unto him which ought him

*ten thousand talents.

25 *But forasmuch as he had not to pay, his lord commanded him to be solde, and his

*wife, and children, and all that he had, and †paiment† to be made.
payment

worshipped
26 *The servant therefore fell downe, and †besought† him, saying, Lorde, have
"worshipped

*patience with me, and I will pay thee all.

"Or, besought him

was compassion and
27 *Then the Lord of that servant, mooved with †pitie,† loosed him, and

*forgave him the debt.

fellowe servants
28 *But the same servant went out, and found one of his †fellowes† which
hee and
*ought him an hundred pence: and †when hee had† laide handes on him, †he† tooke him
me
*by the throte, saying, Pay †<u>me</u>† that thou owest.

servant
29 *And his fellow fell downe at his feete, and besought him, saying,
*Have patience with me, and I will pay thee all.

30 *And he would not: but went and cast him into prison, till he should pay the debt.

fellow servants
31 *So when his †fellowes† sawe what was done, they were very sorie, and
*came, and told unto their lord all that was done.

32 *Then his lord, after that hee had called him, saide unto him, O thou
wicked because
*†ungratious† servant, I forgave thee all that debt †when† thou desiredst me:

servant
33 *Shouldest not thou also have had compassion on thy fellow , even as I
*had pitie on thee?

34 *And his lord was wroth, and delivered him to the tormentors, till he should
*pay all that was due unto him.

35 *So likewise shall my heavenly father doe also unto you, if ye from your hearts
*forgive not every one his brother their trespasses.

The xix. Chapter.

1 *And it came to passe, that when Jesus had finished these sayings, hee
departed
*†gate him† from Galilee, and came into the coastes of †Jury,† beyond Jordane:
Judea

2 *And great multitudes followed him, and he healed them there.

3 *The Pharisees also came unto him, tempting him, and saying unto him, Is it
*lawfull for a man to put away his wife for every cause?

And
4 * He answered, and said unto them, Have ye not read that he which †created†
made them
*at the beginning, made them male and female?

[Delete]
5 *And said, For this cause shall a man leave †his† father and
[Delete] shalbe joyned
*†his† mother, and †shalbe knit† to his wife: and they twaine shalbe
shall cleave
*one flesh.

What therefore God
6 *Wherefore they are no more twaine, but one flesh. †Let not man therfore
hath joyned together let not man put asunder
*put asunder that which God hath coupled together.†

[Delete]
7 *They say unto him, Why did Moses then command to give a †writing†
writing
?
*of divorcement, and to put her away †.†

sayth
8 *He †sayde† unto them, Moses, because of the hardnesse of your hearts, suffered
*you to put away your wives: but from the beginning it was not so.

But
And
9 * I say unto you, Whosoever shall put away his wife, except it be for fornication,
*and shall marrie another, committeth adulterie: and who so marrieth her which
*is †divorced,† doeth commit adulterie.
put away

10 *His disciples say unto him, If the case of the man be so with his wife,
it is
*†then is it† not good to marrie.

11 *But hee sayde unto them, All men can not receive this saying, save they to whom
*it is given.

Eunuches
12 *For there are some †chaste,† which were so borne †out of† their mothers wombe:
from

Eunuches Eunuches
*and there are some †chaste,† which were made †chaste† of men: & there be

Eunuches Eunuches
*†chaste,† which have made themselves †chaste† for the kingdome of heavens sake.
*He that is able to receive it, let him receive it.
13 *Then were there brought unto him †yong† children, that he should put his hands
little
*on them, and pray: and the disciples rebuked them.

[Delete]
[Delete] litle
14 *But Jesus sayd †unto them,† Suffer †the young† children, and

of such is
*forbid them not to come unto me: for †to such belongeth† the kingdome of heaven.

he layd and
15 *And †when he had put† his hands on them, †he† departed thence.
16 *And behold, one came, and said unto him, Good master, what good thing shall
*I doe, that I may have eternall life?

And
17 * He said unto him, Why callest thou mee good? there is none good but one,

[Delete] [Delete]
*†and† that is God: But if thou wilt enter into †that† life,
*keepe the commandements.
18 *He sayth unto him, Which? Jesus sayd, Thou shalt do no murder, Thou shalt not
*commit adulterie, Thou shalt not steale, Thou shalt not beare false witnesse,
19 *Honour thy father and thy mother: and, Thou shalt love thy neighbour as
*thy selfe.

[Delete]
20 *The young man sayeth unto him, All these †things† have I kept from my
things

*youth up: what lacke I yet?

that thou hast
21 *Jesus said unto him, If thou wilt be perfect, goe and sell †thy substance,†

*and give to the poore, and thou shalt have treasure in heaven: and come and

*follow me.

22 *But when the young man heard that saying, he went away †sorie:† for he had
sorrowfull

*great possessions.

23 *Then said Jesus unto his disciples, Verily I say unto you, that a rich

man
*†man† shall hardly enter into the kingdome of heaven.

24 *And againe I say unto you, It is easier for a Camel to go thorow the eie of a

a rich man
*needle, then for †the rich† to enter into the kingdome of God.

And
[Delete] his [Delete]
25 * When †the† Disciples heard †this,† they were exceedingly
it

*amazed, saying, Who then can be saved?

them [Delete]
26 *But Jesus beheld †them,† & said †unto them,† With men this is unpossible,
unto them

*but with God all things are possible.

27 *Then answered Peter, and said unto him, Behold, we have forsaken all, and

*followed thee, what shall we have therefore?

And that ye which have followed
28 * Jesus said unto them, Verily I say unto you, †that when the sonne of man

me in the regeneration, when the sonne of man shall sitt in the throne of
*shall sit in the throne of his majestie, ye that have followed me in the

his glorie, ye also shall sit thrones
*regeneration, shall sit also† upon twelve †seats,† judging the twelve tribes
*of Israel.

houses
29 *And every one that hath forsaken †housen,† or brethren, or sisters, or father,
*or mother, or wife, or children, or lands, for my names sake, shall receive
*an hundred fold, and shall inherite everlasting life.
30 *But many that are first, shall be last, and the last shalbe first.

The xx. Chapter.

1 *For the kingdome of heaven is like unto a man that is an housholder, which
*went out earely in the morning to hire labourers into his Vineyard.

[Delete]
2 *And †when† he had agreed with the labourers for a penie a day, hee
when
*sent them into his Vineyard.

[Delete] and
3 *And †when† hee went out about the third houre, †he† saw †other†
others
*standing idle in the market place,
4 *And said unto them, Goe ye also into the Vineyard, and whatsoever is right,
*I will give you. And they went their way.

[Delete] and
5 *Againe, †when† he went out about the sixth and ninth houre, †he†
*did likewise.

[Delete] and
6 *And about the eleventh houre, †when† he went out, †he† found †other†
others
*standing idle, and saith unto them, Why stand ye here all the day idle?
7 *They say unto him, Because no man hath hired us. He saith unto them, Goe ye
*also into the Vineyard: and whatsoever is right, that shall ye receive.

8 *So when even was come, the lord of the Vineyard saith unto his Steward,
*Call the labourers, and give them their hire, beginning from the last, unto the
*first.

9 *And when they came that were hired about the eleventh houre, they received
*every man a penie.

[Delete]
10 *But when the first came †also,† they supposed that they should have received
*more: and they likewise received every man a penie.

11 *And when they had received it, they murmured against the good man of the
*house,

12 *Saying, These last have wrought †but† one houre, and thou hast made them
"have wrought but
*equall unto us, which have borne the burden and †fervent† heate
[Delete]
*of the day.

"Or, have continued one houre onely

[Delete]
13 *But he answered †to† one of them and said, Friend, I doe thee no wrong:
*diddest †thou not† agree with me for a peny?
not thou

14 *Take that thine is, and go thy way, I wil give unto this last, even as unto
*thee.

what
15 *Is it not lawfull for me to doe †that† I will with mine owne? Is thine eye
*evill, because I am good?

shalbe
[Delete]
16 *So the last shalbe first, and the first †shalbe† last: for many
*be called, but few †be† chosen.
[Delete]

apart
17 *And Jesus going up to Hierusalem, tooke the twelve disciples †aside† in the
*way, and said unto them,
18 *Behold, we go up to Hierusalem, and the sonne of man shall be betrayed unto the
*chiefe priests, and unto the Scribes, and they shal condemne him to death:
19 *And shall deliver him to the Gentiles to †be mocked, & to be scourged, and to
mocke and to scourge, and to crucifie
*be crucified:† and the third day he shall rise againe.
him
20 *Then came to him the mother of Zebedees children, with her sonnes, worshipping
*him, and desiring a certaine thing of him.
sayd sayd
21 *And he †saith† unto her, What wilt thou? She †saith† unto him, Grant, that
saith
*these my two sonnes may sit, the one on thy right hand, and the other on the left,
*in thy kingdome.
[Delete]
said
22 *But Jesus answered, and †said,† Yee †wote† not what ye aske. Are ye able to
know
*drinke of the cup that I shall drinke of, and to be baptized with the baptisme
*that I am baptized with? They say unto him, We are able.
And
23 * He saith unto them, Ye shal drinke indeede of my cup, and be baptized
*with the baptisme that I am baptized with: but to sit on my right hand, and on
*my left, is not mine to give, but to them for whom it is
it shall be given
*prepared of my father.
began to be much displeased with
24 *And when the ten heard †this,† they †disdained at†
it were mooved with indignation against
*the two brethren.

[Delete] and
25 *But Jesus, †when he had† called them unto him, said, Ye knowe that

exercise lordship
*the princes of the Gentiles †have dominion† over them, and they that are
exercise dominion

*great, exercise authority upon them.

But
26 * It shal not be so among you: But whosoever wil be great among you, let him

*be your minister,

27 *And †who so† will be chiefe among you, let him be your servant.
whosoever

28 *Even as the sonne of man came not to be ministred unto, but to minister, and to

*give his life a ransome for many.

a greate multitude
29 *And as they departed from Hiericho, †much people† followed him.

30 *And behold, two blind men sitting by the way side, when they heard that

out
*Jesus passed by, †they† cried, saying, †O Lord, thou sonne of David,
[Delete] Have mercy on us, O Lord, thou

*have mercie on us.†
sonne of David

multitude
31 *And the †people† rebuked them, because they should hold their peace: but they

*cryed the more, saying, Have mercie on us, O Lord, thou sonne of David.

32 *And Jesus stood still, and called them, and said, What will ye that I shall do

*unto you?

33 *They say unto him, Lord, that our eyes may be opened.

34 *So Jesus had compassion on them, and touched their eyes: and immediatly their

*eyes received sight, and they followed him.

The xxi. Chapter.

1 *And when they drewe nigh unto Hierusalem, and were come to Bethphage, unto the

*mount of Olives, then sent Jesus two disciples,

[Delete]

2 *Saying unto them, Goe into the village †that lieth† over against you,

straightway

*and †anon† ye shal find an Asse tied, and a colt with her:

loose and

*†when ye have loosed† †them,† bring †them† unto me.

them them

3 *And if any man say ought unto you, ye shall say, The Lorde hath neede of them,

*and straightway he will †let them goe.†

send them

4 *All this was done, that it might be fulfilled which was spoken by the

*Prophet, saying,

5 *Tell ye the daughter of Sion, Beholde, thy king commeth unto thee, meeke,

*and sitting upon an Asse, and a colt, the foale of †the Asse used to the yoke.†

an Asse

And

6 * The disciples went, and did as Jesus commanded them,

7 *And brought the Asse, and the colt, and put on them their clothes,

*and †he sate thereon.†

they set him thereon

a very greate multitude

8 *And †many of the people† spread their garments in the way, †other†

others

*cut downe branches from the trees, and strawed them in the way.

And followed

9 *†Moreover,† the multitudes that went before, and that †came after,† cried,

*saying, Hosanna to the sonne of David: Blessed is he that commeth in the name of

*the Lord, Hosanna in the highest.

10 *And when hee was come into Hierusalem, all the citie was mooved, saying, Who
*is this?

the
11 *And the multitude saide, This is Jesus †that† Prophet of Nazareth

of
*†a citie in† Galilee.

12 *And Jesus went into the Temple of God, and cast out all them that solde and
*bought in the Temple, and overthrew the tables of the money changers, and the
*seates of them that sold Doves,

13 *And said unto them, It is written, My house shalbe called the house of
*prayer, but ye have made it a denne of theeves.

lame
14 *And the blind and the †halt† came to him in the temple, and he healed them.

And
15 * When the chiefe priests and Scribes saw the †wonders† that he
wonderfull things

*did, and the children crying in the temple, and saying, Hosanna to the sonne of

were sore displeased
*David, they †disdained,†

16 *And sayd unto him, Hearest thou what these say? †But† Jesus saith unto them,
And

*Yea, have ye never read, Out of the mouth of babes and sucklings thou hast

*†ordeined† praise?
perfected

17 *And he left them, and went out of the city †unto† Bethanie, and he lodged there.
into

And
18 * In the morning, as he returned into the citie, he hungred.
Now

a
19 *And when he sawe †one† figge tree in the way, he came to it, and found nothing

Let no fruict growe on the hence
*thereon but leaves onely, and said unto it, †Never fruit grow on thee hence

forward for ever presently
*forward.† And †anon† the figge tree withered away.

presently
20 *And when the Disciples saw it, they marveiled, saying, Howe †soone†
soone

*is the figge tree withered away?

21 *Jesus answered, and said unto them, Verely I say unto you, if ye have faith,

[Delete]
which is done
*and doubt not, ye shall not onely doe this †which is done† to the

*figge tree, but also, if ye shall say unto this mountaine, Be thou removed,

*and be thou cast into the sea, it shalbe done.

22 *And all things whatsoever ye shal aske in prayer, beleeving, ye shall receive.

23 *And when he was come into the temple, the chiefe priests & the elders of the

as he was
*people came unto him teaching, and †say,† By what authority doest
said

authoritie
*thou these things? and who gave thee this †power?†

And thing
24 * Jesus answered, and said unto them, I also will aske you one †question,†

*which if ye tell me, I in likewise will tell you by what authoritie I doe these

*things:

25 *The baptisme of John, whence was it? from heaven, or of men? And they reasoned

*with themselves saying, If we shall say, From heaven, he will say unto us,

*Why did ye not then beleeve him?

[Delete]
26 *But if we shall say, Of men, †then feare we† the people, for all †men†
we feare

*hold John as a Prophet.

[Delete]
27 *And they answered †unto† Jesus, and said, Wee cannot tell. And

*he saide unto them, Neither tell I you by what authority I do these things.

[Delete]
28 *But what thinke you? A certaine man had two sonnes, and †when†

[Delete]
*he came to the first, †he† said, Sonne, go †and† worke to day in my
and

*vineyard.

29 *He answered, and said, I will not: but afterward he repented, and went.

[Delete] and
30 *And †when† he came to the second, †he† sayd likewise: And he answered,

*and said, I <u>goe</u> sir, and went not.

They say
31 *Whether of them twaine did the will of his father? †And they said† unto him,

*The first. Jesus saith unto them, Verely I say unto you, that the Publicanes and

*the harlots go into the kingdome of God before you.

in
32 *For John came unto you †by† the way of righteousnesse, and ye beleeved him not:

*but the Publicanes and the harlots beleeved him. And ye when ye had seene †<u>it</u>,†
it

*†were not mooved afterward with repentance,† that ye might †have beleeved† him.
repented not afterward beleeve

Heare parable
33 *†Hearken† another †similitude.† There was a certaine †man, an† housholder,
[Delete]

*which planted a vineyard, and hedged it round about, and digged a wine presse in

*it, and built a towre, and let it out to husbandmen, and went into a †strange†
farre

*countrey.

34 *And when the time of the fruit drew neere, he sent his servants to the husbandmen,

*that they might receive the fruits of it.

tooke and
35 *And the husbandmen, †when they had taken† his servants, †they† beat one,

and
&
* killed another, and stoned another.

36 *Againe, he sent other servants, moe then the first, and they did unto them

*likewise.

37 *But last of all, he sent unto them his †owne† sonne, saying, They
[Delete]

reverence
*will †stand in awe of† my sonne.

38 *But when the husbandmen saw the sonne, they said among themselves, This is

seaze on
*the heire, come, let us kill him, and let us †season upon† his inheritance.

cast him
39 *And they caught him, and †thrust† him out of the vineyard, and slue †<u>him</u>.†

40 *When the Lorde therefore of the vineyard commeth, what will he doe unto those

*husbandmen?

men
41 *They say unto him, He will miserably destroy those wicked †<u>men</u>,† and will

*let out his vineyard unto other husbandmen, which shall render him the

fruits their
*†fruit† in †due† seasons.

42 *Jesus saith unto them, Did yee never reade in the scriptures, The stone which

rejected
*the builders †disallowed,† the same is become the head of the corner? This

*is the Lords doing, and it is marveilous in our eyes.

43 *Therefore say I unto you, the kingdome of God shall be taken from you, and

*given to a nation bringing foorth the fruits thereof.

44 *And whosoever shall fall on this stone, shalbe broken †in pieces:†
[Delete]

will grinde him to powder
*but on whomsoever it shall fall, it †shal all to grinde him.†

45 *And when the chiefe Priests & Pharisees had heard his parables, they perceived

*that he spake of them.

people
46 *†And† when they sought to lay handes on him, they feared the †multitudes,†
But multitude

*because they tooke him †as† a Prophet.
for

The xxii. Chapter.

1 *And Jesus answered, and spake unto them againe by parables, and said,

2 *The kingdome of heaven is like unto a †man that was a† King, which made a
certaine

*marriage for his sonne,

3 *And sent foorth his servants, to call them that were bidden to the wedding, &

*they would not come.

4 *Againe, he sent foorth other servants, saying, Tell them which are bidden,

*Beholde, I have prepared my dinner, my Oxen and my fatlings are killed, and all

*things are readie: come unto the marriage.

5 *But they made light of it, and went their wayes, one to his farme, another

*to his marchandize:

6 *And the remnant tooke his servants, and intreated them spitefully, and

*slue them.

[Delete]
7 *But when the king heard <u>thereof</u> he was wroth, and †when he had†
he

and
*sent foorth his armies, †hee† destroyed those murderers, and burnt up their citie.

8 *Then saith he to his servants, The †mariage in deede is prepared,†
wedding is ready

*but they which were bidden, were not worthy.

9 *Goe ye therefore †out† into the high wayes, and as many as ye shall
[Delete]

*find bid to the marriage.

10 *†And the† servants went out into the high wayes, and gathered together all as
So those

*many as they found, both †good and bad,† and the wedding was furnished with ghests.
bad and good

And saw
11 * When the king came in to see the ghests, he †spied† there a man, which

*had not on a wedding garment,

12 *And he saith unto him, Friend, howe camest thou in hither, not having a

[Delete]
*wedding garment? And he was †even† speechlesse.

servants Bind
13 *Then sayde the king to the †ministers,† †When yee have bound† him hande and

and away outer
*foote, take him †up,† and cast him into †utter† darkenesse, there shall be

*weeping, and gnashing of teeth.

14 *For many are called, but fewe are chosen.

15 *Then went the Pharisees, and tooke counsaile howe they might entangle him in

*his talke.

16 *And they sent out unto him their disciples with the Herodians, saying, Master,

in truth
*we know that thou art true, and teachest the way of God †truely,† neither

regardest not the person of men
*carest thou for any man, for thou †doest not respect mens persons.†

what
17 *Tell us therefore, †howe† thinkest thou? Is it lawfull to give tribute

*unto Cesar, or not?

perceived And
18 *But Jesus, †when he knew† their wickednesse, sayd, Why tempt ye me,

*ye hypocrites?

19 *Shew mee the tribute money. And they brought unto him a peny.

♣superscription
20 *And he sayth unto them, Whose is this Image and superscription?
"superscription

♣Or, inscription
"Or, inscription

21 *They say unto him, Cesars. Then sayth he unto them, †Give† therefore unto
Render

*Cesar the †things† which are Cesars: and unto God, †those things† that are Gods.
things the things

22 *When they had heard these wordes, they marveiled, and left him, and went their

*way.

23 *The same day came to him the Sadducees, which say that there is no resurrection,

*and asked him,

24 *Saying, Master, Moses sayd, If a man die, having no children, his brother shall

*marrie his wife, and raise up seede unto his brother.

25 * There were with us seven brethren, and the first when he had married a wife,
Now

*deceased, & having no issue, left his wife unto his brother.

26 *Likewise the second also, and the third, unto the seventh.

And
27 * Last of all the woman died also.

28 *Therefore in the resurrection whose wife shall shee bee of the seven? For they

*all had her.

And
29 * Jesus answered, and sayd unto them, Yee doe erre, not knowing
[Delete]

*the Scriptures, nor the power of God.

30 *For in the resurrection they neither marrie, nor are given in marriage, but are

*as the angels of God in heaven.

31 *But as touching the resurrection of the dead, have yee not read that which was

by saying
*spoken unto you †of† God, †which sayth,†

Isaac
32 *I am the God of Abraham, and the God of †Isahac,† and the God of Jacob? God

*is not the God of the dead, but of the living.

multitude astonished
33 *And when the †multitudes† heard this, they were †astonied† at his doctrine.

34 *But when the Pharisees had heard that he had put the Sadducees to silence,

*they were gathered together.

of them
35 *Then one †of them,† which was a lawyer, asked him a question, tempting him, and

*saying,

36 *Master, which is the great commaundement in the lawe?

37 *Jesus sayd unto him, Thou shalt love the Lord thy God with all thy heart,

*and with all thy soule, and with all thy minde.

38 *This is the first and great commandement.

39 *And the second is like unto it, Thou shalt love thy neighbour as thy selfe.

40 *†In† these two commandements hang all the law and the Prophets.
On

41 *†When† the Pharisees were gathered together, Jesus asked them,
While

42 *Saying, What thinke ye of Christ? whose sonne is hee? They †sayd† unto
say

the sonne
*him, †the sonne† of David.

43 *He sayth unto them, How then doeth David in spirit call him Lord, saying,

44 *The Lord sayd unto my Lord, Sit thou on my right hand, till I make thine enemies

*thy footstoole?

[Delete]
45 *If David then call him Lord, how is hee †then† his sonne?

46 *And no man was able to answere him a word, neither durst any man

*(from that day) aske him any moe questions.
forth

The xxiii. Chapter.

multitude
1 *Then spake Jesus to the †multitudes,† and to his disciples,

sit
2 *Saying, The Scribes & the Pharisees †"sate† in Moses seate:

"Beza readeth it, sit

3 *All therefore whatsoever they bid you observe, that observe and doe, but doe

*not yee after their workes: for they say, and do not.

For
4 *†Yea,† they bind †together† heavie burdens, and grievous to be borne, and lay
[Delete]

*them on mens shoulders, but †they themselves† will not moove them with one
they themselves

*of their fingers.

But
5 * All their workes they do, for to be seene of men: they make broade their

*phylacteries, and enlarge the †hemmes† of their garments,
borders

roumes
6 *And love the uppermost †seates† at feasts, and †to sit in†
[Delete]

seates
*the chiefe †place† in the Synagogues,

7 *And greetings in the markets, and to bee called of men, Rabbi, Rabbi.

8 *But be not ye called Rabbi: for one is your master, even Christ, and all ye

*are brethren.

9 *And call no man your father upon the earth: for one is your father, which

*is in heaven.

10 *Neither bee yee called masters: for one is your master, even Christ.

But
11 * He that is greatest among you, shalbe your servant.

And abased and
12 *†But† whosoever shall exalt himselfe shall be †brought lowe,† hee

abaseth
*that †humbleth† himselfe, shalbe exalted.
shall humble

13 * Wo unto you Scribes and Pharises hypocrites, for ye shut up the kingdome
But

For
*of heaven †before† men: ye neither goe in your selves, neither suffer yee
against

would goe in enter
*them that †come,† to †enter in.†
are entring goe in

14 *Woe unto you Scribes and Pharises hypocrites, for ye devoure widowes

[Delete] make
*houses, and †that† †under† a pretence †of† long prayer, therefore ye
for

*shall receive the greater damnation.

[Delete]
15 *Woe unto you Scribes and Pharises hypocrites, for ye compasse †the†

[Delete]
*sea and †the† land to make one proselyte, & when he is †become one,†
made

[Delete] [Delete]
*ye make him two fold more the child of hell then †ye† your selves †are.†

[Delete] [Delete] which
16 *Woe †be† unto you †ye† blinde guides, †for yee† say,
ye

*whosoever shall sweare by the temple, it is nothing, but whosoever shal sweare by

*the gold of the temple, he is a debter.

17 *Ye fooles and blind, for whether is greater. the golde, or the temple that

*sanctifieth the golde?

18 *And whosoever shall sweare by the altar, it is nothing, but whosoever sweareth

*by the gift that is upon it, he is †a debter.†
"guilty

"Or, a debter, or bound

19
†12†*Yee fooles and blinde, for whether is greater, the gift, or the altar that

*sanctifieth the gift?

20 *Who so therefore shal sweare by the altar, sweareth by it, and by all things

*thereon.

21 *And who so shall sweare by the temple, sweareth by it, & by him that dwelleth

*therein.

22 *And he that shall sweare by heaven, sweareth by the †seate† of God,
throne

*and by him that sitteth thereon.

23 *Woe unto you Scribes and Pharisees hypocrites, for ye †tithe†
pay tithe of

omitted
*mint, and annise, & cummine, and have †left† the weightier matters of the

*lawe, judgement, mercie, and faith: these ought ye to have done, and not to

*leave the other undone.

24 *Yee blinde guides, which straine †out† a gnat, and swallow a camell.
at

25 *Woe unto you Scribes and Pharisees hypocrites, for ye make cleane the

outer side
*†utter side† of the cup, and of the platter, but within they are full of
outside

extortion
*†briberie† and excesse.

26 *Thou blinde Pharisee, cleanse first that which is within the cup and platter,

*that the outside of them may be cleane also.

27 *Woe unto you Scribes and Pharisees hypocrites, for yee are like unto
whited
*†painted† sepulchres, which indeed appeare beautiful outward, but are within
[Delete]
mens uncleanesse
*ful of dead †mens† bones, and of all †filthinesse.†

28 *Even so, ye also outwardly appeare righteous unto men: but within ye are full of
*hypocrisie and iniquitie.

29 *Woe unto you Scribes and Pharisees hypocrites, because yee build the tombes of
*the Prophets, and garnish the sepulchres of the righteous,

30 *And say, If we had bene in the dayes of our fathers, we would not have bene
partakers
*†partners† with them in the blood of the Prophets.

31 *Wherefore yee bee witnesses unto your selves, that ye are the children of them
*which killed the Prophets.

32 *†Fulfill yee also† the measure of your fathers.
Fill yee up then

generations can
33 *Ye serpents, ye †generation† of vipers, how †will† ye escape the damnation of hell?
generation

34 *Wherefore behold, I send unto you Prophets, and wisemen, and Scribes, and some
*of them ye shall kill and crucifie, and some of them shall yee scourge in your
*synagogues, and persecute them from citie to citie:

35 *That upon you may come all the righteous blood shed upon the earth, from the
[Delete]
*blood of †that† righteous Abel, unto the blood of Zacharias, sonne of
*Barachias, whom yee slew betweene the temple and the altar.

36 *Verely I say unto you, All these things shall come upon this generation.

37 *O Hierusalem, Hierusalem, thou that killest the Prophets, and stonest them which
are
*†have bene† sent unto thee, how often would I have gathered thy children together,

*even as a hen gathereth her chickens under her wings, and ye would not?

38 *Behold, your house is left unto you desolate.

not
39 *For I say unto you, ye shall †by no meanes† see me henceforth, till yee shall

*say, Blessed is hee that commeth in the name of the Lord.

The xxiiii. Chapter.

1 *And Jesus went out, and departed from the temple: and his disciples came

[Delete]
*†to him for† to shewe him the buildings of the temple.
to him, for

And
2 * Jesus sayd unto them, See ye not all these things? Verely I say unto you,

throwen downe
*there shall not be left here one stone upon another, that shall not be †destroyed.†

3 *And as he sate upon the mount of Olives, the disciples came unto him

privately
*†secretly,† saying, Tel us, when shall these things be? and what shalbe

signe
*the †token† of thy comming, and of the end of the worlde?

4 *And Jesus answered, and said unto them, Take heede that no man deceive you.

5 *For many shall come in my name, saying, I am Christ: and shall deceive many.

And
6 *†It will come to passe, that† ye shall heare of warres, and rumors of warres: See

*that ye be not troubled: for all these things must come to passe, but the end is

*not yet.

kingdome kingdome
7 *For nation shall rise against nation, and †realme† against †realme,† and there

divers
*shall bee famines, and pestilences, and earthquakes in †certaine† places.

8 *All these are the beginning of sorowes.

deliver you up to be afflicted
9 *Then shall they †put you to trouble,† and shall kill you: and ye
*shall be hated of all nations for my names sake.
10 *And then shall many be offended, and shall betray one another, and shal hate
*one another.
11 *And many false prophets shal rise, and shal deceive many.
12 *And because iniquitie shall abound, the love of many shall waxe cold.
13 *But he that shall endure unto the end, the same shall be saved.
14 *And this Gospell of the kingdome shall be preached in all the world, for a
*witnesse unto all nations, and then shall the end come.
15 *When ye therefore shall see the abomination of desolation, spoken of by Daniel
consider
*the Prophet, stand in the holy place, (whoso readeth, let him †understand,†)
understand
16 *Then let them which be in †Jury,† flee into the mountaines.
Judea
17 *†And† let him which is on the house top, not come downe to †fetch†
[Delete] take
*any thing out of his house:
18 *Neither let him which is in the fielde, returne backe to †fetch† his clothes.
take
And [Delete] unto
19 * Woe †shall bee in those dayes† †to† them that are with child, and
in those dayes
*to them that give sucke
20 *But pray ye that your flight be not in the winter, neither on the Sabboth day:
21 *For then shall be great tribulation, such as was not since the beginning of the
neither ever
*world to this time, no, †nor in any wise† shall be.
nor ever
[Delete]
22 *†Yea,† and except those daies should be shortned, there should no flesh

elects
*bee saved: but for the †chosens† sake those dayes shall be shortned.

23 *Then if any man shall say unto you, Loe, here is Christ, or there: beleeve
*it not.

24 *For there shall arise false Christs, and false prophets, and shall shew great
*signes, and wonders: in so much that (if it were possible) they shall deceive the
*very elect.

25 *Behold, I have tolde you before.

26 *Wherefore, if they shall say unto you, Behold, he is in the desert, goe not
*forth: Behold, he is in the secret †pleces,† beleeve it not.
chambers

appeareth
27 *For as the lightning commeth out of the East, and †shineth† †into†
shineth even unto
*the West: so shall also the comming of the sonne of man be.

[Delete]
28 *For wheresoever the †dead† carkeise is, †even† there will the
[Delete]
*Eagles †also† bee gathered together.
[Delete]

29 *Immediatly, after the tribulation of those dayes, shall the Sunne be darkened,
*and the Moone shall not give her light, and the starres shall fall from heaven,
*and the powers of the heavens shalbe shaken.

30 *And then shall appeare the signe of the sonne of man in heaven: and then
tribes
*shall all the †kinreds† of the earth mourne, and they shall see the sonne of
*man comming in the clouds of heaven, with power and great glory.

a trumpet of a great sound
31 *And hee shall send his angels with †the great sound of a trumpet,† and they
"a great sound of a trumpet

elect [Delete]
*shall gather together his †chosen† from the foure winds, †even† from

*one end of heaven to the other.

"Or, with a Trumpet, and a great voyce

Now
32 * Learne a parable of the figge tree: When his branch is yet tender, and

putteth forth leaves
*†the leaves sprung,† ye know that summer is nigh:

know
33 *So likewise ye, when ye shall see all these things, †be sure† that it is neere,

even
*†even† at the dores.

not
34 *Verely I say unto you, this generation shall †in no wise† passe, till all

*these things be fulfilled.

not
35 *Heaven and earth shall passe away, but my words shall †in no wise† passe away.

36 *But of that day and houre knoweth no man, no, not the Angels of heaven, but my

*father onely.

37 *But as the dayes of Noe were, so shall also the comming of the sonne of man be.

38 *For as in the dayes that were before the flood, they were eating, and drinking,

*marying, and giving in mariage, †even† untill the day that Noe entred into
[Delete]

*the arke,

39 *And knewe not untill the flood came, and tooke them all away: so shall also the

*comming of the sonne of man be.

shalbe taken
40 *Then shall two be in the field: the one †is† †received,† and the

[Delete] [Delete]
*other †is† left †alone.†

women shalbe taken
41 *Two †women† shalbe grinding at the mill: the one †is received,† and the

[Delete]
*other left †alone.†

commeth
42 *Watch therefore, for yee know not what houre your Lord †doth come.†
doth come

But know this
43 *†Of this yet be sure,† that if the good man of the house had knowen what
in

*watch the thiefe would come, hee would have watched, and would not have suffered

*his house to bee broken up.

44 *Therefore be yee also ready: for in such an houre as †yee† thinke not, the
you

*sonne of man commeth.

a
45 *Who then is †that† faithfull and wise servant, whome his lord hath made ruler

due
*over his houshold, to give them meat in season?

46 *Blessed is that servant, whome his lorde when he commeth, shall find so doing.

47 *Verely I say unto you, that he shall make him ruler over all his goods.

48 *But and if that evill servant shall say in his heart, My lord

delayeth his
*†will be long a† comming:

shall fellowe servants
49 *And †so† beginne to smite his †fellowes,† †yea,† and to eate
[Delete]

*and drinke with the drunken:

Lord of that servant
50 *The †same servants lord† shal come in a day when hee looketh not for him, and in

*an houre that he is not ware of:

cutt appoynt
51 *And shall †hew† him †in pieces,† and †give† him his portion with the
“asunder

*hypocrites: there shall be weeping and gnashing of teeth.

“Or, cut him off

The xxv. Chapter.

1 *Then shall the kingdome of heaven be likened unto ten virgins, which

tooke and
*†when they had taken† their lamps, went forth to meet the bridegroome.

2 *†But† five of them were wise, and five were foolish.
And

tooke and
3 *They that were foolish, †when they had taken† their lampes, tooke

no
*†none† oyle with them:

[Delete]
4 *But the wise tooke oyle in their vessels, with their lamps †also.†

5 *While the bridegrome taried, they all slumbred and slept.

[Delete]
6 *And †even† at midnight there was a crye made, Behold, the bridegrome

*commeth, goe ye out to meet him.

7 *Then all those virgines arose, and †prepared† their lampes.
trimmed

And
8 *†So† the foolish sayd unto the wise, Give us of your oyle, for our lamps

*are gone out.
"gone out.

"Or, <u>going</u> <u>out</u>

9 *But the wise answered, saying, <u>Not</u> <u>so</u>, least there be not ynough for us and

*you: but goe ye rather to them that sell, and buy for your selves.

10 *And while they went to buy, the bridegrome came, and they that were ready,

[Delete]
*went in with him to the marriage, and the doore was shut †up.†

11 *Afterward came also the other virgines, saying, Lord, Lord, open to us.

12 *But hee answered, and sayd, Verely I say unto you, I know you not.

13 *Watch therefore, for ye know neither the day, nor †yet† the houre,
[Delete]

*wherin the sonne of man commeth.

it is as a certaine taking a farre journey
For as a taking his journey
14 *†Likewise,† †as when a certaine† man †taking his journey†
the kingdome of heaven is as a travailing

[Delete]
*†into a straunge countrey,† called his owne servants, and delivered
into a farre countrey who

*unto them his goods.

15 *And unto one he gave five talents, to another two, and to another one,

according to
*to every man †after† his ability, and straightway tooke his journey.
several

trafficked
16 *Then he that had received the five talents, went and †occupied† with the same,
traded

gained
*and †made them† other five talents.
made them

17 *And likewise he that had received two, he also gained other two.

18 *But hee that had received one, went and digged in the earth, and hid

*his lords money.

time
19 *After a long †season,† the lorde of those servants commeth, and reckoneth with

*them.

20 *And so hee that had received five talents, came and brought other five talents,

*saying, Lorde, thou deliveredst unto mee five talents: behold, I have gained

*besides them, five talents moe.

21 *His lorde sayd unto him, Well done, thou good and faithfull servant, thou

set thee
*hast bene faithfull over fewe things, I will †make thee ruler† over many
a make thee ruler

*things: enter thou into the joy of thy lord.

22 *Hee also that had received two talents, came, and said, Lord, thou deliveredst

gained
*unto me two talents: behold, I have †won† two other talents besides them.

23 *His lord said unto him, Well done, good and faithfull servant, thou hast bene

set thee
*faithfull over few things, I will †make thee ruler† over many things: enter thou
a make thee ruler

*into the joy of thy lord.

24 *Then he which had received the one talent, came, and saide, Lord, I knew thee

*that thou art an hard man, reaping where thou hast not sowen, and gathering

*where thou hast not strawed:

[Delete] I was
25 *And †therefore† †was I† afraid, and went and hid thy talent in the earth:

is thine
*loe, there thou hast that †thine is.†

wicked
26 *His lord answered, and sayde unto him, Thou †evill† and slouthful servant,

*thou knewest that I reape where I sowed not, and gather where I have not strawed:

27 *Thou oughtest therefore to have †delivered† my money to the exchangers, and then
put

usury
*at my comming †should I† have received mine owne with †vantage.†
I should

28 *Take therefore the talent from him, and give it unto him which hath ten talents.

29 *For unto every one that hath shall be given, and he shall have abundance:

*but from him that hath not, shalbe taken away, even that which he hath.

outer
30 *And cast the unprofitable servant into †utter† darkenesse, there shalbe weeping
ye

*and gnashing of teeth.

31 *When the Sonne of man shal come in his glorie, and all the holy angels with him,

*then shall he sit upon the throne of his glory.

32 *And before him shall be gathered all nations, and hee shall separate them one
*from another, as a shepheard devideth his sheepe from the goates.

33 *And hee shall set the sheepe on his right hand, but the goates on the left.

[Delete]
34 *Then shall the king say unto them †which shalbe† on his right hand,

[Delete]
*Come ye blessed of my father, inherite the kingdome, †which hath bene†
*prepared for you from the foundation of the world.

35 *For I was an hungred, and ye gave me meate: I was thirstie, and ye gave me
*drinke: I was a stranger, and ye tooke me in:

36 *Naked, and ye clothed me: I was sicke, and ye visited me: I was in prison, and
*ye came unto me.

37 *Then shall the righteous answere him, saying, Lord, when sawe we thee an hungred,
*and fed thee? or thirstie, and gave thee drinke?

38 *When saw we thee a stranger, and tooke thee in? or naked, and clothed thee?

39 *Or when saw we thee sicke, or in prison, and came unto thee?

40 *And the king shall answere, and say unto them, Verily I say unto you, in as much
*as yee have done it unto one of the least of these my brethren, ye have

it
*done †it† unto me.

41 *Then shall he say also unto them on the left hand, Depart from me, yee cursed,

[Delete] [Delete]
*into †the† everlasting fire, †which is† prepared for the devill and
*his angels.

42 *For I was an hungred, and ye gave me no meat: I was thirstie, and ye gave me no
*drinke.

43 *I was a stranger, and ye tooke me not in: naked, and ye clothed me not: sicke,

*and in prison, and ye visited me not.

44 *Then shall they also answere him, saying, Lord, when saw we thee an hungred, or
*a thirst, or a stranger, or naked, or sicke, or in prison, and did not minister
*unto thee?

45 *Then shall he answere them, saying, Verily I say unto you, in as much as ye did
*it not to one of the least of these, ye did it not to me.

punishment
46 *And these shall go away into everlasting †paine:† but the righteous into
*life eternall.

The xxvi. Chapter.

sayings
1 *And it came to passe, when Jesus had finished al these †things,† he said unto
*his disciples,

the
2 *Yee knowe that after two dayes is the feast of Passeover, and the sonne of
*man is betrayed to be crucified.

3 *Then assembled together the chiefe Priests, and the Scribes, and the Elders
who
*of the people, unto the palace of the high Priest, †which† was called Caiaphas,

by subtilty
4 *And †held a counsell,† that they might take Jesus †subtilly,† and kill him.
consulted

5 *But they said, Not on the feast day, least there be an uproare among the people.

Now
6 * When Jesus was in Bethanie, in the house of Simon the leper,

very
7 *There came unto him a woman, having an alabaster boxe of precious ointment,
meate
*& powred it on his head as he sate †at† †the boord.†
at

8 *But when his disciples saw it, they had indignation, saying, To what purpose

*is this waste?

For
9 * This ointment might have bene sold for much, and given to the poore.

it
10 *When Jesus understood †that,† he said unto them, Why trouble ye the woman?

*for she hath wrought a good worke upon me.

11 *For ye have the poore alwaies with you, but me ye have not alwayes.

she hath powred
12 *For in that †this woman hath cast† this ointment on my body, she did

toward my buriall
it to burie me
*†it to burie me.†
it for my buriall

13 *Verily I say unto you, Wheresoever this Gospel shall be preached in the whole

*world, there shall also this that this woman hath done, bee told for a memoriall

*of her.

14 *Then one of the twelve, called Judas Iscariot, went unto the chiefe Priests,

15 *And said unto them, What wil ye give me, and I will deliver him unto you?

peeces of silver
*And they †appointed unto him† thirtie †silver peeces.†
covenanted with him for

[Delete]
16 *And from that time †foorth,† he sought opportunitie to betray him.

Now day the feaste of unleavend bread
17 * The first †day† of †sweet bread,† the disciples came to

*Jesus, saying unto him, Where wilt thou that we †shall† prepare for thee
[Delete]

*to eate the Passeover?

18 *And he saide, Goe into the citie to such a man, and say unto him, The master

will keepe
*saith, My time is at hand, I †make† the Passeover at thy house with my

*disciples.

19 *And the disciples did as Jesus had appointed them, and they made readie the

*Passeover.

20 * When the even was come, he sate downe with the twelve.
Now

21 *And as they did eate, he sayd, Verely I say unto you, that one of you shall betray

*me.

And
were and
22 *And they †being† exceeding sorowful, began every one of them to say unto

*him, Lord, is it I?

And dippeth
23 * Hee answered, and sayd, He that †hath dipped† his hand with me in the dish,

*the same shall betray me.

indeede goeth
24 *The sonne of man †truely goeth† as it is written of him: but woe unto that man
goeth

*by whom the sonne of man is betrayed: It had bene good for that man if he

*had not bene borne.

25 *Then Judas, which betrayed him, answered, and sayd, Master, Is it I? He

*sayd unto him, Thou hast said.

[Delete]
And as they tooke
26 *†When† †they† were eating, Jesus, †when hee had taken the†

♣blessed and [Delete]
*bread, and †given thankes,† †hee† brake †<u>it</u>† and gave †<u>it</u>† to the disciples,
"blessed it it it

[Delete] [Delete]
*and sayde, Take †ye,† eat †ye,† this is my body.

♣Many Greeke copies have <u>given</u> <u>thankes</u>
"Many Greeke copies have, <u>gave</u> <u>thankes</u>

hee tooke giving
27 *And †when hee had taken† the cup, & †given† thankes, †he† gave it them,
gave & to

*saying, Drinke ye all of it:

28 *For this is my blood of the new testament, †that† is shed for many for
which

*the remission of sinnes.

not
29 *But I say unto you, I will †in no wise† drinke henceforth of this fruite of

[Delete] shall
*the vine †tree,† untill that day when I drinke it newe with
[Delete]

*you in my fathers kingdome.

sung an ♣hymne
30 *And when they had †praised God,† they went out †unto† the mount of Olives.
sung an "hymne into

♣Or, Psalme
"Or, Psalme

31 *Then sayth Jesus unto them, All ye shall be offended because of me this night:

*For it is written, I wil smite the shepheard, & the sheepe of the flocke shalbe

*scattered abroad.

32 *But after I am risen againe, I will goe before you into Galilee.

33 *Peter answered, and sayde unto him, Though all men shalbe offended because of

*thee, yet will I never be offended.

this
34 *Jesus sayd unto him, Verely I say unto thee, that †in this same† night

*before the cocke crow, thou shalt deny me thrise.

35 *Peter sayde unto him, Though I should die with thee, yet wil I

not
*†by no maner of meanes† deny thee. Likewise also said all the disciples.

36 *Then commeth Jesus with them unto a place called Gethsemane, & sayeth unto the

*disciples, Sit ye here while I goe and pray yonder.

he tooke
37 *And †when he had taken† with him Peter, and the two sonnes of Zebedee,

and to be in an ♣agonie
*†hee† began to be sorowfull and †heavy.†
very heavy

♣Or, grievous anguish

sorowfull
38 *Then †said Jesus† unto them, My soule is †exceeding heavie,† even unto †the†
saith he exceeding sorrowfull [Delete]

*death: tary yee here, and watch with me.

he went and [Delete]
39 *And †when he had gone† a little further, †he† fell †flatte† on his face,

and prayed
*†praying, and† saying, O my father, if it be possible, let this cup passe from me:

*neverthelesse, not as I will, but as thou wilt.

40 *And hee commeth unto the disciples, and findeth them asleepe, & saith unto

*Peter, What, could ye not watch with me one houre?

41 *Watch and pray, that yee enter not into temptation: The spirit in deede is

*willing, but the flesh is weake.

42 *He went away againe the second time, and prayed, saying, O my father, if this

*cup may not passe away from me, except I drinke it, thy will

done
*be †fulfilled.†

[Delete] and found
43 *And †when† he came, †he findeth† them asleepe againe: for their

*eyes were heavie.

away
44 *And hee left them, and went againe and prayed the third time, saying the

*same words.

on now
45 *Then commeth he to his disciples, & sayth unto them, Sleepe †henceforth,†
*& take your rest: beholde, the houre is at hand, and the sonne of man is betrayed
*into the hands of sinners.
46 *Rise, let us be going: behold, he is at hand that doth betray me.
And
47 * While he yet spake, loe, Judas one of the twelve came, and with him a great
*multitude with swords and staves from the chiefe Priests and Elders of the
*people.
Now signe
48 *†But† he that betrayed him, gave them a †token,† saying, Whomsoever I shall
*kisse, that same is he, hold him fast.
[Delete] and
49 *And forthwith †when† hee came to Jesus, †he† sayd, Haile master:
*and kissed him.
50 *And Jesus said unto him, Friend, wherefore art thou come? Then came they
*and layde hands on Jesus, and tooke him.
51 *And behold, one of them which were with Jesus, stretched out his hand, & drew
strooke and
*his sword, and †after that he had striken† a servant of the hie priests, †he†
*smote off his eare.
put up
52 *Then sayd Jesus unto him, †Turne backe† thy sword into
againe
his she
the sheathe
*†his place:† for all they that take the sword, shall perish with the sword.
his place
53 *Thinkest thou that I cannot now pray to my father, and he shall
give
*†cause to stand by† me more then twelve legions of angels?
presently give

54 *But howe then shall the scriptures be fulfilled, that thus it must be?

multitude Are ye
55 *In that same houre said Jesus to the †multitudes,† †Ye be† come out
multitudes

against ?
*as †it were unto† a thiefe with swordes and staves for to take me †:†

*I sate dayly with you teaching in the Temple, and yee †tooke me not.†
laid no hold on me

56 *But all this was done that the scriptures of the Prophets might be

forsooke him and
*fulfilled. Then all the disciples †having forsaken him,† fled.

And they tooke Jesus, and
57 *†But they that had taken Jesus,† led him away to Caiaphas the high priest,
And they that had laid hold on Jesus

*where the Scribes and the Elders were assembled.

58 *But Peter followed him afarre off, unto the hie priests palace, and went in,

*and sate with the servants to see the end.

Now
59 * The chiefe priests and elders, and all the counsell, sought false witnesse

*against Jesus, to put him to death,

though
60 *But found none: yea, †when† many false witnesses came, yet found they none.

*At the last came two false witnesses,

61 *And sayd, This fellow sayd, I am able to destroy the Temple of God, and to

*builde it in three dayes.

62 *And the †chiefe† priest arose, and sayd unto him, Answerest thou nothing?
high

Why doe these beare w
Why doe these beare
*†What is that which these† witnes against thee?
What is it, which these

63 *But Jesus helde his peace. And the †chiefe† priest answered, and said unto him,
high

adjure
*I †charge† thee by the living God, that thou tell us whether thou be Christ the
the

*sonne of God?

64 *Jesus sayeth unto him, Thou hast sayde: Neverthelesse, I say unto you, Hereafter

[Delete]
*shall ye see the sonne of man sitting on the right hand of †the† power

[Delete] heaven
*†of God,† and comming in the clouds of †the skie.†

65 *Then the high priest rent his clothes, saying, He hath spoken blasphemy:

neede have we any more of
*what †neede we of any moe† witnesses? Behold, now yee have heard his
further need have we of

*blasphemy.

of death
66 *What thinke ye? They answered and said, He is †worthy† †to die.†
guilty

[Delete] [Delete]
67 *Then did they spit †in† his face, and buffeted him †with fistes,†
in

[Delete] with rods
*and †other† smote him †on the face with the palme of their hands,†
others with "the palmes of their hands

"Or, rods

Thou
68 *Saying, Prophecie unto us, †O† Christ, who is he †thae† smote thee?
that

Now
69 * Peter sate without in the palace: And a damosel came unto him, saying, Thou

*also wast with Jesus of Galilee.

70 *But he denyed before them all, saying, I †wote† not what thou sayest.
know

wench
71 * When he was gone out into the porch, an other †wench† sawe him, and said unto
And maid

*them that were there, This fellow was also with Jesus of Nazareth.

72 *And againe he denied with an othe, I doe not know the man.

73 *And after a while came unto him they that stood by, and said to Peter, Surely

also art
*thou †art even† one of them: for thy speech bewrayeth thee.

74 *Then beganne he to curse and to sweare, saying, I knowe not the man. And

*immediatly the cocke crew.

75 *And Peter remembred the words of Jesu, which sayde unto him, Before the cocke

*crowe, thou shalt deny me thrice. And he went out, and wept bitterly.

The xxvii. Chapter.

1 *When the morning was come, all the chiefe priests and Elders of the people

*†helde a† counsell against Jesus to put him to death.
tooke

2 *And when they had bound him, they ledde him away, and delivered him to Pontius

Governour
*Pilate the †deputie.†

3 *Then Judas, which had betrayed him, when he saw that he was condemned, repented

pieces of silver
*himselfe, and brought againe the thirtie †"silver pieces† to the chiefe priests

*and elders,

"Or, silverlings

4 *Saying, I have sinned, in that I have betrayed the innocent blood. And

*they sayde, What is that to us? see thou to that.

he and
5 *And †when he had† cast downe the pieces of silver in the temple, †he† departed,

[Delete]
*and went †his way,† and hanged himselfe.

peeces
6 *And the chiefe Priests tooke the silver †peeces,† and sayd, It is not lawfull

*for to put them into the treasurie, because it is the price of blood.

they tooke and
7 *And †when they had taken† counsell, †they† bought with them the potters fielde,

*to burie strangers in.

8 *Wherfore that field was called, The field of blood unto this day.

9 *(Then was fulfilled that which was spoken by Jeremie the Prophet, saying, And

pieces of silver
*they tooke the thirtie †silver peeces,† the price of him that was valued,

the children of Israel did value
*whome †they bought of the children of Israel:†
"they of the children of Israel did value

"Or, whom they bought of the children of Israel

10 *And gave them for the potters field, as the Lord appointed me.)

And governour governour
11 * Jesus stood before the †deputie,† & the †deputie† asked him, saying,

*Art thou the king of the Jewes? Jesus †sayth† unto him, Thou sayest.
And said

12 *And when he was accused of the chiefe priests and elders, he answered nothing.

13 *Then sayeth Pilate unto him, Hearest thou not how many things they witnes

*against thee?

governour
14 *And he answered him to never a word: in so much that the †deputy†

*marveiled greatly.

deliver
Now at that governour release
15 *†At that† feast the †deputie† was woont to †let loose† unto the people

*a prisoner, whome they would.

And they
16 *†He† had then a notable prisoner, called Barabbas.

Whome
17 *Therefore when they were gathered together, Pilate sayd unto them, †Whether†

deliver
release
*will ye that I †give loose† unto you Barabbas, or Jesus, which is called Christ?

18 *For he knewe that for envie they had delivered him.

19 *When he was set downe on the judgement seate, his wife sent unto him, saying,

*Have thou nothing to doe with that just man: For I have suffered many things this

*day in a dreame because of him.

multitude
20 *But the chiefe priests and elders perswaded the †people† that they should

*aske Barabbas, and destroy Jesus.

governour
21 *The †deputie† answered, and sayde unto them, Whether of the twaine will ye that

deliver
release
*I †let loose† unto you? They sayd, Barabbas.

22 *Pilate sayde unto them, What shall I doe then with Jesus, which is called

*Christ? They all sayd unto him, Let him be crucified.

And the governour out
23 *†The deputie† sayd, What evill hath hee done? But they cryed
Why

*†exceedingly,† saying, Let him be crucified.
the more

a greater tumult
that rather tumult
24 *When Pilate sawe that he could prevaile nothing, but †that more businesse†
that rather a tumult

hee
and multitude
*was made, hee tooke water, †and† washed his handes before the †people,†

*saying, I am innocent of the blood of this just person: see ye to it.

be
25 *Then answered all the people, and sayd, His blood †be† on us, and on our

*children.

released he Barabbas
26 *Then †let he Barabbas loose† unto them, and when he had scourged Jesus,

*hee delivered him to be crucified.

governour tooke
27 *Then the souldiers of the †deputie,† †when they had taken† Jesus into the

and the whole
*common hall, gathered unto him †all the† band <u>of</u> <u>souldiers</u>.
"common hall

"Or, <u>Governours</u> <u>house</u>

and
they and
28 *And †when they had† stripped him, †they† put on him a scarlet robe:

29 *And when they had platted a crowne of thornes, they put it upon his head,

[Delete]
they the knee
*and a reed in his right hand: and †when they had† bowed †the knee†

and
*before him, †they† mocked him, saying, Haile king of the Jewes.

they and
30 *And †when they had† spitte upon him, †they† tooke the reed, and smote

*him on the head.

from
31 *And after that they had mocked him, they tooke the robe off him, and put his

*owne rayment on him, and led him away to crucifie him.

32 *And as they came out, they found a man of Cyrene, Simon by name: him they

*compelled to beare his crosse.

33 *And when they were come unto a place called Golgotha, that is to say,

*a place of a skull,

34 *They gave him vineger to drinke, mingled with gall: and when he had tasted

*thereof, he would not drinke.

And they and
35 *†When they had† crucified him, †they† parted his garments, casting lots: that
*it might be fulfilled which was spoken by the Prophet, They parted my garments
[Delete]
vesture
*among them, and upon my †vesture† did they cast lots.
36 *And sitting downe, they watched him there:
37 *And set up over his head, his accusation written, This Is Jesus, The King Of The
*Jewes.
were
38 *Then †are† there two theeves crucified with him: one on the right hand,
*and another on the left.
And
39 * They that passed by reviled him, wagging their heads,
40 *And saying, Thou that destroyest the temple, and buildest it in three dayes,
*save thy selfe: If thou be the sonne of God, come downe from the crosse.
41 *Likewise also the †high† Priestes mocking him, with the Scribes and
chiefe
*Elders, sayd,
others
42 *He saved †other,† himselfe †can he not† save: If hee be the king of Israel, let
he cannot
*him now come downe from the crosse, and we will beleeve him.
[Delete]
43 *Hee †hath† trusted in God, let him deliver him now if he will have
*him: for hee sayd, I am the sonne of God.
And
44 * The theeves also which were crucified with him, cast the same in
[Delete]
*his teeth.

Now their was
45 * From the sixth houre †was their† darknes over all the land, unto the

*ninth houre.

greate
46 *And about the ninth houre, Jesus cryed with a †loud† voice, saying,
loud

*<u>Eli</u>, <u>Eli</u>, <u>Lamasabachthani</u>, that is to say, My God, my God, why hast thou

*forsaken me?

And
47 * Some of them that stood there, when they heard that, sayd, This man
[Delete]

*calleth for Elias.

[Delete]
48 *And straightway one of them ranne, and tooke a spunge, and †when he had†

[Delete]
it with and
*filled †it† †full of† vineger, & put it on a reed, †he† gave him to drinke.

49 *The rest sayde, Let be, let us see whether Elias will come to save him.

greate
50 *Jesus, when hee had cryed againe with a †loud† voice, yeelded up the ghost.
loud

twayne
51 *And behold, the vaile of the temple was rent in †two parts,† from the top to the

rockes
*bottome, and the earth did quake, and the †stones† rent,

52 *And graves were opened, and many bodies of saints which slept, arose,
the

came
53 *And †after that they were come† out of the graves after his resurrection,

& went
*†came† into the holy citie, and appeared unto many.

Now
54 * When the Centurion, and they that were with him watching Jesus, saw the

*earthquake, and those things that were done, they feared greatly, saying, Truly *this was the son of God.

55 *And many women were there (beholding †him† afarre off) which followed
[Delete]

*Jesus from Galilee, ministring unto him.

56 *Among which was Mary Magdalene, and Mary the mother of James and Joses, and

*the mother of Zebedees children.

[Delete]
57 *When the Even was come, there came a rich man †from the citie† †of†
of

who
*Arimathea, named Joseph, †which† also himselfe was Jesus disciple.

58 *He went to Pilate, and begged the bodie of Jesus: then Pilate commaunded the

*body to be delivered.

59 *And when Joseph had taken the body, he wrapped it in a cleane linnen cloth,

owne
60 *And layd it in his new tombe which hee had hewen out in the rocke: and

hee and
*†when hee had† rolled a great stone to the doore of the sepulchre, †he† departed.

61 *And there was Mary Magdalene, & the other Mary, sitting over against the

*sepulchre.

Now the preparation
62 * The next day that followed the day of †preparing,† the †high†
chiefe

*Priestes and Pharises came together unto Pilate,

63 *Saying, Sir, we remember that †this† deceiver said while hee was yet alive, After
that

will
*three dayes I rise againe.

64 *Command therefore, that the sepulchre be made sure untill the third day, least

*his disciples come by night, and steale him away, and say unto the people, He is

*risen from the dead: †and† the last errour shall be worse then the first.
so

[Delete]
65 *Pilat said unto them, Ye have †the† watch, goe your way, make it †as†
a as

can
know
*sure as †ye† †know.†
you can

[Delete] and
66 *So they went, and †when they had† †sealed up the stone, †they† made the
made the sepulchre sure, sealing the

*sepulchre sure with the† watch.
stone, and setting a

The xxviii. Chapter.

1 *In the †latter end of the Sabboth day, which dawneth† the first †day†
end of the Sabbath, as it beganne to dawne towards day

*of the weeke, came Mary Magdalene, and the other Mary to see the sepulchre.

2 *And behold, there was a great earthquake, for the Angel of the Lorde descended
"was

*from heaven, and came and rolled backe the stone from the doore, and sate upon it.

"Or, had bin

3 *His countenance was like lightning, and his raiment white as snow.

4 *And for feare of him the keepers did shake, and became as dead men.

And not yee
5 * The Angel answered, and sayde unto the women, Feare †ye not:† for I know

*that ye seeke Jesus, which was crucified.

for
6 *He is not here, he is risen, as he said, Come, see the place where

the Lord lay.
*†that the Lord was laid,†

7 *And go quickely, and tell his disciples that he is risen from the dead. And

*behold, hee goeth before you into Galilee, there shal ye see him: loe, I have
*told you.
8 *And they departed quickely from the sepulchre, with feare and great joy, and did
*run, to bring his disciples word.
9 *And as they went to tell his disciples, beholde, Jesus met them, saying, All
*haile. And they came, and helde him by the feete, and worshipped him.
10 *Then sayde Jesus unto them, Be not afraid: goe tell my brethren that they go into
*Galilee, and there shall they see me.

[Delete]
Now were goeing
11 * When they †were† †gone,† behold, some of the watch came into the
*city, and shewed unto the †high† Priests all the things that were done.
chiefe

12 *And when they were assembled with the elders, and had taken counsell, they
*gave large money unto the souldiers,

that
[Delete]
13 *Saying, Say yee, His disciples came by night, and stole him away
*while we slept.

governours eares
14 *And if this come to the †deputies† †eares,† wee will perswade him, and

secure you
*†make you carelesse.†

[Delete] they tooke and
15 *So they †,† †when they had taken† the money, did as they were taught.
tooke

is commonly reported
*And this saying †was noysed† among the Jewes untill this day.
16 *Then the eleven disciples went away into Galilee, into a mountaine where Jesus
*had appointed them.
17 *And when they saw him, they worshipped him: but some doubted.

18 *And Jesus came, and spake unto them, saying, All power is given unto me in
*heaven and in earth.
19 *Goe yee therefore, and teach all nations, baptizing them in the Name of the
*Father, and of the Sonne, and of the holy Ghost:
20 *Teaching them to observe all things, whatsoever I have commanded you: and loe,
*I am with you alway, even unto the ende of the world. Amen

Bishops' Bible

The Gospel by S. Marke

Annotation

holy
[Delete]

*The Gospel according to St. Marke

Authorized Version

The Gospel according to S. Marke

The first Chapter.

1 *The beginning of the Gospel of Jesus Christ, the Sonne of God,

is
2 *As it †hath bene† written in the Prophets, Beholde, I sende my messenger
*before thy face, which shall prepare thy way before thee.

The voyce of one cryinge
3 *†A voyce of him that cryeth† in the wildernesse, Prepare ye the way of the
[Delete]
*Lord, †and† make his paths straight.

did baptise preache
4 *John †was baptizing† in the wildernesse, and †preaching† the baptisme of

♣for
*repentance for the remission of sinnes.
"for

♣Or, unto
"Or, unto

there went out unto him all the land of Jury, and they of Hierusalem
5 *And †all the land of †Jury,† and they of Hierusalem, went out unto him,†
Judea

*and were all baptized of him in the river of Jordane, confessing their sinnes.

And
6 * John was clothed with camels haire, and with a girdle of a skinne about his

*loynes: and he did eate locusts and wilde hony,

theare commeth one stronger then I
7 *And preached, saying, †Hee that is stronger then I, commeth† after mee,
There commeth one mightier then I

the latchet of whose shooes
*†whose shooe latchet† I am not worthy to stoupe downe, and unloose.

indeede
8 *I have baptized you with water: but he shall baptize you with the holy

*Ghost.

9 *And it came to passe in those dayes, that Jesus came from Nazareth

[Delete]
*†a citie† of Galilee, and was baptized of John in Jordane.

strayght waye comming up heavens ♣opened
10 *And †assoone as he was come up† out of the water, he sawe †heaven open,†
the heavens "opened

like a Dove descending upon him
*and the Spirit †descending upon him like a Dove.†

♣Or, cloven or rent
"Or, cloven, or rent

beloved
11 *And there came a voyce from heaven, Thou art my †deare† Sonne, in
saying

*whom I am wel pleased.

the
12 *And immediatly the Spirit driveth him into wildernesse.

13 *And he was there in the wildernesse fourtie dayes tempted of Satan, and was

*with the wilde beastes, and the Angels ministred unto him.

Now delivered up
14 * After that John was †delivered to prison,† Jesus came into Galilee,
put in prison

*preaching the Gospel of the kingdome of God,

fulfilled
15 *And saying, The time is †come,† and the kingdome of God is at hand: repent

*ye, and beleeve the Gospel.

Now
16 * As he walked by the Sea of Galilee, he saw Simon, and Andrew his brother,

a nette
*casting †nets† into the Sea (for they were fishers.)

Come yee after
17 *And Jesus said unto them, †Follow† mee, and I wil make you to become

*fishers of men.

18 *And straightway they forsooke their nets, and followed him.

the sonne
19 *And when hee had gone a little further thence, hee sawe James †the sonne†

whoe
*of Zebedee, and John his brother, †which† also were in the ship mending their nets.

straightway
20 *And †anon† hee called them: and they left their father Zebedee in the ship

went after
*with the hired servants, and †followed† him.

went
21 *And they †came† into Capernaum, and straightway on the Sabboth †dayes,†
day

*hee entred into the Synagogue, and taught.

teaching
astonished doctrine
22 *And they were †astonied† at his †learning:† for hee taught them as one that had
*authoritie, and not as the Scribes.

[Delete]
23 *And there was in their Synagogue, a man †vexed† with an uncleane spirit,
out
*and he cried †alowd,†

♣Let us alone
24 *Saying, Let us alone, what have wee †to do† with thee, thou Jesus of Nazareth?
to doe

whoe the
*Art thou come to destroy us? I know thee †what† thou art, †even that† holy One
*of God.

♣Or, Awaye

it
25 *And Jesus rebuked †him,† saying, Holde thy peace, and come out of him.
him

it
26 *And when the uncleane spirit had torne him, and cried with a lowde voyce, †he†
hee
*came out of him.

questioned
27 *And they were all amazed, insomuch that they †demaunded one of another†
*among themselves, saying, What thing is this? What new doctrine is this? For
even the uncleane
*with authoritie commandeth he †the fowle† spirits, and they doe obey him.
28 *And immediatly his fame spread abroad throughout all the region
round about
*†bordering on† Galilee.
29 *And foorthwith, when they were come out of the Synagogue, they entered into
*the house of Simon, and Andrewe, with James and John.
30 *But Simons wives mother lay sicke of a fever: and anon they tell him of her.

31 *And hee came and tooke her by the hand, and lift her up: and immediately the

*fever †forsooke† her, and she ministred unto them.
left

did sett
32 *And at Even, when the Sunne †was downe,† they brought unto him all that were

possessed
*diseased, and them that were †vexed† with devils:

33 *And all the citie was gathered together at the doore.

34 *And hee healed many that were sicke of divers diseases, and cast out many devils,

say that
♣speake, because
*and suffered not the devils to †speake, because† they knew him.
"to speake, because

♣Or, say that
"Or, to say that they knew him

rising up, a greate while before day, hee
35 *And in the morning †very early before day, Jesus when hee was risen up,†

*went out, and departed into a solitarie place, and there prayed.

36 *And Simon, and they that were with him, followed after him:

37 *And when they had found him, they saide unto him, All men seeke for thee.

38 *And he said unto them, Let us goe into the next townes, that I may preach

came I forthe
*there also: for therefore †am I come.†

through out
39 *And he preached in their Synagogues, †in† all Galilee, and cast

out devils
*†the devils out.†

40 *And there came a leper to him, beseeching him, and kneeling downe to him, &

*saying unto him, If thou wilt, thou canst make me cleane.

putting
moved with [Delete] put
41 *And Jesus, †having† compassion †on him,† †when he had put† foorth his

and
*hand, touched him, and saith unto him, I will, be thou cleane.

42 *And as soone as he had spoken, immediatly the leprosie departed from him,

clensed
*and he was †made cleane.†

he straightly charged him, & forthwith sent him away
43 *And †after he had given him a strait commandement, he sent him away forthwith:†

goe thy way
44 *And saith unto him, See thou say nothing to any man: but †get thee hence,†

*shew thy selfe to the Priest, and offer for thy cleansing those things which Moses

testimonye
*commanded, for a †witnes† unto them.

when he was gone
went out and to proclame
45 *But he, †as soone as he was departed,† beganne †openly to declare† †many things,†
to publish it much

Jesus
the matter Jesus
*and to †publish† †this rumor:† insomuch, that †Jesus† could no more openly
blase abroad

*enter into the citie, but was without in desert places: and they came to him from

*every quarter.

The ii. Chapter.

And againe, he entered into Capernaum after some dayes,
1 *†After a few dayes also, he entered into Capernaum againe,† and it was noysed

*that hee was in the house.

straight way insomuch [Delete]
2 *And †anon† many were gathered together, †insomuch† that †now†

*there was no roome to receive them, no not so much as about the doore: and he

[Delete]
*preached the word †of the Gospel† unto them.

3 *And they come unto him, bringing one sick of the palsie, which was borne of

[Delete]
*foure †men.†

4 *And when they could not come nigh unto him for preasse, they uncovered the

where he was it up
*roofe †of the house that he was in:† and when they had broken †up the roofe,†

[Delete]
*they †do with cords† let downe the bed wherein the sicke of the palsie lay.

5 *When Jesus saw their faith, he said unto the sicke of the palsie, Sonne, thy

*sinnes be forgiven thee.

6 *But there were certaine of the Scribes sitting there, and reasoning in their

*hearts,

this man
7 *Why doeth †he† thus speake blasphemies? Who can forgive sinnes but God

*onely?

reasoned
8 *And immediatly, when Jesus perceived in his spirit that they so †reason† within

theise thinges things
said theise things
*themselves, he †saith† unto them, Why reason ye †such things†

*in your hearts?

9 *Whether is it easier to say to the sick of the palsie, Thy sinnes be forgiven

and
*thee: or to say, Arise, take up thy bed and walke?

to forgive sinnes on earth
on earth to forgive sinnes
10 *But that ye may know that the Sonne of man hath power †in earth to forgive sinnes,†

*(He saith to the sicke of the palsie,)

goe thy way
11 *I say unto thee, Arise, and take up thy bed, and †get thee hence† into thine

*house.

12 *And immediatly he arose, tooke up the bed, and went foorth before them all,

*insomuch that they were all amazed, and glorified God, saying, We never saw it on
*this fashion.

forth multitude
13 *And he went againe by the Sea side, and all the †people† resorted unto
*him, and hee taught them.

hee the sonne ♣receite
14 *And as †Jesus† passed by, He saw Levi †the sonne† of Alphee sitting at the receite
"at the receit
*of Custome, and said unto him, Follow me. And he arose, and followed him.

♣Or, at the place where the custome was received
"Or, at the place where the Custome was received

as Jesus
as Jesus
15 *And it came to passe, that †when Jesus† sate at meate in his house, many Publicanes
[Delete]
*and sinners sate also together †at meate† with Jesus and his disciples: for
*there were many, and they followed him.

16 *And when the Scribes & Pharisees sawe him eat with Publicanes and sinners,
*they said unto his Disciples, How is it that he eateth and drinketh with Publicanes
*and sinners?

it are strong
17 *When Jesus heard †that,† hee sayeth unto them, They that †be whole,†
are whole
*have no neede of the Physition, but they that are sicke: I came not to call the
*righteous, but sinners to repentance.

♣were fasters
18 *And the disciples of John, and of the Pharisees †did fast:†
used to fast
*and they come and say unto him, Why doe the disciples of John, and of the Pharisees
*fast, but thy Disciples fast not?

♣Or, used to fast

19 *And Jesus saide unto them, Can the children of the Bride-chamber fast, while
*the Bridegrome is with them? As long as they have the Bridegrome with them,
*they cannot fast.

20 *But the dayes wil come, when the Bridegrome shalbe taken away from them, and then
*shall they fast in those dayes.

♣newe on els the
21 *No man also soweth a piece of newe cloth †unto† an olde garment: †otherwayes, his†
"new

that filled it up taketh away from the olde, & the
*newe piece †taketh away somewhat from the olde garment, and so the† rent is made worse.

♣Or, rawe, or unwrought
"Or, raw, or unwrought

putteth bottels
22 *And no man †powreth† new wine into olde †vessels,† else the new wine doth burst

bottels bottels
*the †vessels,† and the wine †runneth out,† and the †vessels† will be marred:
is spilled

bottels
*But new wine must be put into new †vessels.†

23 *And it came to passe, that hee went thorow the corne fields on the Sabboth †dayes,†
day

as they went
*and his Disciples began †by the way† to plucke the eares of corne.

24 *And the Pharisees said unto him, Behold, why do they on the Sabboth †dayes†
day

*that which is not lawfull?

25 *And he said unto them, Have yee never read what David did, when hee had neede,

[Delete] were
*and was an hungred, †both† hee, and they that †were† with him?

26 *How he went into the house of God in the dayes of Abiathar the high Priest,
*and did eate the Shew-bread, which is not lawfull to eate but for the Priests, and
*gave also to them which were with him?

27 *And he said unto them, The Sabboth was made for man, & not man for the Sabboth.

the Sonne of man is
28 *Therefore †is the Sonne of man† Lord also of the Sabboth.

The iii. Chapter.

there was a man
1 *And he entered againe into the Synagogue, and †a man was† there which had
*a withered hand:

2 *And they watched him, whether hee would heale him on the Sabboth day, that they
*might accuse him.

sayth
3 *And he †sayd† unto the man which had the withered hand,
Stand forth
*†Arise, <u>and</u> <u>stand</u> in the midst.†

4 *And hee sayeth unto them, Is it lawfull to doe good on the Sabboth dayes, or
*to doe evill? to save life, or to kill? But they helde their peace.

mourning withall
5 *And when he had looked round about on them with anger, †mourning† for the
being grieved
*hardnesse of their hearts, hee saith unto the man, Stretch foorth thine hand. And
"hardnesse
[Delete]
*hee stretched it out: and his hand was restored †as† whole as the other.
"Or, <u>blindnesse</u>

went forth consulted
6 *And the Pharisees †departed,† and straightway †gathered a counsell† with the
tooke counsell
how
*Herodians against him, †that† they might destroy him.

withdrewe himselfe
7 *But Jesus †avoyded† with his disciples, to the Sea: and a great

from Galilee, followed him
*multitude †followed him from Galilee,† and from †Jury,†
Judea

from
8 *And from Hiersualem, and from Idumea, and †from the region which is† beyond

[Delete]
*Jordane, and they †that dwelt† about Tyre and Sidon, a great multitude,

*when they had heard what things he did, came unto him.
great

he spake to smale
9 *And †Jesus commanded† his disciples that a ship should wait on him,

multitude
*because of the †people,† lest they should throng him.

in so much ♣preassed
10 *For he had healed many, †in so much† that they preassed upon him for to touch
"preassed

*him, as many as had plagues.

♣Or, rushed
"Or, rushed

[Delete] [Delete]
11 *And †the† uncleane spirits, when they saw him, †they† fell downe

[Delete]
*before him †at his feete,† and cryed, saying, Thou art the Sonne of God.

12 *And hee straitly charged them, that they should not make him knowen.

13 *And hee goeth up into a mountaine, and calleth unto him whom hee would: and they

*came unto him.

14 *And he ordeined twelve, that they should be with him, and that he might send

*them forth to preach:

to
15 *And †that they might† have power to heale sickenesses, and to cast out devils.

Simon he surnamed
16 *And †he gave unto Simon to name† Peter.

[Delete] the brother of James
17 *And †he called† James the sonne of Zebedee, and John †James brother†

he surnamed them [Delete]
*(and †gave them names,† Boanerges, which is †to say,† The sonnes of thunder.)

18 *And Andrew, and Philip, and Bartholomew, and Matthew, and Thomas, and James

*the sonne of Alphee, and Thaddeus, and Simon the Chanaanite,

went ♣into an house
19 *And Judas Iscariot, which also betrayed him: and they †come† into an house.
"into an house

♣Or, home
"Or, home

multitude
20 *And the †people† commeth together againe, so that they could not so much as

*eate bread.

his ♣frends
21 *And when †they that belonged unto him,† heard of it, they went out to lay
his "friends

holde on beside him selfe
*†hands upon† him, for they said, He is †madde.†

♣Or, kinsmen
"Or, kinsmen

22 *And the Scribes which came downe from Hierusalem, sayde, Hee hath Beelzebub,

*and by the prince of the devils, casteth hee out devils.

he and
23 *And †when he had† called them unto him, †he† said unto them in parables, How

*can Satan cast out Satan?

kingdome kingdome stande
24 *And if a †realme† be divided against it selfe, that †realme† cannot †endure.†

stande
25 *And if a house bee divided against it selfe, that house cannot †continue.†

rise up
26 *And if Satan †make insurrection† against himselfe, and be divided, he cannot

stande
*†continue,† but hath an ende.

rifle his stuffe
27 *No man can enter into a strong mans house, and †take away his goods,† except
spoile his goods

will he rifle
*he will first binde the strong man, and then †will spoyle† his house.
hee will spoyle

sonnes
28 *Verely I say unto you, All sinnes shalbe forgiven unto the †children† of men,

*and blasphemies, wherewithsoever they shall blaspheme:

29 *But he that shall blaspheme against the holy Ghost, hath never forgivenes,

guiltie of
lyable to
*but is †in danger of† eternall damnation.
in danger of

Because
30 *†For† they said, He hath an uncleane spirit.

then his brethren, and his mother
31 *There came †his mother, and his brethren,† and standing without, sent unto him,

*calling him.

multitude they
32 *And the †people† sate about him, and saide unto him, Beholde, thy mother,

without seeke for thee
*and thy brethren, †and thy sisters seeke for thee without.†

33 *And he answered them, saying, Who is my mother, or my brethren?

he and
34 *And †when he had† looked round about on them which sate about him, †he† said,

*Behold my mother and my brethren.

35 *For who so ever shall doe the will of God, the same is my brother, and my

*sister, & mother.

The iiii. Chapter.

was
1 *And hee began againe to teach by the Sea side: and there gathered unto him

a greate multitude
*†much people,† so that hee entred into a ship, and sate in the Sea: and

the whole multitude Sea lande
*†all the people† was by the †Sea side† on the †shore.†

2 *And hee taught them many things by parables, and said unto them in

teaching
doctrine
*his †doctrine,†

3 *Hearken, Behold, there went out a sower to sowe:

came to passe [Delete] waye
4 *And it †fortuned† as he sowed, †that† some fell by the †wayes†

*side: and the foules of the aire came, and devoured it up.

And
5 * Some fell on stonie ground, where it had not much earth: and immediately

*it sprang up, because it had no depth of earth.

risen
when up was scorched
6 *But †as soone as† the Sunne was †up,† it †caught heate,† and because it had

*no roote, it withered away.

7 *And some fell among thornes, and the thornes grewe up, and choked it, and

yeelded
*it †gave† no fruit.

other increased
8 *And †some† fell on good ground, and did yeeld fruite that sprang up, & †grew,†

*and brought foorth some thirtie, and some sixtie, and some an hundred.

9 *And he said unto them, He that hath eares to heare, let him heare.

10 *And when hee was alone, they that were about him, with the twelve, asked of

*him the parable.

11 *And he sayd unto them, Unto you it is given to knowe the mysterie of the kingdome

in
*of God: but unto them that are without, al things are done †by† parables,
these

seeing perceyve hearing
12 *That †when they see,† they may see, and not †discerne:† and †when they heare,†

convert
*they may heare, and not understand, least at any time they should †turne,†
bee converted

*and their sinnes should be forgiven them.

13 *And hee saide unto them, Knowe yee not this parable? And howe then will †yee†
you

*know all parables?

14 *The Sower soweth the word.

Now theise are they by the way side
15 *†And† †they that received seed by the way side, are those† where the word is
And

*sowen, but when they have heard, Satan commeth immediatly, and taketh away the

*worde that was sowen in their hearts.

theise are they likewise which are sowen on stonie ground
16 *And †likewise they that receive seede into the stonie ground, are they,†

whoe
who immediately
*†which† when they have heard the worde, †at once† receive it with gladnesse:

but last but a while
And but endure for a time
17 *†Yet† have no root in themselves, †and so endure but a time:† †and†
and so endure but for a time [Delete]

after affliction or
*†anon† when †trouble and† persecution ariseth for the words sake, immediatly
afterward

*they are offended.

theise are such
theise are they which are sowen such
18 *And †those bee they that receive seede† among thornes: †and they are such†

*as heare the word,

this
19 *And the cares of †the† world, and the deceitfulnesse of riches, & the lusts of

fruitlesse
becommeth unfruitfull
*other things entring in, choke the word, and it †is made† †unfruitfull.†

theise are they which are sowen on good ground
20 *And †they which received seede into good ground, are† such as heare the word,

and bring forth fruit some thirty folde, and some sixtie, and
*and receive it, †so that one corne doth bring forth thirty, some sixtie,†
and bring foorth fruit, some thirty fold, some sixty, &

*some an hundred.

a brought ♣bushell
21 *And hee saide unto them, Is †the† candle †lighted† to bee put under a bushell,
"bushel

a bed
*or under †the table?† and not to be †put† on a candlesticke?
set

♣the word in the originall signifyeth a less measure
"The word in the originall signifieth a lesse measure, as mat. 5.15

hid, which manifested
22 *For there is nothing †so privie, that† shall not be †opened:† neither

was it
*†hath it bene so† secret, but that it †shall† come abroad.
was any thing kept should

23 *If any man have eares to heare, let him heare.

24 *And he said unto them, Take heed what †ye† heare: With what measure yee mete,
you

it shall be measured to you
*†with the same shall it be measured to you againe:† And unto you that heare, shall

*more be given.

25 *For †unto him that hath, shall it† be given: and †from him that hath not,
hee that hath, to him shall he that hath not, from

*shalbe taken away,† even that which he hath.
him shall be taken

as cast
26 *And hee sayde, So is the kingdome of God, †even as† if a man should †sowe†

on
*seede †in† the ground,
into

spring
27 *And should sleepe, and rise night and day, and the seed should †sping† and grow

*up, he knoweth not how.

28 *For the earth bringeth foorth fruite of her selfe, first the blade, then the

*eare, after that the full corne in the eare.

♣brought foorth immediately he putteth
29 *But when the fruite is brought foorth, †anon he thrusteth† in the sickle,
"brought forth

*because the harvest is come.

♣Or, ripe
"Or, ripe

30 *And hee saide, Whereunto shall we liken the kingdome of God? Or with what

*comparison shall we compare it?

[Delete]
31 *†It is† like a graine of mustard seed: which when it is sowen in the
It is

*earth, is lesse then all seedes that be in the earth:
the

becommeth
32 *†And† when it is sowen, it groweth up, and †is† greater then all herbes,
But

shooteth out
*and †beareth† great branches, so that the fowles of the aire may

lodge
*†make their nestes† under the shadow of it.

spake
33 *And with many such parables †preached† he the worde unto them, as they were

[Delete]
*able to heare †it.†
it

in private
34 *But without parable spake hee not unto them: †but† †when they were alone,†
a and when they were alone

*he expounded all things to his disciples.

35 *And the same day when the Even was come, he saith unto them, Let us passe over

side
*unto the other †side.†

when they had sent away the multitude they
36 *And †they left the people, and† tooke him, even as he was in the

*ship, and there were also with him other little ships.

beate
37 *And there arose a great storme of winde, and the waves †dashed† into the

*shippe, so that it was now full.

awaked
hinder part of the ship awoke
38 *And hee was in the †sterne† asleepe on a pillow: and they †awake†
awake

*him, and say unto him, Master, carest thou not that we perish?

being awaked he
he arose and [Delete]
39 *And †he arose, and† rebuked the winde, and saide unto the Sea, Peace, †and†

was
*be still: and the winde ceassed, and there †followed† a great calme.

in this sort
40 *And he said unto them, Why are ye fearefull ?
so [Delete]

*How is it that †ye† have no faith?
you

What maner of man
41 *And they feared exceedingly, and saide one to another, †Who†

*is this, that †both† the wind and the sea obey him?
even

The v. Chapter.

side
1 *And they came over unto the other †side† of the Sea, into the countrey of the
*Gadarenes.

out of
2 *And when he was come out of the ship, immediately there met him †from among†
with
*the tombes, a man †possessed of† an uncleane spirit,

Whoe dwelling
3 *†Which† had his †abiding† among the tombs, and no man could binde him, no not with
*chaines:

4 *Because that hee had bene often bound with fetters and chaines, and the chaines
*had bene plucked asunder by him, and the fetters broken in pieces: neither coulde
*any man tame him.

5 *And alwayes, night and day, he was in the mountaines, and in the tombes, crying,
[Delete]
*and †all to† cutting himselfe with stones.

sawe
6 *But when hee †had spied† Jesus afarre off, he †ranne,† and worshipped him,
came

7 *And cryed with a loude voyce, and sayde, What have I to do with thee, Jesus,
highe adjure by
*thou sonne of the most †highest† God? I †require† thee †in the Name of†
*God, that thou torment me not.

uncleane
8 *(For hee saide unto him, Come out of the man, thou †foule† spirit.)

9 *And he asked him, What is thy name? And he answered, saying, My name is Legion:
*for we are many.

besought him much
10 *And he †praied him instantly† that he would not send them away out of the countrey.

Now
11 *†But† there was there nigh unto the mountaines, a great heard of swine, feeding.

12 *And all the devils besought him, saying, Send us into the swine, that wee may

*enter into them.

forthwith
13 *And †anon† Jesus gave them leave. And the uncleane spirits went out,

rushed violently from a steepe place
*and entred into the swine, and the heard †ranne headlong†
ranne violently downe a steepe place

*into the sea (they were about two thousand) and were choked in the sea.

they that fed the swyne
14 *And †the swineheards† fled, and tolde it in the city, and in the

[Delete] it was that
*countrey. And they went out †for† to see what was done:

possessed with the devil
15 *And they come to Jesus, and see him that was †vexed with the feend,† and

*had the Legion, sitting, and clothed, and in his right minde: and they were afraid.

was with
befell to
16 *And they that sawe †it,† tolde them howe it †came to passe to† him that was
it

concerning
*possessed with the devil, and also †of† the swine.

17 *And they began to pray him to depart out of their coasts.

18 *And when he was come into the ship, hee that had bene possessed with the devil

*praied him that he might be with him.

to thy house to thine friendes
19 *Howbeit, Jesus suffered him not, but saith unto him, Goe †home to thy friendes,†
home to thy friends

tell hath
*and †shew† them how great things the Lord hath done for thee, and had

*compassion on thee.

20 *And he departed, and began to publish in Decapolis, how great things Jesus had

to
*done †for† him: and all men did marvaile.
for

passed side
21 *And when Jesus was †come† over againe by ship unto the other †side,†

*much people gathered unto him, and he was nigh unto the sea.

22 *And behold, there commeth one of the rulers of the synagogue, Jairus by name: &

[Delete]
*when he saw him, he fell †downe† at his feete,

Because My
My little
23 *And besought him greatly, saying, †My† †yong† daughter lieth

wouldest thou
I pray thee
*at point of death, †I pray thee† come and lay thy hands on her that she
the

healed
*may bee †safe,† and she shal live.

Jesus
24 *And †Jesus† went with him, and much people followed him, and thronged him.

[Delete] [Delete]
25 *And †there was† a certaine woman, which had †beene diseased of†

*an issue of blood twelve yeeres,

26 *And had suffered many things of many Phisicians, and had spent al that she had,

was nothing bettered grew worse;
*and †felt none amendement at all,† but rather †the worse.†
grew worse,

[Delete] [Delete]
27 *When she had heard of Jesus, †she† came in the preasse behind †him,†

*& touched his garment.

touch but
28 *For she said, If I may †but touch† his clothes, I shall be whole.

29 *And straightway the fountain of her blood was dried up: and shee felt in her

that
*body that shee was healed of †the† plague.

had gone out of
30 *And Jesus immediatly knowing in himselfe that vertue †proceeded from† him,
*turned him about in the preasse, and sayd, Who touched my clothes?

multitude thronging thee & sayest
31 *And his disciples sayde unto him, Thou seest the †people thrust thee, and askest†
touched
*thou, Who †did touch† me?

[Delete]
32 *And he looked round about, †for† to see her that had done this thing.

in
33 *But the woman fearing, and trembling, knowing what was done †within† her,
*came and fel down before him, and told him all the trueth.

made thee whole
34 *And he sayd unto her, Daughter, thy faith hath †saved thee,† go in peace, and
*be whole of thy plague.

35 *While he yet spake, there came from the ruler of the synagogues house, certaine
troublest
*which sayd, Thy daughter is dead, why †diseasest† thou the master any further?

36 *As soone as Jesus heard the worde that was spoken, he saith unto the ruler of
*the synagogue, Be not afraid, onely beleeve.

37 *And he suffered no man to follow him, save Peter, and James, and John, the
*brother of James.

38 *And he commeth to the house of the ruler of the synagogue, & seeth the tumult,
*and them that wept and wailed greatly.

39 *And when he was come in, he sayth unto them, Why make ye this adoe, and weepe?
*the damosell is not dead, but sleepeth.

when he he
when he
40 *And they laughed him to scorne: but †hee, after that he† had put them all out,

hee
* taketh the father and the mother of the Damosell, and them that were with him:

was laying
was lying
*and entreth in where the Damosel †lay.†

hee tooke & sayd
41 *And †when hee had taken† the Damosel by the hand, †he sayth† unto her,

*Talitha cumi, which is, being interpreted, Damosell (I say unto thee) arise.

42 *And straightway the Damosel arose, and walked, for she was of the age of twelve

astonished with a greate astonishment
*yeeres: and they were †astonied out of measure.†

[Delete]
43 *And hee charged them straitly that no man should know †of† it: and

that some thing should be given her to eate
*commanded †to give her meate.†

The vi. Chapter.

went out from
1 *And he †departed† thence, and came into his owne countrey, and his disciples

*follow him.

2 *And when the Sabboth day was come, he beganne to teach in the synagogue: And

astonished
*many hearing him, were †astonied,† saying, From whence hath †hee† these things?
this man

that even
which that
*And what wisedome is this †that† is given unto him, †and† such mighty workes
that even

[Delete]
*†that† are wrought by his hands?

the sonne of Marie
3 *Is not this the carpenter, †Maries sonne,† the brother of James and Joses,

*and of Juda and Simon? And are not his sisters here with us? And they were

in
*offended †at† him.
at

dishonoured
But without honour
4 * Jesus said unto them, A Prophet is not †without honour,† but in his owne

*countrey, and among his owne kinne, and in his owne house.

5 *And he could there doe no mighty worke: †but† layd his hands upon a
save that hee

them
*fewe sicke folke, and healed †them:†

6 *And he marveiled because of their unbeliefe. And he went

about the villages in circuit
round about the villages
*†about by the villages that lay on every side,† teaching.

unto him by
7 *And he calleth the twelve, and began to send them foorth,

over
against
*two and two, and gave them power †against† uncleane spirits,
over

for
8 *And commanded them that they should take nothing †in† their journey, save

rodde
staffe
*a †staffe† onely: no scrip, no bread, no money in their purse:

be shod [Delete]
9 *But †should be shooed† with sandales: and †that they should† not put

*on two coates.

in what place soever
10 *And he sayd unto them, †Wheresoever† yee enter into an house, there

from that place
*abide till yee depart †thence.†

11 *And whosoever shall not receive you, nor heare you, when ye depart thence, shake

from
[Delete] testimonie
*off the dust †that is† under your feete, for a †witnesse† against them:

verely I say more tolerable
*†I say verely† unto you, it shall bee †easier† for

Sodom & Gomorrha
*†the Sodomites and the Gomorrheans† in the day of judgement, then for that citie.

12 *And they went out, and preached, that men should repent:

13 *And they cast out many devils, and anointed †many that were sicke, with oyle,†
with oyle, many that were sicke

*and healed them.

14 *And king Herod heard <u>of him</u>, (for his name was spred abroad:) and he sayd that

Baptizer
the Baptist
*John †Baptist† was risen from the dead, and therefore mighty works do shew

*forth themselves in him.

And other
15 *†Other† said, That it is Elias. †Some† said, That it is a Prophet, or as one
Others And others

*of the Prophets.

[Delete] <u>thereof</u>
16 *But when Herod †had† heard †of him,† hee sayd, It is John, whom I beheaded,

the deade
*he is risen from †death.†

holde
17 *For Herod himselfe had sent foorth and laid †hands† upon John, and bound him

*in prison for Herodias sake, his brother Philips wife, †because† he had
for

*married her.

had
18 *For John said unto Herod, It is not lawfull for thee to have thy

*brothers wife.

had a quarrell to
♣layd waite for
19 *Therefore Herodias †layd waite for† him, and would have killed him,
had “a quarrell against

*but she could not.

♣Or, had a quarrell to
“Or, an inward grudge

20 *For Herod feared John, knowing that he was a just man, and an holy, and

reverenced him
*†gave him reverence:† and when hee heard him, hee did many things, and heard him
“observed him

*gladly.

“Or, kept him or saved him

21 *And when a convenient day was come, that Herod on his birth day made a supper

his
*to †the† lords, high captaines, and chiefe estates of Galilee:

sayd
22 *And when the daughter of the †same† Herodias came in, and danced, and

with him
*pleased Herode, and them that sate †at boord also,† the king sayd unto the

*Damosel, Aske of me, whatsoever thou wilt, and I will give it thee.

23 *And he sware unto her, Whatsoever thou shalt aske of me, I wil give it thee,

[Delete] [Delete]
*†even† unto the †one† halfe of my kingdome.

And
24 *And she went forth, and sayd unto her mother, What shall I aske? She

the head of John the Baptist
*sayd, †John Baptists head.†

25 *And shee came in straightway with haste unto the king, and asked, saying, I wil

the
*that thou give me by and by in a charger, the head of John Baptist.

yet
26 *And the king was exceeding sory, †howbeit† for his oaths sake, and for their sakes

frustrate her
with him reject her
*which sate †at supper also,† he would not †cast her off.†

one of his gard
27 *And immediatly the king sent †the hangman,† and commanded his head to be
"an executioner

[Delete]
*brought †in,† and he went and beheaded him in the prison,

"Or, one of his guard

28 *And brought his head in a charger, and gave it to the Damosel, and the Damosel

*gave it to her mother.

corpse
29 *And when his disciples heard of it, they came & tooke up his †body,† and layd

*it in a tombe,

30 *And the Apostles gathered themselves together unto Jesus, and told him all

*things, both what they had done, and what they had taught.

your selves apart a desert place
31 *And he sayd unto them, Come †ye alone out of the way† into †the wildernesse,†
ye your selves apart

comming and going
*and rest a while. For there were many †commers and goers,† and they had no

fit tyme
leasure
*†leasure† so much as to eate.

into a desert place by shippe privately
32 *And they departed †by ship out of the way into a desert place.†

saw them departing
33 *And the people †spied them when they departed,† and many knew him, and ranne afoote

came before
*thither out of all cities, and †came thither before† them, and came together unto
outwent

*him.

was moved with
34 *And Jesus when he came out, saw much people, and †had† compassion

toward as
*†on† them, because they were †like† sheepe not having a shepheard: and he began

*to teach them many things.

came and sayd
35 *And when the day was now farre spent, his disciples †come† unto him, †saying,†

*This is a desert place, and now the time is farre passed:

Send them away
36 *†Let them depart,† that they may goe into the countrey round about, and into the

them selves
*villages, and buy †them† bread: for they have nothing to eate.

37 *He answered, and said unto them, Give ye them to eate. And they say unto him,

Should wee ♣two hundred peniworth
*†Shall we† go and buy two hundred peniworth of bread, and give them to eate?
Shall wee two hundred "peny-worth

♣The wordes in the originall import about 25 ounces of silver
"The Romaine penie is seven pence halfe-penie, as mat. 18.28

see
38 *Hee sayth unto them, Howe many loaves have yee? goe and †looke.† And when

knew
*they †had searched,† they say, Five, and two fishes.

[Delete]
39 *And hee commanded them to make †them† all sitte downe by companies upon

*the greene grasse.

in ranckes by by
40 *And they sate downe, †here a rowe, and there a rowe,† †by† hundreds, and †by†

*fifties.

he
41 *And when hee had taken the five loaves, and the two fishes, †and† looked up to

and
*heaven, †hee† blessed, and brake the loaves, and gave them to his disciples to

*set before them: and the two fishes divided he among them all.

all did eate filled
42 *And they †did eate,† and were †satisfied.†
did all eat

broken peeces
43 *And they tooke up twelve baskets full of the †fragments,† and of the fishes.
fragments

of
44 *And they that did eate the loaves, were about five thousand men.

get up
45 *And straightway he constrained his disciples to †goe† into the ship, and
get

♣to the other side ♣unto sent
*to goe †over the sea† before unto Bethsaida, while he †should send†
"unto

*away the people.

♣Or, [Cancelled, illegible]
♣Or, over against
"Or, over against Bethsaida

46 *And when he had sent them away, hee departed into a mountaine to pray.

47 *And when Even was come, the ship was in the midst of the sea, and he alone
*on the land.

toyled
toyled
toyling
48 *And hee sawe them †troubled† in rowing (for the winde was contrary unto them:)
*and about the fourth watch of the night, hee commeth unto them, walking upon the
*sea, and would have passed by them.

49 *But when they sawe him walking upon the sea, they supposed it had bene a spirit,
*and cried out.

50 *(For they all saw him, & were troubled.) and †anon† he talked with them, and
immediatly
*sayth unto them, Be of good cheare, It is I, be not afraid.

51 *And he went up unto them into the ship, and the winde ceased, and they were

wondered
*sore amazed in themselves beyond measure, and †marveiled.†

considered not the miracle for
52 *For they †understood not what was done† of the loaves, †because† their heart

*was hardened.

53 *And when they had passed over, they came into the land of Genezareth, and

*†drew up into the haven.†
drew to the shore

54 *And when they were come out of the ship, straightway they knew him,

[Delete] through that whole
55 *And ran †foorth† †throughout all the† region round about, and began to

[Delete]
*carrie about in beds, those that were sicke, †thither† where they heard

[Delete]
*†that† he was.

countrie
56 *And whithersoever he entred, into villages, or cities, or †fields,† they

[Delete] besought
*layd the sicke †folkes† in the streetes, and †prayed† him that they might

if ♣him
*touch †&† it were but the †hemme† of his garment: and as many as touched †it,†
border "him

*were made whole.

♣Or, it
"Or, it

The vii. Chapter.

Then gathered unto him the Pharisees
1 *†And the Pharisees come together unto him,† and certaine of the Scribes,
Then came together unto him the Pharisees

*which came from Hierusalem.

common
2 *And when they saw some of his disciples eate bread with †defiled† (that is to
"defiled

*say, with unwashen) hands, they found fault.

"Or, <u>common</u>

♣oft
3 *For the Pharisees and all the Jewes, except they wash their hands oft,
"oft

holding
*eate not, †observing† the tradition of the elders.

♣Or, <u>diligently</u>, <u>in</u> <u>the</u> <u>originall</u>, <u>with</u> <u>the</u> <u>fist</u> <u>Theophy</u>: <u>up</u> <u>to</u> <u>the</u> <u>elbow</u>
"Or, <u>diligently</u>, <u>in</u> <u>the</u> <u>Originall</u>, <u>with</u> <u>the</u> <u>fist</u>. <u>Theophilact</u>, <u>up</u> <u>to</u> <u>the</u> <u>elbow</u>

abroade
the market
4 *And when they come from †the market,† except they wash, they eate not. And many

received to hold
*other things there bee which they have †taken upon them to observe,† <u>as</u> the washing

♣tables
*of cups and pots, brasen vessels, and of tables.
"tables

♣Or, <u>beds</u>
"Or, <u>beds</u>

the Pharisees & Scribes asked him
5 *Then †asked him the Pharisees & Scribes,† Why walke not thy disciples according

*to the tradition of the elders, but eate bread with unwashen hands?

Well hath Esaias prophesied
6 *He answered and said unto them, †Surely Esaias hath prophesied well†

*of you hypocrites, as it is written, This people honoreth me with their lips,

*but their heart is farre from me.

7 *Howbeit in vaine do they worship me, teaching doctrines, the commandements
for

*of men.

laying aside the commandement of God hold
8 *For, †the commandement of God being laid apart,† yee †observe† the tradition of

*men, as the washing of pots and cups: and many other such like things ye do.

frustrate
♣reject
9 *And he sayd unto them, Full well ye †cast aside† the commandement of God, that
"reject

*yee may keepe your owne tradition.

♣Or, frustrate
"Or, frustrate

10 *For Moses sayd, Honour thy father and thy mother: and whoso curseth father

*or mother, let him die the death.

11 *But ye say, If a man shal say to his father or mother,

that is, the offeringe whatsoever is from me by it thou mayst
that is the gift offered of me by it thou mayst
*†Corban† †(that is, by the gift) that is offered of me, thou shalt
It is Corban, that is to say, a gift, by whatsoever thou mightest bee

be benefited
be benefited
*be helped.†
profited by me: he shall be free

12 *And †so† ye suffer him no more to doe ought for his father, or his mother,
[Delete]

13 *Making the word of God of none effect through your tradition, which ye have

delivered
*†ordeined:† And many such things do ye.
like

14 *And when hee had called all the people unto him, he sayd unto them, Hearken

♣understand
*unto me every one of you, and understand.

♣Or, consider

from entring into him can defile him
†25†*There is nothing without a man that †can defile him, when it entreth into him:†
15

proceed out of him
come out of him
*but the things which †proceed out of a man,† those are they that defile the man.

16 *If any man have eares to heare, let him heare.

was entred [Delete]
17 *And when hee †came† into the house †away† from the people, his disciples

concerning the parable
*asked him †of the similitude.†

18 *And hee sayth unto them, Are yee †also so without understanding?† Doe yee
so without understanding also

*not perceive that whatsoever thing from without entreth into the man, it can not

*defile him,

19 *Because it entreth not into his heart, but into the belly, and goeth out into

♣draught [Delete]
*the draught, purging all †the† meats?

♣the naturall passage. Suidas

that
20 *And he sayd, That which commeth out of the man, defileth the man.

[Delete]
21 *For from within, †even† out of the heart of men, proceed evill thoughts,

*adulteries, fornications, murders,

an evill
22 *Thefts, covetousnesse, wickednesse, deceit, †wantonnesse,† †a wicked† eye,
lasciviousnesse

*blasphemie, pride, foolishnesse:

23 *All these evill things come from within, and defile the man.

24 *And from thence hee arose, and went into the borders of Tyre and Sidon, and entred

have knowe it
*into an house, and would †that† no man †should have knowen,† but he could not be hid.

little
[Delete]
25 *For a certain woman, whose †yong† daughter had an uncleane spirit,
yong

[Delete] and
*†when she had† heard of him, came and fell at his feet.

a Syrophenician by birth
26 *(The woman was a Greeke, †out of the nation of Syrophenissa:†) & she besought him
"Greeke a Syrophenician by nation

foorth out of
*that he would cast †out† the devill †from† her daughter.

"Or, <u>Gentile</u>

filled
27 *But Jesus sayd unto her, Let the children first be †fed:† for it is not meet to

[Delete]
the litle
*take the childrens bread, and to cast it unto †the litle† dogges.
the

Truth
Yet even [Delete]
And Yes yet little
28 * She answered, and sayd unto him, †Yes† lord, †for† the †little†
[Delete]

under the table eate
*dogges †also eat under the table† of the childrens crummes.

29 *And he sayd unto her, For this saying, goe thy way, the devill is gone out of

*thy daughter.

owne
[Delete] [Delete]
30 *And when shee was come †home† to her house, shee found

[Delete] gone out layed upon
*†that† the devill †was departed,† and her daughter †lying on† the bed.

againe departing
31 *And †when hee was departed againe† from the coasts of Tyre and Sidon, he

*came unto the sea of Galilee, thorow the mids of the coasts of Decapolis.

32 *And they bring unto him one that was deafe, and had an impediment in his speech:

beseeche hand
*and they †pray† him to put his †hands† upon him.

hee tooke multitude and
33 *And †when hee had taken† him aside from the †people, he† put his fingers

*into his eares, and †when he had† spet, touched his tongue,
he and

looking he sayeth
34 *And †when hee had looked† up to heaven, sighed, and †said† unto him,

[Delete] [Delete]
*Ephphatha, that is †to say,† Be †thou† opened.

35 *And straightway his eares were opened, and the string of his tongue was loosed,

*and hee spake plaine.

charged
36 *And he †commanded† them that they should tell no man: but the more he

charged
*†commanded† them, so much the more a great deale they published it,

astonished
37 *And were beyond measure †astonied,† saying, He hath done all things well:

maketh
*he †hath made† both the deafe to heare, and the dumbe to speake.

The viii. Chapter.

multitude
1 *In those dayes, the †company† being very great, and having nothing to eat,

Jesus and
*†when Jesus had† called his disciples unto him, †he† sayth unto them,

multitude
2 *I have compassion on the †people,† because they have now beene with mee three

*dayes, and have nothing to eat:

house
houses will
3 *And if I send them away fasting to their owne †houses,† they †shall† faint by

came
*the way: for divers of them †come† from farre.

4 *And his Disciples answered him, From whence can a man satisfie these men with

*bread here in the wildernesse?

And
5 *And hee asked them, How many loaves have ye? They sayd, Seven.

6 *And he commanded the people to sit down on the ground: and hee tooke the

gave and
*seven loaves, and †when he had given† thanks, †he† brake, & gave to his disciples

*to set before them: and they did set them before the people.

he and
7 *And they had a few small fishes: and †when he had† blessed, †he† commanded to

*set them also before them.

filled of the overplus of the
8 *So they did eat, and were †sufficed:† and they tooke up †of the broken meat that
of the broken meat that

broken pieces [Delete]
*was left,† seven baskets †full.†
was left

9 *And they that had eaten, were about foure thousand: And he sent them away.

straightway hee and
10 *And †anon,† †when hee had† entred into a ship with his disciples, †he†

*came into the parts of Dalmanutha.

question
11 *And the Pharisees came foorth, and began to †dispute† with him, seeking of him

*a signe from heaven, tempting him.

he and
12 *And †when he had† sighed deeply in his spirit, †he† sayth, Why doth this generation

after
*seeke a signe? Verely I say unto you, There shall no signe be given unto

*this generation.

he entring [Delete]
13 *And †when he had† left them, and †entred† into the ship againe, †he†

to the other side
*departed †over the water.†

Now [Delete]
14 *†And† †they† had forgotten to take bread †with them,† neither
the disciples

*had they in the shippe with them more then one loafe.

15 *And he charged them, saying, Take heed, beware of the leaven of the Pharisees,

*and of the leaven of Herode.

Because
16 *And they reasoned among themselves, saying, We have no bread.
It is because

17 *And when Jesus knewe it, hee saith unto them, Why reason ye, because ye have

*no bread? Perceive ye not yet, neither understand? Have ye your heart yet hardened?

And
18 *Having eyes, see yee not? and having eares, heare ye not? Doe ye not

*remember?

[Delete]
19 *When I brake the five loaves among five thousand †men,† how many baskets

fragments
broken pieces
*ful of †broken meate† tooke yee up? They say unto him, Twelve.
fragments

And [Delete] full
20 * When †I brake† the seven among foure thousand, howe many baskets

[Delete] fragments
of the leavings broken pieces And
*†of the leavings† of †the† †broken meat† tooke ye up? They
[Delete] [Delete] fragments

*said, Seven.

is
21 *And he said unto them, How †happeneth† it, that ye doe not understand?

22 *And hee commeth to Bethsaida, and they bring a blinde man unto him, and

besought
*†desired† him to touch him:

he tooke man and
23 *And †when he had caught† the blinde by the hand, †he† led him out of the towne:

on
*and when he had spit †in† his eyes, and put his handes upon him, he asked him if

*he saw ought.

24 *And he looked up, and said, I see men: †for I perceive them walke as they were trees.†
as trees, walking

look up
25 *After that, he put his hands againe upon his eyes, and made him †see:†

*and he was restored, and saw every man clearely.

towne
26 *And he sent him †home† to his house, saying, Neither goe into the †village,†
away

towne
*nor tell it to any in the †village.†

of
27 *And Jesus went out, and his disciples, into the †villages† †that long to†
townes

*Cesarea Philippi: and by the way he asked his disciples, saying unto them, Whom

*do men say that I am?

the and some
28 *And they answered, John Baptist, †and some say,† Elias:
but some say

And others,
*†Againe, some say that that thou art† one of the Prophets.

sayeth And
29 *And he †said† unto them, But whom say ye that I am? Peter answereth, and

that
*sayeth unto him, Thou art †very† Christ.
the

of him
30 *And he charged them that they should tell no man .

31 *And hee beganne to teach them that the Sonne of man must suffer many things,

rejected
*and be †reproved† of the Elders, and of the †high† Priestes and Scribes, and be
chiefe

*killed, and after three daies rise againe.

[Delete]
32 *And he spake that saying openly. And Peter tooke him †aside,† and began

*to rebuke him.

33 *But when he had turned about, and looked on his disciples, hee rebuked Peter,

mindest
savourest
*saying, †Go after† me, Satan: for thou †savourest† not the things that †be†
Get thee behind be

*of God, but the things that be of men.

34 *And when hee had called the people unto him, with his disciples also, hee said

deny
*unto them, Whosoever will come after me, let him †forsake† himselfe, and take up

*his crosse, and follow me.

35 *For whosoever will save his life, shal lose it: but whosoever shall lose his life

*for my sake and the Gospels, the same shall save it.

gaine the whole
36 *For what shall it profite a man, if hee shall †winne all the† world,

be punished with the losse of his owne soule
suffer losse of his owne soule
*and †lose his owne soule?†
lose his owne soule

for his owne
what exchange for his
37 *Or †what† shal a man give †for a ransome of his† soule?
what in exchange for his

38 *Whosoever therefore shall be ashamed of me, and of my words, in this adulterous

*and sinfull generation, of him also shall the Sonne of man be ashamed, when he

*commeth in the glory of his Father, with the holy Angels.

The ix. Chapter.

1 *And he said unto them, Verely I say unto you, that there be some of them that stand
*here, which shall †in no wise† taste of death, till they have seene the kingdome
not
*of God come with power.
2 *And after sixe dayes, Jesus taketh with him Peter, and James, and John, and
apart by them selves
*leadeth them up into an high mountaine †out of the way alone:† and he was
*transfigured before them.
became shining exceeding white
3 *And his raiment †did shine, and became very white, even† as snow: so as no
on
*Fuller †upon the† earth can white them.
4 *And there appeared unto them Elias with Moses: and they were talking with Jesus.
it is good for us to be here
5 *And Peter answered, and saide to Jesus, Master, †there is good being for us:†
*and let us make three Tabernacles, one for thee, and one for Moses, and one for
*Elias.
hee spake
6 *For he wist not what †hee should say:† for they were sore afraid.
to say
7 *And there was a cloude that †shadowed† them: and a voyce came out of the
overshadowed
*cloud, saying, This is my beloved Sonne: heare him.
any save
8 *And suddenly when they had looked round about, they saw no man, more †then†
*Jesus onely with themselves.
mountaine
9 *And as they came downe from the †hill,† hee charged them that they should
what things
*tell no man †those things that† they had seene, till the Sonne of man were risen

*from the dead.

them selves questioning with
10 *And they kept that saying with †them,† †and demanded† one †of† another, what

*the rising from the dead should meane.

[Delete]
11 *And they asked him, saying, Why †then† say the Scribes, that Elias

*must first come?

And comming
12 * He answered, and †said unto them,† Elias verely †when he commeth† first,
told them commeth and

shall restore as it is written of the sonne of man hee shall
*†restoreth† al things: and †the Sonne of man, as it is written of him, shall†
restoreth how it is written of the Sonne of man, that hee must

*suffer many things, and be set at nought.

13 *But I say unto you, that Elias is come, and they have done unto him
indeed

listed
*whatsoever they †would,† as it is written of him.

a greate multitude
14 *And when hee came to his disciples, hee saw †much people† about them, and

reasoning
questioning
*the Scribes †disputing† with them.

15 *And straightway all the people, when they behelde him, were greatly amazed,

*and running to him, saluted him.

reason
question ♣among your selves
16 *And he asked the Scribes, What †dispute† ye †"among your selves?†
"with them

♣Or, with them
"Some reade, with them
"Or, among your selves

multitude
17 *And one of the †company† answered, and said, Master, I have brought unto thee

*my son, which hath a dumbe spirit:

it it he
18 *And wheresoever †hee† taketh him, †hee† teareth him, and †he† fometh, and
he hee "teareth

*gnasheth with his teeth, and pineth away: and I spake to thy disciples that

it
*they should cast †him† out, and they could not.
him

"Or, dasheth him

generation
19 *He answereth him, and saith, O faithlesse †nation,† how long shall I be with

indure
*you, how long shall I †suffer† you? Bring him unto me.
suffer

20 *And they brought him unto him: and when hee saw him, straightway the spirit tare

he fell and
*him, and †when he fell downe† on the ground, †he† wallowed, foming.

21 *And he asked his father, How long is it agoe since this came unto him? And

*he sayd, Of a childe.

22 *And oft times it hath cast him into the fire, and into the waters, to destroy

compassion
*him: but if thou canst do any thing, have †mercy† on us, and helpe us.

[Delete]
23 *Jesus sayd unto him, †This thing† if thou canst beleeve, all things are

*possible to him that beleeveth.

the father of the childe cried out & sayd with teares
24 *And straightway, †when the father of the childe had cried with teares, he sayd,†

*Lord, I beleeve, helpe thou mine unbeliefe.

25 *When Jesus sawe that the people came running together, hee rebuked the foule

it
*spirit, saying unto †him,† Thou dumbe and deafe spirit, I charge thee come out of
him

*him, & enter no more into him.

[Delete] and
26 *And †the† spirit †when he had† cried, and rent him sore, came out of
the

[Delete]
*him, and hee was as one †that had beene† dead, insomuch that many sayd, He

*is dead.

tooke and
27 *But Jesus, †when hee had caught† him by the hand, lifted him up: and

*he arose.

privately
28 *And when he was come into the house, his disciples asked him †secretly,†

it
*Why could not we cast †him† out?
him

29 *And he sayd unto them, This kinde can come forth by nothing, but by prayer

*& fasting.

[Delete] and passed
30 *And †after† they departed thence, †they tooke their journey† thorow

*Galilee, & he would not that any man should know †it†.
it

31 *For he taught his disciples, and sayd unto them, The sonne of man is delivered

*into the hands of men, and they shall kill him, and after that he is killed, he

*shall rise the third day.

32 *But they understood not that saying, and were afrayd to aske him.

and being in
being in
33 *And he came to Capernaum: and †when he was come into† the house, he asked them,

reasoned
*What was it that yee †disputed† among your selves by the way?
disputed

But disputed
34 *†And† they held their peace: For by the way they had †reasoned† among themselves,

greatest
*who should be the †chiefest.†

he sate and
35 *And †when he was set† downe, †he† called the twelve, and sayth unto them, If

of
*any man desire to be first, the same shalbe last of all, and servant †unto† all.

little
he tooke [Delete] and
36 *And †when he had taken† a †yoong† childe, †he† set him in the middest of

*them: and when he had taken him in his armes, he sayd unto them,

one of such little children
one of such children
37 *Whosoever shall receive †any such a yoong childe† in my Name, receiveth me:

*and whosoever shall receive me, receiveth not me, but him that sent me.

And
38 * John answered him, saying, Master, we saw one casting out devils in thy

*Name, and he followeth not us, and we forbade him, because he followeth †us not.†
not us

shall
39 *But Jesus sayd, Forbid him not, for there is no man, which †if he† do a

by & by
*miracle in my name, can †lightly† speake evill of me.
that lightly

40 *For hee that is not against us, is on our part.

For give you a cuppe of water to drinke in my name
41 * Whosoever shall †in my Name give you a cuppe of colde water to drinke,†

*because ye belong to Christ: Verely I say unto you, he shall not lose his reward.

42 *And whosoever shall offend one of these litle ones that beleeve in me, it is

*better for him †if† a milstone were hanged about his necke, and he were cast
that

*into the sea.

43 *And if thy hand offend thee, cut it off: It is better for thee to enter into
"offend thee

*life maimed, then having two hands, to go into hell, into the fire

unquencheable
*†that never shalbe quenched:†
that never shall bee quenched

"Or, cause thee to offend

44 *Where their worme dieth not, and the fire is not quenched.

45 *And if thy foot offend thee, cut it off: it is better for thee to enter halt

[Delete]
*into life, then having †thy† two feet, to be cast into hell, into the fire

unquencheable
*†that never shalbe quenched:†
that never shalbe quenched

46 *Where their worme dieth not, and the fire is not quenched.

47 *And if thine eye offend thee, plucke it out: it is better for thee to enter
"offend thee

*into the kingdome of God with one eye, then having two eyes, to be cast into

*hell fire:

"Or, cause thee to offend

48 *Where their worme dieth not, and the fire is not quenched.

one salted
49 *For every †man† shalbe salted with fire, and every sacrifice shalbe †seasoned†

*with salt.

have lost his saltnes wherewith will
50 *Salt is good: but if the salt †be unsavery,† †with what thing shall†

[Delete] [Delete]
*you season it? Have †ye† salt in your selves, and have peace †among your

*selves† one with another.

The x. Chapter.

[Delete] and
1 *And †when† he rose from thence, †he† commeth into the coasts of †Jurie,†
Judea

by the farther side of againe
*†thorow the region that is beyond† Jordan: and the people resort unto him †afresh,†

*& as he was woont, he taught them againe.

to him
2 *And the Pharisees came , and asked him, Is it lawfull for a man to put

*away his wife? tempting him.

[Delete]
3 *And hee answered, and sayd unto them, What did Moses command you †to do?†

bill
4 *And they sayd, Moses suffered to write a †booke† of divorcement, and to put

*her away.

5 *And Jesus answered, and said unto them, For the hardnesse of your heart, hee

you this precept
*wrote †this precept unto you.†

6 *But from the beginning of the creation, God made them male and female,

[Delete]
7 *†And sayd,† For this cause shal a man leave his father and mother, and

shall be joyned to
*†bide by† his wife,
cleave to

they are
8 *And they twaine shalbe one flesh: so then †are they† no more twaine, but one flesh.

What Therefore joyned not put asunder
9 *†Therefore what† God hath †coupled† together, let †no† man †separate.†

10 *And in the house his disciples asked him againe of the same matter.

11 *And he sayth unto them, Whosoever shal put away his wife, and marry another,

*committeth adultery against her.

12 *And if a woman shall put away her husband, and be married to another, she committeth

*adultery.

little
[Delete]
13 *And they brought †yong† children to him, that he should touch them: and
yong

*his disciples rebuked those that brought them.

[Delete]
14 *But when Jesus saw it, he was †sore† displeased, and sayd unto them,
much

little of such
*Suffer †the yoong† children to come unto me, and forbid them not: for †to such
the little

is
*belongeth† the kingdome of God.

15 *Verily I say unto you, Whosoever shall not receive the kingdom of God as a

little not
*†yong† child, he shall †in no wise† enter therein.

hee tooke putt
16 *And †when hee had taken† them up in his armes, †putting† his hands upon them,

and
*†he† blessed them.

17 *And when hee was gone foorth into the way, there came one running, and kneeled

*to him, and asked him, Good master, what shall I do that I may inherit

*eternall life?

And
18 * Jesus sayd unto him, Why callest thou me good? There is no man

even
that is
*good, but one, †which is† God.

19 *Thou knowest the commandements, Do not commit adulterie, Doe not kill, Doe not

not
*steale, Do not beare false witnesse, Defraud †no man,† Honour thy father and mother.

And
20 * He answered, and sayd unto him, Master, all these have I observed from

*my youth.

Then Jesus beholding him,
21 *†Jesus beheld him, and† loved him, and sayd unto him, One thing thou lackest:

*Go thy way, sell whatsoever thou hast, and give to the poore, and thou shalt have

take up the crosse and followe me
*treasure in heaven, & come †follow me, when thou hast taken up the crosse.†

word
And he was stricken sad at saying
22 *†But hee was discomforted† †because of† that †saying,† and went away †mourning:†
And hee was sad grieved

*for hee had great possessions.

Jesus and
23 *And †when Jesus had† looked round about, †he† sayth unto his Disciples, How

*hardly shall they that have riches, enter into the kingdome of God?

astonished
24 *And the Disciples were †astonied† at his words. But Jesus answereth againe,

*and saith unto them, Children, how hard is it for them that trust in riches, to

*enter into the kingdome of God?

a rich man
25 *It is easier for a camel to goe thorow the eye of a needle, then for †the rich†

*to enter into the kingdome of God.

astonished
26 *And they were †astonied† out of measure, saying among themselves, Who then can

*be saved?

And Jesus looking
27 *†Jesus, when hee had looked† upon them, sayth, With men it is †unpossible,†
impossible

*but not with God: for with God all things are possible.

Then left
28 *†And† Peter beganne to say unto him, Loe, we have †forsaken† all, and have

*followed thee.

And
29 * Jesus answered, and sayd, Verily I say unto you, There is no man that hath

left
*†forsaken† house, or brethren, or sisters, or father, or mother, or wife, or children,

*or lands, for my sake and the Gospels,

in this tyme
30 *But he shall receive an hundred folde now †at this present,† houses, and

*brethren, and sisters, and mothers, and children, and lands, with persecutions, and

*in the world to come eternall life.

that are
31 *But many †that are† first, shall be last: and the last, first.
that are

32 *And they were in the way going up to Hierusalem: and Jesus went before them, and

they
*they were amazed, and as they followed, were afraid: and

he tooke againe and
*†when he had againe taken with him† the twelve, †he† began to tell them what things

*should happen unto him,

For
33 *†Saying,† Beholde, we go up to Hierusalem, and the sonne of man shall be delivered
Saying

*unto the †high† Priests, and unto the Scribes: and they shall condemne him to
chiefe

*death, and shall deliver him to the Gentiles.

shall shall
34 *And they shal mocke him, and scourge him, and spit upon him,

shall rise againe
*and kill him: and the third day he shall †arise.†

35 *And James and John the sonnes of Zebedee come unto him, saying, Master, we

aske
desire
*†will† that thou shouldest doe for us whatsoever wee shall †desire.†
would

And
36 * He sayd unto them, What †will† yee that I should do for you?
would

37 *They sayd unto him, Grant unto us that we may sit, one on thy right hand,

*and the other on thy left hand, in thy glory.

38 *But Jesus sayd unto them, Ye †wote† not what ye aske: Can ye drinke of the
know

*cuppe that I drinke of? and be baptized with the baptisme that I am baptized with?

[Delete] And
39 *And they sayd unto him, †That† we can. Jesus sayd unto them, Ye

*shall indeed drinke of the cuppe that I drinke of: and with the baptisme that I am

*baptized withall, shall ye be baptized:

40 *But to sit on my right hand, and on my left hand, is not mine to give, but

[Delete] to
*†it shalbe given† †unto† them for whom it is prepared.
it shall be given

[Delete] be much displeased with
41 *And when the †other† ten heard it, they began to †disdaine at†

*James and John.

[Delete] and
42 *But Jesus, †when hee had† called them to him, saith unto them, Ye

are accompted rule over
*know that they which †seeme† to †beare rule among† the Gentiles,
"are accompted

exercise Lordship theyr greate ones
*†reigne as lordes† over them: and †they that be great among them,†

*exercise authoritie upon them.

"Or, thinke good

[Delete]
43 *But so shal it not be among you: but whosoever †of you† will be great

*among you, shall be your minister:

44 *And whosoever of you will be the chiefest, shalbe servant of all.

even the sonne of man
45 *For †the sonne of man also† came not to be ministred unto, but to minister,

*and to give his life a ransome for many.

[Delete]
46 *And they came to Jericho: and as hee went out of †the city of† Jericho

good
[Delete]
*with his Disciples, and a †great† number of people, blinde Bartimeus,
great

*the sonne of Timeus, sate by the high wayes side, begging.

out
47 *And when hee heard that it was Jesus of Nazareth, he began to crie ,

*and say, Jesus thou sonne of David, have mercy on me.

48 *And many †rebuked† him, that hee should holde his peace: But hee
charged

out
[Delete]
*cried the more a great deale, Thou sonne of David, have mercy on me.

49 *And Jesus stood still, and commanded him to be called: and they call

man
*the blinde , saying unto him, Be of good comfort, rise, hee calleth thee.

he casting away his garment
50 *And †when he had throwen away his cloke, he† rose, and came to Jesus.

should
51 *And Jesus answered, and sayd unto him, What wilt thou that I do

man Lord that I might receive my sight
*unto thee? The blind sayd unto him, †Master, that I might see.†

♣made thee whole
52 * Jesus sayd unto him, Goe thy way, thy faith hath †saved thee.†
And "made thee whole

*And immediatly he received his sight, and followed Jesus in the way.

♣Or, saved the
"Or, saved thee

The xi. Chapter.

1 *And when they came nigh to Hierusalem, unto Bethphage and Bethanie, at the
*mount of Olives, hee sendeth foorth two of his Disciples,

village
2 *And sayth unto them, Go your way into the †towne that is† over against you,
*and assoone as ye be entred into it, ye shall finde a colt tied, whereon never
[Delete]
*man sate, loose him, and bring him †hither.†

this
3 *And if any man say unto you, Why doe ye †so?† Say ye that the Lord hath
*need of him: and straightway he will send him hither.

4 *And they went their way, and found the colt tied by the doore without,
*in a place where two wayes met: and they loose him.

certayne
5 *And †divers† of them that stood there, sayd unto them, What do ye loosing
*the colt?

[Delete]
6 *And they sayd unto them †even† as Jesus had commanded: and they let them
even
*go.

7 *And they brought the colt to Jesus, and cast their garments on him, & he sate
*upon him.

8 *And many spread their garments in the way: & †other† cut downe branches off
others
[Delete]
them
*the trees, and strawed †them† in the way.

9 *And they that went before, and they that followed, cried, saying, Hosanna,
*blessed is he that commeth in the name of the Lord.

that commeth in the Name of the Lord of
10 *Blessed be the kingdome †that commeth in the Name of him that is Lord of
of our father David, that commeth in the

our father David
*our father David,† Hosanna in the highest.
Name of the Lord

11 *And Jesus entred into Hierusalem, and into the Temple, and when he had looked

*round about upon all things, and now the eventide was come, hee went out unto

*Bethanie with the twelve.

12 *And on the morow, when they were come from Bethanie, he †hungred.†
was hungry

seeing
13 *And †when he had spied† a figge tree afar off, having leaves, he came

if happily
*†to see if† he might find any thing thereon: and when he came to it, hee found

it was not the season of figges
*nothing but leaves: for †the time of figges was not yet.†
the time of figs was not yet

it, No
14 *And Jesus answered, and sayd unto †the figge tree, Never† man eat fruit of thee

for ever
*hereafter †while the world standeth.† And his disciples heard it.

[Delete]
15 *And they come to Hierusalem, and †when† Jesus went into the Temple,

and
*†he† beganne to cast out them that solde and bought in the Temple, and overthrew

*the tables of the money changers, and the seats of them that solde doves,

vessell
16 *And would not suffer that any man should cary any †stuffe† thorow the Temple.

17 *And he taught, saying unto them, Is it not written, My house shalbe called

*†the house of prayer unto all nations?† but ye have made it a denne of theeves.
of all nations the house of prayer

18 *And the Scribes and †high† Priests heard it, and sought how they might destroy
chiefe

astonished
*him: for they feared him, because all the people was †astonied† at his doctrine.

hee
19 *And when even was come, †Jesus† went out of the citie.

20 *And in the morning, as they passed by, they saw the figge tree dried up from

*the roots.

calling to remembrance
21 *And Peter †having remembred,† sayth unto him, Master, beholde, the figge

*tree which thou cursedst, is withered away.

♣Have faith in God
22 *And Jesus answering, sayth unto them, Have faith in God.
"Have faith in God

♣Or, have the faith of God
"Or, have the faith of God

23 *For verily I say unto you, that whosoever shall say unto this mountaine, Be thou

*remooved, and be thou cast into the sea, and shall not doubt in his heart, but shall

he shall have
*beleeve that those things which he sayth shall come to passe: †whatsoever he shall

whatsoever he sayth
*say, shalbe unto him.†

24 *Therefore I say unto you, What things soever ye desire when ye pray, beleeve

[Delete] [Delete]
them them
*that ye receive †them,† and ye shall have †them.†

and pray [Delete]
25 *And when ye stand †praying,† forgive, if ye have ought against any †man:†
praying

*that your father also which is in heaven, may forgive you your trespasses.

26 *But if you do not forgive, neither wil your father which is in heaven forgive

[Delete]
*†you† your trespasses.

was walking
27 *And they come againe to Hierusalem: and as hee †walked† in the Temple,

*there come to him the †high† Priests, and the Scribes, and the Elders,
chiefe

28 *And say unto him, By what authoritie doest thou these things? and who gave thee

*this authoritie to do these things?

And
29 * Jesus answered, and sayd unto them, I will also aske of you one

♣thing
thing
*†question,† and answere me, and I will tell you by what authoritie I do these things.
"question

♣Or, word
"Or, thing

of
[Delete] from
30 *The baptisme of John, †whether† was it †from† heaven, or of men?

*Answere me.

considered of
reasoned From
31 *And they †reasoned† with themselves, saying, If we shall say, †From† heaven,

*he will say, Why then did ye not beleeve him?

they feared
32 *But if we shall say, Of men, †[a]we feare† the people: for all men counted John

[Delete] indeede
*that he was a †very† Prophet .

[a]This is the third person in Greeke

33 *And they †answering, say† unto Jesus, We cannot tell. And Jesus answering,
answered and said

*sayth unto them, Neither do I tell you by what authoritie I do these things.

The xii. Chapter.

1 *And he began to speake unto them by parables. A certaine man planted a vineyard,

a place for the wine-fate
*and †he† set an hedge about it, and digged †a wine presse,† and built
[Delete]

then tooke a farre journey
went into a strange countrey
*a tower, and let it out to husbandmen, and †went into a strange countrey.†
went into a farre countrey

at the season
2 *And †when the time was come,† he sent to the husbandmen a servant that hee

*might receive †of† the husbandmen of the fruit of the vineyard.
from

3 *And they caught him, and beat him, and sent him away emptie.

4 *And againe, he sent unto them another servant: and at him they cast stones,

shamefully handled
*and †brake his† head, and sent him away †all to reviled.†
wounded him in the

5 *And againe he sent another, and him they killed: and many †other,† beating
others

*some, and killing some.

Having yet therefore one sonne his wellbeloved
6 *†And so when hee had yet but† †one beloved sonne,† he sent him also

[Delete] reverence
*†at the† last unto them, saying, They will †stand in awe of† my sonne.

those
7 *But †the† husbandmen said amongst themselves, This is the heire, come, let us

*kill him, and the inheritance shalbe ours.

8 *And they tooke him, and killed him, and cast him out of the vineyard.

9 *What shall therefore the Lord of the vineyard do? He †shall† come and destroy
will

*the husbandmen, and will give the vineyard unto †other.†
others

And rejected
10 * Have ye not read this Scripture? The stone which the builders †disallowed,†

heade
*is become the †chiefe stone† of the corner?

11 *This was the Lords doing, and it is marvellous in our eyes.

multitude
And they sought to lay holde on him but people
12 *†They went about also to take him, and† feared the †people:† for they knew that

*he had spoken the parable against them: and they left him, and went their way.

send
13 *And they †sent† unto him certaine of the Pharisees and of the Herodians,

catche
*to †take† him in his words.

14 *And when they were come, they say unto him, Master, we know that thou art true,

regardest person
*and carest for no man: for thou †considerest† not the †persons† of men, but teachest

♣tribute
tribute
*the way of God in trueth: Is it lawfull to give †tribute† to Cesar, or not?

♣Or, poll monye

15 *Shall we give, or shall we not give? But hee knowing their hypocrisie, sayd

♣penie
*unto them, Why tempt yee mee? Bring mee a penie, that I may see it.
"penny

♣About the eyght part of an ounce; see Ca. 6, 37
"Valewing of our money seven pence halfe peny, as Mat. 18.28

16 *And they brought it: and hee sayeth unto them, Whose is this image and

*superscription? And they sayd unto him, Cesars.

17 *And Jesus answering, sayd unto them, †Give† to Cesar the things that
Render

are Cesars that are Gods
*†belong to Cesar:† and to God, the things †which pertaine to God.†

*And they marvelled at him.

Then come
18 *†There come also† unto him the Sadducees, which say there is no resurrection,

*& they asked him, saying,

19 *Master, Moses wrote unto us, If †any† mans brother die, and leave his wife
a

*behinde him, and leave no children, that his brother should take his wife, and raise

*up seed unto his brother.

Now dyinge
20 * There were seven brethren: and the first tooke a wife, and †when he died,†

[Delete]
*left no seed †behinde him.†

21 *And the second tooke her, and died, neither left he any seed: and the

*third likewise.

the [Delete]
22 *And seven had her, and left no seed †behind them:† last of all the

woman
*†wife† died also.

23 *In the resurrection therefore, when they shall rise, whose wife shall she be

the
*of them? for seven had her to wife.

24 *And Jesus answering, sayd unto them, Doe ye not therefore erre, because ye

*know not the Scriptures, neither the power of God?

25 *For when they shall rise from the dead, they neither marry, nor are given

*in marriage: but are as the Angels which †are† in heaven.
are

And
26 * As touching the dead, that they rise: have yee not read in the booke of Moses,

am
*how in the bush God spake unto him, saying, I †am† the God of Abraham, and

Isaak
*the God of †Isahac,† and the God of Jacob?
Isahac

the
27 *He is not the God of the dead, but God of the living: ye therefore do greatly

*erre.

one of the scribes, came having reasoning
28 *And †when there came one of the scribes,† and †had† heard them †disputing†

perceiving [Delete]
*together, †and perceived† that he had answered them well, †he† asked him
and perceiving

*which is the first commandement of all.

And
29 * Jesus answered him, The first of all the commandements is, Heare, O

*Israel, the Lord our God is one Lord:

30 *And thou shalt love the Lord thy God with all thy heart, and with all thy soule,

*and with all thy minde, and with all thy strength. This †is† the first commandement:
is

namely this
31 *And the second is like †unto this,† Thou shalt love thy neighbour as thy selfe:

*there is none other commandement greater then these.

32 *And the Scribe sayd unto him, Well, master, thou hast sayd the trueth: for there

*is one God, and there is none other but he.

33 *And to love him with all the heart, and with all the understanding, and with

*all the soule, and with all the strength, and to love †a mans† neighbour as
his

more [Delete]
*himselfe, is †greater† then all †the† burnt offerings and sacrifices.
whole

34 *And when Jesus saw that hee answered discreetly, he sayd unto him, Thou art not

*farre from the kingdome of God. And no man after that durst aske him any question.

answered and
35 *And Jesus †answering,† sayd, †teaching† in the Temple, How say the Scribes
while he taught

*that Christ is the sonne of David?

sayd by the holy Ghost
36 *For David himselfe †inspired with the holy Ghost, sayd,† The Lord sayd to my

thou
*Lord, Sit on my right hand, till I make thine enemies thy footstoole.

therefore
37 *David himselfe calleth him Lorde, and whence is he then his sonne?

*And †much† people heard him gladly.
the common

teaching
hee doctrine
38 *And †hee† sayd unto them in his †doctrine,† Beware of the Scribes, which

love to goe
*†desire to walke† in long clothing, and love salutations in the market places,

39 *And the chiefe seats in the Synagogues, and the uppermost roumes at feasts.

40 *Which devoure widowes houses, and †under† a pretence make long prayers:
for

*These shall receive greater damnation.

[Delete] and
41 *And †when† Jesus sate over against the treasurie, †he† beheld how the

cast
*people †put† money into the treasurie: and many that were rich, cast in much.

42 *And there came a certaine poore widow, and shee threw in two mites, which

*make a farthing.

he and
43 *And †when he had† called unto him his disciples, †he† sayeth unto them,

*Verily I say unto you, that this poore widow hath cast more in, then all they

*which have cast into the treasurie.

44 *For all they did cast in of their †superfluity:† but shee of her want,
abundance

*did cast in all that shee had, even all her living.

The xiii. Chapter.

sayeth
1 *And as he went out of the temple, one of his disciples †sayd† unto him,

maner of maner of [Delete]
*Master, see what stones and what buildings †are here.†
[Delete] are here

2 *And Jesus answering, sayd unto him, Seest thou these great buildings?

*there shall not be left one stone upon another, that shall not be throwen downe.

3 *And as he sate upon the mount of Olives, over against the temple, Peter,

privately
*and James, and John, and Andrew, asked him †secretly,†

4 *Tell us, when shall these things be? And what shalbe the signe when all these

*things shal be fulfilled?

5 *And Jesus answering them, began to say, Take heed lest any man deceive you.

6 *For many shall come in my name, saying, I am Christ: and shall deceive many.

And rumors
7 * When ye shall heare of warres, & †tidings† of warres, be yee not

*troubled: For such things must needs be, but the end shall not be yet.

nation shall
8 *For †there shall nation† rise against nation, and kingdome against kingdome:

there shall be famines
*and there shal be earthquakes in divers places, and †famines shall there be,†

♣sorowes
*and troubles: these are the beginnings of sorowes.
"sorrowes

♣the word in the originall importeth the paynes of a woman in travaile
"The word in the originall, importeth, the paines of a woman in travaile

9 *But take heed to your selves: for they shal deliver you up to councels,

in the ye shalbe scourged yee
*and †to† synagogues, †and ye shalbe whipped, yea,† and shalbe brought
ye shall be beaten

[Delete] testimonie
*before rulers & kings for my sake, †that this might be† for a †witnesse†

*against them.

10 *And the Gospel must first be published among all nations.

take no carefull thought
take no thought
11 *But when they shall leade you, †delivering† you up, †be not carefull
and deliver

before hand what ye shall speake neither doe ye premeditate
*aforehand,† †neither take thought what ye shall speake:† but whatsoever shall

that
*be given you in †the same† houre, that speake ye: for it is not ye that speake,

*but the holy Ghost.

Now
12 * The brother shall betray the brother to death, and the father the sonne:

up parents
*and children shall rise against their †fathers and mothers,† and

cause them to dye
cause them to be put to death
*shall †put them to death.†

13 *And yee shall be hated of all men for my names sake: but hee that shall

saved
*endure unto the end, the same shalbe †safe.†

But when you shall spoken of
14 *†Moreover, when ye† see the abomination of desolation, †whereof is spoken†
But when ye shal

*by Daniel the Prophet, standing where it ought not (let him that readeth,

consider
*†understand†) then let them that be in †Jurie,† flee to the mountaines:
understand Judea

upon [Delete]
on top
15 *And let him that is †on† the house †top,† not go downe into the

*house, neither enter therein, to †fetch† any thing out of his house.
take

up his garment

16 *And let him that is in the field, not turne backe againe for to
*take †his garment with him.†

But woe to
But woe
17 *†Woe shall be then† to them that are with child, and to them that give sucke
*in those dayes.

And
18 *†But† pray yee that your flight be not in the Winter:

those dayes shalbe affliction such
19 *For †there shall be in those dayes† †such tribulation,† as was not from the
in those dayes shall be
*beginning of the creation which God created, unto this time, neither

[Delete]
*shalbe †in any wise.†

20 *And except that the Lord had shortened those dayes, no flesh should be saved:
*but for the elects sake whom he hath chosen, he hath shortened

the
*†those† dayes.

21 *And then, if any man shall say to you, Loe, here is Christ, or loe, he is there:

[Delete]
him
*beleeve †him† not.

22 *For false Christs, and false prophets shall rise, and shall shew signes and
*woonders, to †deceive,† if it were possible, even the elect.
seduce

foretold [Delete]
23 *But take ye heed: beholde, I have †shewed† you all things †before.†

affliction
But tribulation
24 *†Moreover,† in those dayes, after that †tribulation,† the Sunne shall be darkened,
*and the Moone shall not give her light:

that
25 *And the Starres of heaven shall fall, and the powers †which† are in heaven
*shalbe shaken.
26 *And then shall they see the Sonne of man comming in the clouds, with great
*power and glory.
27 *And then shall he send his angels, and shal gather together his elect from the
uttermost part
*foure winds, from the †end† of the earth, to the uttermost part of
*heaven.
Now
28 * Learne a parable of the figge tree. When her branch is yet tender, and
putteth
*†hath brought† forth leaves, ye know that Summer is neere:
knowe
29 *So ye in like maner, when ye shal see these things come to passe, †understand†
[Delete]
it even
*that †it† is nigh, †even† at the doores.
not
30 *Verily I say unto you, that this generation shal †in no wise† passe, till all
*these things be done.
not
31 *Heaven and earth shall passe away: but my words shall †in no wise† passe away.
32 *But of that day and that houre knoweth no man, no not the Angels which are in
[Delete] but [Delete]
*heaven, neither the Sonne †himselfe,† †save† the Father †onely.†
33 *Take yee heed, watch and pray: for yee know not when the time is.
taking a farre journye
34 * "As a man †which is gone into a strange countrey,†
For the Sonne of man is
leaveth giveth
*†and hath left† his house, and †given† authoritie to his servants, and to every
who left gave

*man his worke, and commanded the porter to watch:

"For the sonne of man is

35 *Watch ye therefore (for ye know not when the master of the house commeth, at

or morning
*even, or at midnight, †whether† at the cocke crowing, or in the †dawning†)

comming
36 *Lest †if he come† suddenly, he finde you sleeping.

what
37 *And †that† I say unto you, I say unto all, Watch.

The xiiii. Chapter.

1 *After two dayes was the feast of the Passeover, and of unleavened bread: and

lay hold on
take
*the †high† Priests, and the Scribes sought howe they might †take† him
chiefe

*by craft, and put him to death.

there be a tumult of
on there be an uprore of
2 *But they said, Not †in† the feast day, lest †any businesse arise among†

*the people.

beeing [Delete]
3 *And †when hee was† in Bethanie, in the house of Simon the leper, †even†

[Delete]
*as hee sate at meat, there came a woman, having an Alabaster boxe of †very

of ♣Nard very precious
*precious† ointment, †called† †Nard† †pisticke† :
"spikenard [Delete]

she brake the boxe and
*and †when she had broken the boxe, shee† powred it on his head.

♣Or, Spikenarde, or Pure Nard, or Liquid Nard
"Or, pure nard: or liquid nard

4 *And there †was† some that had indignation within themselves, and sayd, Why
were

*was this waste of the ointment made?

♣three hundred pence
5 *For it might have bene sold for more then three hundred pence, and have
three hundred "pence

murmured
*bene given to the poore. And they †grudged† against her.

♣about 37 ounces and an halfe of silver
"See Matth. 18.28

wrought
6 *And Jesus sayd, Let her alone, why trouble †ye† her? She hath †done†
you

*a good worke on me.

the
7 *For ye have poore with you alwayes, and whensoever ye will, ye may do them

*good: but me †have ye not† alwayes.
ye have not

what is come
8 *She hath done †that† she could: she †came† aforehand to anoint my body to

*the burying.

9 *Verely I say unto you, Wheresoever this Gospel shall be preached thorowout

spoken of
*the whole world, this also that she hath done, shalbe †rehearsed†

for a memoriall
*†in remembrance† of her.

[Delete]
10 *And Judas Iscariot, one of the twelve, went †away† unto the †high†
chiefe

*Priests, to betray him unto them.

And it to
11 * When they heard †that,† they were glad, and promised †that they would†

*give him money. And hee sought how hee might conveniently betray him.

♣killed
12 *And the first day of unleavened bread, when they †did kill† the Passeover,
"killed

*his disciples sayd unto him, Where wilt thou that we go and prepare, that thou
*mayest eat the Passeover?

♣Or, sacrificed
"Or, sacrificed

13 *And he sendeth forth two of his disciples, and sayth unto them, Goe ye into
*the citie, and there shall meet you a man bearing a pitcher of water: follow him.

wheresoever
14 *And †whithersoever† he shall goe in, say ye to the good man of the house,
*The master sayth, Where is the ghest-chamber, where I shall eat the
*Passeover with my disciples?

♣paved
roome furnished
15 *And he will shew you a large upper †chamber,† †paved† and prepared: there
*make readie for us.

♣Or, trimmed, or furnished

16 *And his disciples went forth, and came into the citie, and found as he had sayd
*unto them: and they made ready the Passeover.

in the evening
17 *And †when it was now even tide,† he commeth with the twelve.

[Delete]
18 *And as they sate †at boord,† and did eat, Jesus sayd, Verily I say unto

which
*you, one of you †that† eateth with me, shall betray me.

sorowfull
19 *And they began to be †sory,† and to say unto him, one by one, Is it I?
*And another sayd, Is it I?

And [Delete]
20 * He answered, and sayd unto them, †It is† one of the twelve, †even†
It is

dish
*†he† that dippeth with me in the †platter.†
[Delete]

indeede
21 *The Sonne of man †truely† goeth, as it is written of him: but woe to that man
*by whom the Sonne of man is betrayed: Good were it for that man, if he had never
*bene borne.

tooke and
22 *And as they did eat, Jesus, †when he had taken† bread, and blessed, †he†
*brake it, and gave to them, and sayd, Take, eat: this is my body.

hee tooke when he had
23 *And †when he had taken† the cup, and given thanks, he gave it to
*them: and they all dranke of it.

24 *And he sayd unto them, This is my blood of the new Testament, which is shed
*for many.

25 *Verily I say unto you, I will drinke no more of the fruit of the vine, untill
*that day that I drinke it new in the kingdome of God.

sung an ♣hymne
26 *And when they had †praised God,† they went out into the mount of Olives.
sung an "hymne

♣Or, Psalme
"Or, Psalme

27 *And Jesus sayth unto them, All ye shall be offended because of me this night:
*for it is written, I will smite the shepheard, & the sheepe shalbe scattered.

before you into Galilee
28 *But after that I am risen, I will goe †into Galilee before you.†

But [Delete]
29 * Peter sayd unto him, Although all †men† shalbe offended,
*yet will not I.

to day
this day
30 *And Jesus sayth unto him, Verily I say unto thee, that †this day,†

[Delete]
even
*†even† in this night, before the cocke crow twise, thou shalt denie mee

thrise
*†three times.†

exceedingly the more
the more vehemently
31 *But he spake †more vehemently,† If I shuld die with thee, I will not denie

[Delete]
*thee †in any wise.† Likewise also sayd they all.
in any wise

to
32 *And they came †into† a place which was named Gethsemani, and he saith to his

*disciples, Sit ye here, while I shall pray.

33 *And he taketh with him Peter, & James, and John, and began to be sore amazed,

in an ♣agony
*and to be †in an agony,†
very heavy

♣Or, grievous anguish

sorowfull [Delete]
34 *And sayth unto them, My soule is †exceeding heavy,† †even†
exceeding sorowfull

[Delete]
*unto †the† death: tary ye heere, and watch.

he went and
35 *And †when he had gone† forward a litle, †he† fell on the ground, and prayed,

*that if it were possible, the houre might passe from him.

36 *And he sayd, Abba, father, all things are possible unto thee, take away this cup

*from me: Neverthelesse, not that I will, but †that† thou
what

[Delete]
*wilt, †be done.†

37 *And hee commeth and findeth them sleeping, and sayeth unto Peter, Simon, sleepest

*thou? Couldest not thou watch one houre?

[Delete]
38 *Watch †ye† and pray, lest ye enter into temptation: The spirit truely
ye

*is ready, but the flesh is weake.

away
39 *And againe he went †aside,† and prayed, and spake the same words.

40 *And when he returned, he found them asleepe againe (for their eyes were heavy)

*neither wist they what to answere him.

on now
41 *And he commeth the third time, and sayth unto them, Sleepe †henceforth,†

rest
*and take your †ease:† it is enough, the houre is come, beholde, the Sonne of man

*is betrayed into the hands of sinners.

42 *Rise up, let us goe: Loe, he that betrayeth me, is at hand.

[Delete]
43 *And immediatly, while he yet spake, commeth Judas, †being† one of the

multitude
*twelve, and with him a great †number of people† with swords and staves, from

the the
*the †high† Priests, and Scribes, and Elders.
chiefe

[Delete]
44 *And he that betrayed him, had given them a †generall† token, saying,

lay hold on
whomesoever take
*†Whosoever† I shall kisse, that same is he: †take† him, and leade him

safely
*away †warily.†

[Delete]
45 *And assoone as hee was come, he goeth straightway to him, and sayeth †unto him,†

*Master, master: and kissed him.

46 *And they layed their hands on him, and tooke him.

drew a and
47 *And one of them that stood by, †when hee had drawen out his† sword, smote

*a servant of the high Priest, and cut off his eare.

Are Yee against
48 *And Jesus answered, and sayd unto them, †Yee be† come out as †unto† a

[Delete] ?
*thiefe, with swords and with staves †for† to take me †.†

49 *I was dayly with you in the Temple, teaching, and ye tooke me not:

Delete]
*but †these things come to passe† †that† the Scriptures †should†
[Delete] must

*be fulfilled.

left
forsooke fled
50 *And they all †forsooke† him, and †ran away.†

wrapped in linnen
clothed in linnen
wrapped in linnen
51 *And there followed him a certaine yoong man, †clothed in linnen†
having a linnen cloth cast

body layd hold on
*†upon the bare :† and the yoong men †caught† him.
about his naked body

[Delete]
52 *And hee left †his† linnen †garment,† and fled from them naked.
the cloth

were assembled
53 *And they ledde Jesus away to the high Priest, and with him †came†

chiefe
*all the †high† Priests, and the Elders, and the Scribes.

farre [Delete]
54 *And Peter followed him a †great way† off, even †till he was come† into the

himselfe
*palace of the high Priest: and he sate with the servants, and warmed †himselfe†

*at the fire.

55 *And the †high† Priests and all the councel sought for witnesse against Jesus,
chiefe

*to put him to death, and found none:

56 *For many bare false witnesse against him, but their witnesse agreed not together.

bore
57 *And there arose certaine, and †brought† false witnesse against him, saying,
bare

58 *Wee heard him say, I will destroy this Temple that is made with handes, and

*within three dayes I will build another made without hands.

neither so did their witnesse agree
59 *But †yet their witnesse agreed not so† together.

60 *And the high Priest stood up in the mids, and asked Jesus, saying, Answerest thou

Why doe
*nothing? †How is it that† these †beare† witnesse against thee?
What is it which [Delete]

61 *But hee held his peace, and answered nothing. Againe, the high Priest asked him,

*and sayd unto him, Art thou Christ the sonne of the blessed?
the

62 *And Jesus sayd, I am: and yee shall see the sonne of man sitting on the right

power with
*hand of †the power of God,† and comming †in† the clouds of heaven.
in

[Delete] and
63 *Then the high Priest, †having† rent his clothes, sayth, What need we

*any further witnesses?

64 *Ye have heard the blasphemy: what thinke ye? And they all condemned him to

*be †worthy† of death.
guilty

spit on buffet him
65 *And some began to †spet at† him, and to cover his face, and to †beat him with fists,†

*and to say unto him, Prophecie: And the servants did

*†beat him with rods.†
strike him with the palmes of their hands

66 *And as Peter was beneath in the palace, there commeth one of the †wenches†
maids

*of the high Priest.

shee
67 *And when shee saw Peter warming himselfe, †after shee had† looked upon him,

and sayd
*†shee sayth,† And thou also wast with Jesus of Nazareth.

[Delete] understand
68 *But he denied, saying, I know †him† not, neither †wote†

*I what thou sayest. And he went out into the porch, and the cocke crew.

the wench when she saw him againe, began
69 *And †a damosell,† †when she saw him, began againe† to say to them that stood by,
a maid saw him againe, and began

*This is †one† of them.
one

a little
70 *And he denied it againe. And †anon† after, they that stood by sayd againe

[Delete]
one a Galilean
*to Peter, Surely thou art †one† of them: for thou art †of Galilee,†

is like
agreeth thereto
*and thy speech †agreeth thereto.†

[Delete]
saying
71 *But he began to curse and to sweare, †saying,† I know not this man

*of whom ye speake.

called to minde
72 *And the second time the cocke crew: and Peter †remembred† the word

*that Jesus sayd unto him, Before the cocke crow twise, thou shalt deny me

thrice he fell a weeping
*†three times:† And †he began to weepe.†
when he thought thereon, “he wept

“Or, he wept abundantly, or he began to weepe

The xv. Chapter.

straightway in the morning [Delete] [Delete]
1 *And †anon in the dawning,† †when† the †high† Priests †had†
chiefe

consultation [Delete]
*held a †councel† with the Elders & †the† Scribes, and the whole

Councell [Delete] and
*†congregation,† and †had† bound Jesus, †they† caried him away, and

*delivered him to Pilate.

2 *And Pilate asked him, Art thou the king of the Jewes? And hee answering, sayd

*unto him, Thou sayest it.

[Delete]
3 *And the †high† Priests accused him of many things, †but he answered nothing.†
chiefe but he answered nothing

And
4 *†So† Pilate asked him againe, saying, Answerest thou nothing? behold how many

*things they witnesse against thee.

But [Delete]
5 * Jesus yet answered nothing †at all,† so that Pilate marvelled.

[Delete]
Now at the he released one
6 * †At† †that† feast †Pilate did deliver† unto them †one† prisoner,
that

*whomsoever they desired.

[Delete]
7 *And there was one †that was† named Barabbas, which lay bound with them

whoe [Delete]
*that made insurrection with him, †which men† had committed murder †also†
had

sedition
insurrection
*in the †insurrection.†

multitude him to doe
8 *And the †people† crying aloud, began to desire †that hee would doe according†

*as hee had ever done unto them.

But   release
9 * Pilate answered them, saying, Wil ye that I †let loose† unto you the king

*of the Jewes?

10 *(For he knew that the †high† Priests had delivered him for envy.)
chiefe

release
11 *But the †high† Priests mooved the people, that hee should rather †deliver†
chiefe

*Barabbas unto them.

But
And   answered and   againe
12 * Pilate †answering againe,† said   unto them, What will ye then that

*I shall do unto him whom ye call the king of the Jewes?

out
13 *And they cried   againe, Crucifie him.

For What evill
Then   What evill
14 * Pilate sayd unto them, †What evill† hath he done? And they
Why, what evill

out   exceedingly
*cried   the more †fervently,† Crucifie him.

released
15 *And so Pilate, willing to content the people, †let loose† Barabbas unto them,

[Delete]   [Delete]
*and delivered †up† Jesus, when he had scourged him, †for†

*to be crucified.

16 *And the souldiers led him away into the hall, called Pretorium, and they call

*together the whole band.

17 *And they clothed him with purple, and platted a crowne of thorns, and put

*it about his head,

[Delete]
18 *And beganne to salute him, †saying,† Haile king of the Jewes.

19 *And they smote him on the head with a reed, and did spet upon him, and bowing

*their knees, worshipped him.

20 *And when they had mocked him, they tooke off the purple from him, & put his owne

*clothes on him, and led him out to crucifie him.

Simon a Cyrenian whoe passed by [Delete]
21 *And they compell one †that passed by, called Simon of Cyrene† †(†

cuntrye [Delete]
*comming out of the †field,† the father of Alexander and Rufus †)†

*to beare his crosse.

unto the [Delete]
22 *And they bring him †to a† place †named† Golgotha, which is,

beeing interpreted, the
*†if a man interpret it, a† place of a skull.

23 *And they gave him to drinke, wine mingled with myrrhe: but he received it not.

24 *And when they had crucified him, they parted his garments, casting lots upon

*them, what every man should take.

25 *And it was the third houre, and they crucified him.

superscription
26 *And the †title† of his accusation was written over, THE KING OF THE

*JEWES.

with him they crucifye his
27 *And †they crucified with him† two thieves, the one on †the† right hand, and

his
*the other on †the† left.

And reputed
28 *And the Scripture was fulfilled, which sayth, He was †counted†
numbred

*†among the wicked.†
with the transgressours

passed
29 *And they that †went† by, railed on him, wagging their heads, and saying,

[Delete] thou
*Ah †wretch,† †thou† that destroyest the temple, and buildest it in

*three dayes,

30 *Save thy selfe, and come downe from the crosse.

sayd among themselves, with the
31 *Likewise also the †high† Priests mocking †him among themselves, with the
chiefe

Scribes others
*Scribes, said,† He saved †other men,† himselfe he cannot save.

32 *Let Christ the king of Israel descend now from the crosse, that we may see,

reviled him
*and beleeve: And they that were crucified with him, †checked him also.†

there was darkenes the whole
33 *And when the sixth houre was come, †darkenesse arose† over †all the†

♣earth
*†earth,† untill the ninth houre.
land

♣Or, Land

mighty
greate
34 *And at the ninth houre, Jesus cried with a †loud† voice, saying, Eloi, Eloi,
loud

beeing interpreted,
*lama sabachthani? which is, †if one interpret it,† My God, my God, why hast

*thou forsaken me?

it
35 *And some of them that stood by, when they heard †that,† sayd, Behold, he

[Delete]
*calleth †for† Elias.

[Delete]
36 *And one ranne, and †after hee had† filled a spunge full of vineger,

about and [Delete]
*and put it †on† a reed, †he† gave him to drinke, saying, Let †him†
on

will comme
*alone, let us see whether Elias †commeth† to take him downe.

mighty
And [Delete] greate and
37 *†But when† Jesus †had† cried with a †loud† voice, †he† gave up the ghost.
loud

in twayne
38 *And the vaile of the Temple was rent †into two pieces,† from the top to the
*bottome.

[Delete]
39 *And when the Centurion, which stood over against him, saw, that †when†
[Delete] out and
*he †had† so cried , †he† gave up the ghost, he sayd, Truely this man
*was the sonne of God.

looking on afarre of also
40 *There were also women †a good way off, beholding him,† among whom was
[Delete]

[Delete]
*Mary Magdalene, and Mary the mother of James the little †,†
lesse,

Joses, and of
*and of †Joses and† Salome:
Joses, and

41 *†Which† also when he was in Galilee, followed him, and ministred unto him, and many
Who
*other women which came up with him unto Hierusalem.

Preparation, that is, the day
42 *And now when the even was come, (because it was the †day of preparing, that goeth†
*before the Sabboth)

[Delete] an honorable
43 *Joseph †<u>of</u> <u>the</u> <u>citie</u>† of Arimathea, †a noble† counseller, which
*also †looked† for the kingdome of God, came and went in boldly unto Pilate, and
waited

[Delete]
*†begged† †of him† the body of Jesus.
craved

calling
44 *And Pilate marvelled if he were alreadie dead, and †when he had called†

hee [Delete]
*unto him the Centurion, asked †of† him whether hee had beene any

*while dead.

the trueth
45 *And when he knew †the trueth† of the Centurion, he gave the body to Joseph.
it

hee tooke and
46 *And †when hee had† bought †a linnen cloth,† and †taken† him downe, †hee†
fine linnen

*wrapped him in the linnen †cloth,† and layed him in a sepulchre
[Delete]

which a
*†that† was hewen out of †the† rocke, and rolled a stone unto the doore of the

*sepulchre.

the mother of
47 *And Mary Magdalene, and Mary "Joses beheld where he was layed.

"The mother of

The xvi. Chapter.

[Delete]
1 *And when the Sabboth †day† was past, Mary Magdalene, and Marie

had spices
*†the mother† of James and Salome, bought sweet †smelling ointments,†
the mother

*that they might come and anoint him.

2 *And very early in the morning, the [a]first day of the †Sabboths,† they came
weeke

*unto the sepulchre, †when the sunne was risen.†
at the rising of the Sunne

[a]That is, Sunday, the first day of the weeke

3 *And they sayd among themselves, Who shall roll us away the stone from the doore
*of the sepulchre?

see
saw
4 *(And when they looked, they †saw how† that the stone was rolled away) for it
*was very great.

entring
5 *And †when they went† into the sepulchre, they saw a yoong man sitting on the
*right side, clothed in a long white garment, and they were
afrighted
*†greatly amazed.†

afrighted
6 *And hee sayth unto them, Be not †greatly amazed,† ye seeke Jesus of Nazareth,
*which was crucified, he is risen, he is not here, beholde the place where they
*†had put† him.
laid

[Delete]
7 *But goe your way, †and† tell his disciples, and Peter, that he goeth
*before you into Galilee, there shall ye see him, as he sayd unto you.

8 *And they went out quickly, and fled from the sepulchre, for they trembled, and
*were amazed, neither sayd they any thing to any man, for they were afrayd.

Now hee day of the week
9 * When Jesus was risen early, the first †day after the Sabboth,†
[Delete]

[Delete]
*†hee† appeared first to Marie Magdalene, out of whom he had cast seven
he
*devils.

had beene
10 *And shee went and tolde them that †were† with him, as they mourned and wept.

11 *And they, when they had heard that he was alive, and had bene seene of her,

[Delete]
*beleeved †it† not.

12 *After that, he appeared in another forme, unto two of them, as they walked,

*and went into the countrey.

neither beleeved they them
13 *And they went and tolde it unto the residue: †and <u>they</u> beleeved not these also.†

♣at meat
14 *Afterward, he appeared unto the eleven as they sate at meat, and
"at meat

upbrayded
*†cast in their teeth† their unbeliefe and hardnesse of heart, because they
them with

*beleeved not them, which had seene †that† he was risen.
him after

♣Or, <u>together</u>
"Or, <u>together</u>

15 *And he sayd unto them, Go ye into all the world, and preach the Gospel

every creature
*to †all creatures.†

beleeveth, & is beleeveth
16 *He that †shall beleeve, and be† baptized, shall be saved, but he that †shall not

not
*beleeve,† shall be damned.

signes
17 *And these †tokens† shall follow them that beleeve, In my name shall they cast

*out devils, they shall speake with new tongues,

18 *They shall †drive away† serpents, and if they drinke any deadly thing,
take up

not
*it shall †in no wise† hurt them, they shal lay hands on the sicke, and they

*shall recover.

after up
19 *So then, †when† the Lord had spoken unto them, he was received into heaven,

[Delete]
*and sate †him downe† on the right hand of God.

20 *And they went foorth, and preached every where, the Lord working with them,

Amen
*and confirming the word with signes following.

Bishops' Bible

The Gospel by S. Luke

Annotation

holy
[Delete]

*The Gospell according to St. Luke

Authorized Version

The Gospel according to S. Luke

The first Chapter.

a
1 *Forasmuch as many have taken in hand to set forth in order †the† declaration of
*those things which are most surely beleved among us,
2 *Even as they delivered them unto us, which from the beginning
were eye witnesses and
*†sawe them themselves with their eyes, and were† ministers of the word:
exactly atteyned unto
3 *It seemed good to me also, having †perfect understanding of† †al† things
had perfect understanding of [Delete]
very first
*from the †beginning,† to write unto thee in order, most excellent Theophilus,

better knowe
acknowledge
4 *That thou mightest †knowe† the certaintie of those things †whereof†
know wherein

*thou hast bene †taught by mouth.†
instructed

5 *There was in the dayes of Herode the king of †Jury,† a certaine Priest, named
Judea

*Zacharias, of the course of Abia, and his wife †was† of the daughters of Aaron, and
was

*her name was Elizabeth.

And
6 * They were both righteous before God, walking in all the commaundements

*and ordinances of the Lord, blamelesse.

7 *And they had no childe, because that Elizabeth was barren, and they both were

yeares
*nowe well striken in †age.†

hee
8 *And it came to passe, that †when† †Zacharias† executed the Priests office before
while

in the order of his course
*God †as his course came,†

9 *According to the custome of the Priests office, his lot was to burne incense when

*he went into the temple of the Lord.

praying without at the time of
10 *And the whole multitude of the people were †without in prayer, while the incense

incense
*was burning.†

11 *And there appeared unto him an Angel of the Lord, standing on the right side

*of the altar of †the† incense.
[Delete]

12 *And when Zacharias saw him, hee was troubled, and feare fell upon him.

13 *But the Angel sayd unto him, Feare not, Zacharias, for thy prayer is heard,

*and thy wife Elizabeth shal beare thee a sonne, and thou shalt call his name John.

For
And
14 *†And† thou shalt have joy and gladnesse, and many shall rejoice at his birth:

before
For in the sight of drinke neither
15 *†And† he shalbe great †in the sight of† the Lord, and shall †neither drinke†

*wine nor strong drinke, and he shall be filled with the holy Ghost, even from

*his mothers wombe.

And theyr God
16 *†For† many of the children of Israel shall he turne to the Lord .

in
17 *And he shall goe before him †with† the spirit and power of Elias, to turne the

by
♣to
*hearts of the fathers to the children, and the disobedient †to† the wisedome of
"to

[Delete] people prepared
*the just †men,† to make readie a †perfect people† for the Lord.

♣Or, by the wisedome of the just
"Or, by

Whereby
18 *And Zacharias sayde unto the Angel, †By what token† shal I know this?

an old man
*For I am †old,† and my wife well striken in yeres.

19 *And the Angel answering, sayd unto him, I am Gabriel that stand in the presence

I was
am
*of God, and †was† sent to speake unto thee, and to shewe thee these glad tidings.

[Delete]
20 *And behold, thou shalt be dumbe, and not †be† able to speake, until the

*day that these things shall be performed, because thou beleevedst not my words,

*which shalbe fulfilled in their season.

21 *And the people waited for Zacharias, and marveiled that he taried so long in

*the temple.

22 *And when he came out, he could not speake unto them: and they perceived that he

*had seene a vision in the temple: for hee beckened unto them, and remained

*speechlesse.

ministring
23 *And it came to passe, that as soone as the dayes of his †office†
ministration

expired
accomplished to
*were †out,† he departed †into† his owne house.

24 *And after those dayes, his wife Elizabeth conceived, and hid her selfe five

*moneths, saying,

25 *Thus hath the Lord dealt with me in the dayes wherein he looked on me, to take

reproche
*†from me† my †rebuke† among men.
away

26 *And in the sixt moneth, the Angel Gabriel was sent from God, unto a citie of

*Galilee, named Nazareth,

27 *To a virgin, †spoused† to a man whose name was Joseph of the house of David,
espoused

*and the virgins name was Marie.

[Delete] went and
28 *And †when† the Angel †was come† in unto her, †he† sayd, Haile
came

graciously accepted
[Delete] ♣full of grace
*†thou that art† †in high favour,† the Lord is with thee: Blessed art thou
thou that art "highly favoured

*among women.

♣Or, graciously accepted
"Or, graciously accepted, or much graced, see vers. 30

29 *And when she saw him, shee was troubled at his saying, and cast in her mind

*what maner of salutation this should be.

grace
30 *And the Angel sayd unto her, Feare not Marie, for thou hast found †favour†
favor

*with God.

And
31 *†For† beholde, thou shalt conceive in thy wombe, and †beare† a sonne,
bring forth

*and shalt call his name Jesus.

32 *He shall be great, and shall bee called the sonne of the Highest, and the Lord

throne
*God shal give unto him the †seate† of his father David.

33 *And he shall reigne over the house of Jacob for ever, and of his kingdome there

no
*shall bee †none† end.

34 *Then sayd Marie unto the Angel, Howe shall this be, seeing I know not a man?

answered &
35 *And the Angel †answering,† said unto her, The holy Ghost shall come upon thee, and

*the power of the Highest shall overshadowe thee. Therefore also that holy thing

*which shall bee borne , shall be called the sonne of God.
of thee

36 *And behold, thy cousin Elizabeth, she hath also conceived a sonne in her old

the sixt moneth unto her
her sixt moneth whoe
*age, and this is †her sixt moneth,† †which† was called barren.
the sixt moneth with her

shall ♣no word
no thing shall
37 *For with God †shall no word† be unpossible.

♣Or, no thing

handmaide
38 *And Marie sayd, Behold the †handmaiden† of the Lord, be it unto me according

*to thy word: and the Angel departed from her.

39 *And Mary arose in those dayes, and went into the hill countrey with haste,

*into a citie of Juda,

40 *And entred into the house of Zacharie, and saluted Elizabeth.

41 *And it came to passe, that when Elizabeth heard the salutation of Marie, the

leaped
*babe †sprang† in her wombe, and Elizabeth was filled with the holy Ghost.

42 *And she spake out with a loude voice, and sayd, Blessed art thou among women,

blessed is the fruite of thy wombe
*and †the fruite of thy wombe is blessed.†

is
43 *And whence †commeth† this to me, that the mother of my Lord should come to me?

44 *For loe, assoone as the voice of thy salutation sounded in mine eares, the

leaped
*babe †sprang† in my wombe for joy.

♣that beleeved there shall be a performance of those things
45 *And blessed is she that beleeved, for †those things shall be performed†
"that beleeved

*which were tolde her from the Lord.

♣Or, which beleeved that there
"Or, which beleeved that there

doth magnifie
46 *And Marie sayd, My soule †magnifieth† the Lord.

47 *And my spirit hath rejoyced in God my saviour.

regarded lownesse behold
48 *For he hath †looked on† the †lowlinesse† of his handmaiden: for †loe, now†
low estate

all generations shall
*from henceforth †shall all generations† call me blessed.

For
49 *†Because† he that is mighty hath done to me great things, and holy is his name.

50 *And his mercie is on them that feare him, from generation to generation.

the
51 *Hee hath shewed strength with his arme, he hath scattered †them that are†

*proud, in the imagination of their hearts.

them of low degree
52 *He hath put downe the mighty from their seates, and exalted †the lowly.†

the rich he hath sent empty away
53 *Hee hath filled the hungry with good things, and †sent away the rich empty.†

holpen
54 *He hath †helped† his servant Israel, in remembrance of his mercie,

[Delete] [Delete] to
55 *†(† † Even† as he spake to our fathers Abraham, and

[Delete]
*to his seede †)† for ever.

[Delete]
56 *And Marie abode with her about three moneths, & †afterward† returned

*to her own house.

time was fulfilled
Now full time came
57 * Elizabeths †time† †came† that she should bee delivered, and she

*brought forth a sonne.

magnifyed his
had shewed great
58 *And her neighbours and her cousins heard howe the Lord †had shewed great†

*mercie upon her, and they rejoiced with her.

59 *And it came to passe, that on the eight day they came to circumcise the child,

they
*and called him Zacharias, after the name of his father.

answered &
60 *And his mother †answering,† sayd, Not so, but he shall be called John.

of
61 *And they sayd unto her, There is none †in† thy kinred that is called

this
*by †that† name.

how
62 *And they made signes to his father, †what† he would have him called.

demanding a writing table he
he asked for writing tables and
63 *And †when he had asked for† †writing tables,† †he† wrote, saying, His name is
a writing table

*John: and they marveiled all.

[Delete]
64 *And his mouth was opened immediatly, and his tongue †loosed,†
loosed

and praysed
*and hee spake, †praysing† God.

[Delete]
65 *And feare came on all †them† that dwelt round about them, and all

*these sayings were noised abroad thorowout all the hill countrey of †Jurie.†
"sayings Judea

"Or, things

66 *And all they that had heard them, layde them up in their hearts, saying, What

*maner of childe shall this bee? And the hand of the Lord was with him.

67 *And his father Zacharias was filled with the holy Ghost, and prophesied, saying,

Blessed
68 *†Praised† be the Lord God of Israel, for he hath visited and redeemed his people,

for
69 *And hath raised up an horne of salvation †unto† us, in the house of his

*servant David:

(As have bene
70 *†Even as† he spake by the mouth of his holy Prophets, which †were† since
As

began)
*the world began.
began

we should be saved
71 *That †he would save us† from our enemies, and from the hand of all that

*hate us.

72 *†That he would deale mercifully with† our fathers, and remember his holy
To performe the mercy promised to to

*covenant:

[Delete]
73 *†And that hee would performe† the othe which he sware to our father

; to grant us
*Abraham †,† †for to give us.†
,

74 * That we being delivered out of the hands of our enemies,
That he would grant unto us

,
*might serve him without feare †.†

75 *In holinesse and righteousnesse before him, all the dayes of our life.

76 *And thou child shalt be called the Prophet of the highest: for thou shalt goe

*before the face of the Lord to prepare his wayes.

♣by
77 *To give knowledge of salvation unto his people, by the remission of their sinnes,
"by

♣Or, for
"Or, for

Sunne-rising
♣day spring on
78 *Through the tender mercie of our God, whereby the day spring from †an†
"tender mercy "day spring

*high hath visited us,

♣Or, Sunne-rising
"Or, bowels of the mercy
"Or, Sunne-rising, or branch

79 *To give light to them that sit in darkenes, and in the shadowe of death, to

*guide our feete into the way of peace.

the deserts
80 *And the childe grew, and waxed strong in spirit, and was in †wildernesse†

[Delete] Israel
*till the day †came† of his shewing unto †the Israelites.†

The ii. Chapter.

out decree
1 *And it came to passe in those dayes, that there went a †commaundement†

Cesar Augustus ♣taxed
*from †Augustus Cesar,† that all the world should be taxed.
"taxed

♣Or, inrolled
"Or, inrolled

Governour
2 *(And this †first taxing was† made when Cyrenius was †Lieutenant† of Syria.)
taxing was first

one
3 *And all went to be taxed, every †man† into his owne citie.

4 *And Joseph went up from Galilee, out of the citie of Nazareth, into
also

*†Jurie,† unto the citie of David, which is called Bethlehem, (because he was of the
Judea

*house and linage of David,)

5 *To bee taxed with Marie his espoused wife, being great with childe.

6 *And so it was, that while they were there, the dayes were accomplished that shee

*should be delivered.

borne wrapped him in swadling
7 *And shee brought foorth her first †begotten† sonne, and †swadled him,†

clothes
* & layd him in a manger, because there was no roume for them in the Inne.

laying
And abiding
8 * There were in the same countrey shepheards †abiding† in the field,

the night watches [Delete]
♣watch by night
*keeping †watch† over their flocke †by night.†
"watch

♣Or, the night watches
"Or, the night watches

came upon
9 *And loe the Angel of the Lord †stoode hard by† them, and the glorie of the
*Lord shone round about them, and they were sore afraid.

Feare not
10 *And the Angel sayde unto them, †Bee not afraid:† For behold, I bring you good
which
*tidings of great joy, †that† shall be to all people.

11 *For unto you is borne this day, in the citie of David, a saviour, which is
*Christ the Lord.

this shall be a signe unto you babe
12 *And †take this for a signe,† Ye shall finde the †childe†
laying
wrapped in swadling clothes lying
*†swadled,† †laid† in a manger.

13 *And suddenly there was with the Angel a multitude of
the heavenly army
the heavenly hoste
*†heavenly souldiers,† praising God, and saying,

on earth peace
14 *Glorie to God in the highest, and †peace on the earth,†
good will towards men
*†and among men a good will.†

[Delete]
15 *And it came to passe, †assoone† as the Angels were gone away from them
[Delete]
*into heaven, †the men† the shepheards sayd one to another, Let us
[Delete]
now goe even
*†goe nowe† †even† unto Bethlehem, and see this thing which is come to passe,
made knowen
*which the Lord hath †shewed† unto us.

16 *And they came with haste, & found Marie and Joseph, and the babe

laying
lying
*†laydt† in a manger.

made knowen
they made knowen thing
17 *And when they had seene it, †they published† abroade the †saying† which
saying

concerning
*was told them †of† this childe.

18 *And all they that heard it, woondered at those things which were tolde them

by
*†of† the shepheards.

theise ♣sayings pondering them
theise things and pondered them
19 *But Marie kept all †those sayings,† †and pondered them† in her heart.

♣Or, things

20 *And the shepheards returned, glorifying and praising God for all the things that

[Delete]
*they had heard and seene, †even† as it was tolde unto them.

eight dayes were accomplished for the circumcising of the childe
21 *And when †the eight day was come,† †that the childe should be circumcised,†

*his name was called Jesus, which was so named of the Angel before he was conceived

*in the wombe.

♣her
♣theyr
22 *And when the dayes of †her† purification, †after† the law of Moses,
her according to

*were accomplished, they brought him to Hierusalem, to present him to the Lord,

♣Or, theyr
♣Or, her

male [Delete]
23 *(As it is written in the lawe of the Lord, Every †man child† that †first†

*openeth the wombe, shalbe called holy to the Lord.)

[Delete] a sacrifice according to that which
24 *And to offer †,† †as it† is sayd in the
*lawe of the Lord, a paire of turtle doves, or two yong pigeons.
25 *And beholde, there was a man in Hierusalem, whose name was Simeon, and the same
devoute
*man was just and †godly,† †looking† for the consolation of Israel: and the holy
waiting
*Ghost was upon him.
it was revealed unto him by that he should not
26 *And †a revelation was given him of† the holy Ghost, †not to†
*see death, before he had seene the Lords Christ.
the spirit
27 *And he came by †inspiration† into the temple: and when the parents brought in
*the childe Jesus, to doe for him after the custome of the lawe,
blessed
28 *Then tooke he him up in his armes, and †praised† God, and sayd,
word
29 *Lord, now lettest thou thy servant depart in peace, according to thy †promise.†
30 *For mine eyes have seene thy salvation,
31 *Which thou hast prepared before the face of all people.
lighten
32 *A light to †be revealed to† the Gentiles, and the glory of thy people Israel.
Joseph
33 *And †his father† and his mother marveiled at those things which were spoken
*of him.
34 *And Simeon blessed them, and said unto Marie his mother, Behold, this childe
for rising
*is set †to be† the fall and †uprising† againe of many in Israel: and for a signe
*which †is† spoken against,
shalbe

[Delete] thorow

35 *(†And† †moreover,† †the† sworde shall pearce thy soule)
Yea a owne also

revealed
*that the thoughts of many hearts may be †opened.†

36 *And there was †a Prophetesse one Anna,† the daughter of Phanuel, of the
one Anna a Prophetesse

; shee
*tribe of Aser †,† †which† was of a great age, and had lived with an husband seven

*yeeres from her virginitie.

was of
37 *And shee †had bene† a widowe about foure score and foure yeres, which departed

God
*not from the temple, but served †God† with fastings and prayers night and day.

in at that instant upon them
in at that instant
38 *And she comming †at the same instant upon them,† gave thankes likewise unto
in that instant

*the Lord, and spake of him to all them that looked for redemption

♣Hierusalem
*in Hierusalem.
"Hierusalem

♣Or, Israel
"Or, Israel

39 *And when they had performed all things according to the law of the Lord, they

*returned into Galilee, to their owne citie Nazareth.

[Delete]
40 *And the childe grew, and waxed strong in spirit, †and was† filled

*with wisedome, and the grace of God was upon him.

yearely
every yere
41 *Now his parents went to Hierusalem †every yere,† at the feast of the Passeover.

went
42 *And when he was twelve yeres old, they †ascended† up to Hierusalem, after the

[Delete]
*custome of the feast †day:†

[Delete]
43 *And when they had fulfilled the dayes, as they returned †home,† the

*childe Jesus †abode still† in Hierusalem, and Joseph & his mother knewe not of it.
taried behind

went
44 *But they supposing him to have bene in the company, †came† a dayes journey,

they
*and sought him among their kinsfolke and acquaintance.

45 *And when they found him not, they turned backe againe to Hierusalem, seeking him.

46 *And it came to passe, that after three dayes they found him in the temple, sitting

both asking them questions
*in the middest of the Doctors, hearing them, and †posing them.†

astonished
47 *And all that heard him, were †astonied† at his understanding and answeres.

48 *And when they saw him, they were amazed: and his mother said unto him, Sonne,

*why hast thou thus dealt with us? Behold, thy father and I have sought thee sorowing.

49 *And he sayd unto them, How is it that yee sought me? Wist yee not that I

bee
*must †goe† about my fathers businesse?

the
50 *And they understood not †that† saying which he spake unto them.

subject
51 *And hee went downe with them, and came to Nazareth, and was †obedient† unto them:

*But his mother kept all these sayings in her heart.

♣increased
52 *And Jesus increased in wisedome and stature, and in favour with God and man.
"stature

♣Or, proffitted
"Or, age

The iii. Chapter.

1 *Nowe in the fifteenth yeere of the reigne of Tiberius Cesar, Pontius Pilate being
Governor
*†lieutenant† of †Jurie,† and Herode being Tetrarch of Galilee, and his brother Philip
Judea
Trachonitis
*Tetrarch of Iturea, and of the region of †Trachonites,† and Lysanias the Tetrarch
*of Abilene,
Annas and Caiaphas beeing God
2 *†When Annas and Caiaphas were† the high Priests, the word of †the Lord†
*came unto John, the sonne of Zacharias, in the wildernesse.
countrie
3 *And hee came into all the †coastes† about Jordane, preaching the baptisme of
*repentance, for the remission of sinnes,
4 *As it is written in the booke of the words of Esaias the Prophet, saying, The
one crying
*voyce of †a cryer† in the wildernesse, Prepare ye the way of the Lord, make his
*pathes straight.
5 *Every valley shalbe filled, and every mountaine and hill shall be brought lowe,
the
*and †things that be† crooked, shall be made straight, and the rough wayes shalbe
smoothe
*made †plaine.†
6 *And al flesh shall see the salvation of God.
multitude came
7 *Then saide he to the †people† that †were come† forth to be baptized of him,
generations warned
*O †generation† of vipers, who hath †forewarned† you to flee from the wrath to come?
generation
fruits ♣worthy
8 *Bring forth therefore †due fruits of† repentance, and begin not to say within
fruites "worthy of

*your selves, We have Abraham to our father: For I say unto you, that God is able

[Delete]
up
*of these stones to raise †up† children unto Abraham.

♣Or, <u>answearable</u> <u>to</u> <u>amendment</u> <u>of</u> <u>life</u>
"Or, <u>meet</u> <u>for</u>

And now also the axe is
And now the axe is
And now also the axe is
9 *†Now also is the axe† layed unto the roote of the trees: Every tree therefore

*which bringeth not foorth good fruit, is hewen downe, and cast into the fire.

10 *And the people asked him, saying, What shall we do then?

11 *He answereth and saith unto them, Hee that hath two coates, let him

impart to
*†part with† him that hath none, and he that hath meate, let him do likewise.

there Publicanes
also Publicanes
12 *Then came †Publicanes also† to bee baptized, and saide unto him, Master, what shall

*we doe?

Exact
13 *And hee said unto them, †Require† no more then that which is appointed

[Delete]
*†unto† you.

And
14 * The souldiers likewise demanded of him, saying, And what shall we do?

*And he said unto them, Doe violence to no man, neither accuse any falsely,
"Doe violence to no man

♣wages
*and be content with your wages.
"wages

♣Or, <u>allowance</u>
"Or, <u>put</u> <u>no</u> <u>man</u> <u>in</u> <u>feare</u>
"Or, <u>allowance</u>

as the people were in expectation
15 *And †the people waited,† and all men mused in their hearts of
as the people were "in expectation "mused

Christ or not
*John, whether hee were †very Christ.†
the Christ or not

"Or, in suspence
"Or, reasoned or debated

I in deede
16 *John answered, saying unto them all, †In deede I† baptize you with water, but

the latchet of whose shooes
*one †stronger† then I commeth, †whose shooes latchet† I am not worthy to
mightier

*unloose, he shal baptize you with the holy Ghost, and with fire.

Whose fanne is hee
17 *†Which hath his fanne† in his hand, and will thorowly purge his floore,

garner hee will
*and will gather the wheat into his †barne,† but the chaffe †will hee† burne

*with fire unquenchable.

18 *And many other things in his exhortation preached he unto the people.

But being reproved by
19 *†Then† Herode the Tetrarch, †when hee was rebuked of† him for Herodias his

had done
*brother Philips wife, & for al the evils which Herod †did,†

yet that hee
20 *Added this above all, †and† shut up John in prison.

21 *Nowe †it came to passe, as all the people were baptized, and†
when all the people were baptized, and it came to passe that

Jesus also being praying
*†when Jesus was† baptized, and †did pray,† †that† the heaven was
[Delete]

*opened:

22 *And the holy Ghost †came downe† in a bodily shape like a Dove upon him, and a
descended

*voice came from heaven, which said, Thou art my beloved Sonne, in thee I am well

*pleased.

23 *And Jesus himselfe beganne to be about thirtie yeeres of age, being

[Delete] sonne the sonne
*(as †he† was supposed) the †son† of Joseph, which was †the sonne†
the sonne

*of Heli,

24 *Which was †the sonne† of Matthat, which was †the sonne† of Levi, which was
the sonne the sonne

*†the sonne† of Melchi, which was †the sonne† of Janna, which was †the sonne†
the sonne the sonne the sonne

*of Joseph,

25 *Which was †the sonne† of Matthathias, which was †the sonne† of Amos, which was
the sonne the sonne

Esly
*†the sonne† of Naum, which was †the sonne† of †Hesly,† which was †the sonne†
the sonne the sonne the sonne

*of Nagge,

26 *Which was †the sonne† of Maath, which was †the sonne† of Matthathias, which was
the sonne the sonne

*†the sonne† of Semei, which was †the son† of Joseph, which was †the sonne†
the sonne the sonne the sonne

*of Juda,

27 *Which was †the sonne† of Joanna, which was †the sonne† of Rhesa, which was
the sonne the sonne

*†the sonne† of Zorobabel, which was †the son† of Salathiel, which was
the sonne the sonne

*†the sonne† of Neri,
the sonne

28 *Which was †the sonne† of Melchi, which was †the sonne† of Addi, which was
the sonne the sonne

*†the sonne† of Cosam, which was †the son† of Elmodam, which was †the sonne†
the sonne the sonne the sonne

*of Er,

29 *Which was †the sonne† of Jose, which was †the sonne† of Eliezer, which was
the sonne the sonne

*†the sonne† of Jorim, which was †the sonne† of Matthat, which was †the sonne†
the sonne the sonne the sonne

*of Levi,

30 *Which was †the sonne† of Simeon, which was †the sonne† of Juda, which was
the sonne the sonne

*†the sonne† of Joseph, which was †the sonne† of Jonan, which was †the sonne†
the sonne the sonne the sonne

Eliakim
*of †Eliacim,†

31 *Which was †the son† of Melea, which was †the sonne† of Menam, which was
the sonne the sonne

Mattatha
*†the sonne† of †Matthathia,† which was †the sonne† of Nathan, which was
the sonne the sonne

*†the sonne† of David,
the sonne

32 *Which was †the sonne† of Jesse, which was †the sonne† of Obed, which was
the sonne the sonne

*†the son† of Booz, which was †the sonne† of Salmon, which was †the sonne†
the sonne the sonne the sonne

*of Naasson,

33 *Which was †the son† of Aminadab, which was †the sonne† of Aram, which was
the sonne the sonne

Esrom
*†the sonne† of †Esron,† which was †the sonne† of Phares, which was †the sonne†
the sonne the sonne the sonne

*of Juda,

34 *Which was †the son† of Jacob, which was †the sonne† of Isahac, which was
the sonne the sonne

*†the sonne† of Abraham, which was †the sonne† of Thara, which was †the sonne†
the sonne the sonne the sonne

*of Nachor,

35 *Which was †the sonne† of Saruch, which was †the sonne† of Ragau, which was
the sonne the sonne

Palec Eber
Phaleg Heber
*†the sonne† of †Phaleg,† which was †the son† of †Heber,† which was †the sonne†
the sonne the sonne the sonne

*of Sala,

of Cainan which was the sonne
36 *Which was †the sonne† of Arphaxad, which
the sonne of Cainan, which was the sonne

*was †the sonne† of Sem, which was †the sonne† of Noe, which was †the sonne†
the sonne the sonne the sonne

*of Lamech,

37 *Which was †the son† of Mathusala, which was †the sonne† of Enoch, which was
the sonne the sonne

Maleleel
Malaleel
*†the sonne† of Jared, which was †the sonne† of †Malaleel,† which was †the sonne†
the sonne the sonne Maleleel the sonne

*of Cainan,

Enos
Henos
38 *Which was †the sonne† of †Henos,† which was †the sonne† of Seth, which was
the sonne Enos the sonne

*†the sonne† of Adam, which was †the Sonne† of God.
the sonne the sonne

The iiii. Chapter.

And
And
1 * Jesus beeing full of the holy Ghost, returned from Jordan, and

[Delete] the
*was ledde by the †same† Spirit into wildernesse,

2 *Being fourtie dayes tempted of the devill, and in those dayes †did he† eat nothing:
he did

*and when they were ended, he afterward hungred.

3 *And the devil saide unto him, If thou bee the Sonne of God, command this stone
*that it be made bread.

[Delete]
that
4 *And Jesus answered him, saying, It is written, †that† man shall not live
alone
*by bread †onely,† but by every word of God.

the devill taking
5 *And †when the devill had taken† him up into an high mountaine,
and
[Delete] unto
*†hee† shewed him all the kingdomes of the worlde in a moment of time.

[Delete]
6 *And the devil said unto him, Al this power will I give thee †every whit,†
*and the glory of them, for that is delivered unto mee, and to whomsoever I wil,
*I give it.

before me all shall be
7 *If thou therefore wilt worship †me,† †it shall be all† thine.
"worship me

"Or, <u>fall</u> <u>downe</u> <u>before</u> <u>me</u>

And answered &
8 * Jesus †answering,† said unto him, Get thee †hence† behinde mee,
[Delete]
*Satan: for it is written, Thou shalt worship the Lord thy God, and him
alone
onely
*†onely† shalt thou serve.

brought
9 *And hee †caried† him to Hierusalem, and set him on a pinacle of the Temple, and
*sayd unto him, If thou be the Sonne of God, cast thy selfe downe from hence.

[Delete] concerning
10 *For it is written, †that† hee shall give his Angels charge †over†
over

*thee, to keepe thee.

that
[Delete]
11 *And in their handes they shall beare thee up,

least at any time thou dash thy foote
*†that thou dash not thy foote at any time† against a stone.

12 *And Jesus answering, sayde unto him, It is saide, Thou shalt not tempt the Lord

*thy God.

13 *And when the devil had ended al the temptation, he departed from him for a

*season.

14 *And Jesus returned †by† the power of the Spirit into Galilee, and there
in

out through
*went a fame of him †throughout† all the region round about.

[Delete]
15 *And he taught in their Synagogues, being glorified of all †men.†

brought up
16 *And he came to Nazareth, where he †was† †nursed,† and as his custome was,
had bene

*hee went into the Synagogue on the Sabboth day, and stood up for to reade.

17 *And there was delivered unto him the booke of the Prophet Esaias: and when he had

was
*opened the booke, he found the place where it †is† written,

for which cause
18 *The Spirit of the Lord upon me, †because† he hath anointed me,
is because

.
*to preach the Gospel to the poore †:† he hath sent me, to heale the broken hearted,
,

captives
*to preach deliverance to the †captive,† and recovering of sight to the blinde,

[Delete]
*†freely† to set at libertie them that are bruised,

19 *†And† to preach the acceptable yeere of the Lord.
[Delete]

he gave
20 *And †when he had closed† the booke, †and given† it againe to the minister,
he closed & he gave

and
*†he† sate downe: and the eyes of al them that were in the Synagogue were fastened

*on him.

21 *And he began to say unto them, This day is this Scripture fulfilled in your eares.

22 *And all bare him witnesse, and wondered at the gracious wordes, which proceeded

*out of his mouth. And they said, Is not this Josephs sonne?

doubtlesse ye will
Ye will utterly
23 *And he saide unto them, †Ye will utterly† say unto me this proverbe, Physition,
Ye will surely

*heale thy selfe: Whatsoever wee have heard done in Capernaum, doe

also here in thy
*†the same here likewise in thine owne† countrey.

24 *And hee saide, Verely I say unto you, no Prophet is accepted in his owne

*countrey.

25 *But I tell you of a trueth, many widowes were in Israel in the dayes of Elias,

so that great famine
up when great famine
*when the heaven was shut three yeeres and sixe moneths, †when great famishment†

*was throughout all the land:

[Delete]
26 *†And† unto none of them was Elias sent, save unto Sarepta †a citie†
But a citie

widow woman
*of Sidon, unto a †woman that was a widow.†
woman that was a widow

27 *And many lepers were in Israel in the time of Elizeus the Prophet: and none of

*them was cleansed, saving Naaman the Syrian.

28 *And all they in the Synagogue, when they heard these things, were filled with

*wrath,

[Delete]
29 *And rose up, and thrust him out of the city, and led him †even† unto

brow
*the †"top† of the hil (whereon their city was built) that they might cast him
"brow

*downe headlong.

"The Greek readeth, brow of the hill
"Or, edge

30 *But hee passing thorow the mids of them, went his way:

[Delete]
31 *And came downe to Capernaum, a citie of Galilee, and †there† taught

*them on the Sabboth dayes.

astonished word
32 *And they were †astonied† at his doctrine: for his †preaching† was with power.

an uncleane
33 *And in the Synagogue there was a man, which had a spirit of †a fowle† devil,

*and cried out with a lowd voyce,

♣Let us alone
34 *Saying, Let us alone, what have wee to do with thee, thou Jesus of Nazareth?
"Let us alone

thee [Delete]
*art thou come to destroy us? I know who thou art, †even† the holy

*One of God.

♣Or, Away
"Or, away

it
35 *And Jesus rebuked †him,† saying, Hold thy peace, and come out of him. And when
him

[Delete]
hee
*the devil had throwen him in the mids, †hee† came out of him, and hurt

*him not.

they were all amazed [Delete]
36 *And †feare came on them all,† and †they† spake among themselves, saying,

maner of ♣saying
*What †maner of saying† is this? For with authoritie and power he commaundeth the
a word

uncleane
*†fowle† spirits, and they come out.

♣Or, thing

37 *And the fame of him went out into every place of the countrey round about.

hee arose and
38 *And †when hee was risen† out of the Synagogue, †hee† entred into Simons house:

besought
*and Simons wives mother was taken with a great fever, and they †made intercession to†

*him for her.

standing over her hee
he stood over her, and
39 *And †he stood over her, and† rebuked the fever, and it left her. And immediatly

*shee arose, and ministred unto them.

Now setting
40 * When the Sunne was †downe,† all they that had any sicke with divers diseases,

hee
*brought them unto him: and †when he had† layd his handes on every one of them,

and
*†hee† healed them.

out [Delete]
41 *And devils also came out of many, crying , and saying, Thou art †that†

*Christ the Sonne of God. And he rebuking them, suffered them not to
"to

say that they knew him to be Christ
♣speake: for they knew that hee was
*†speake: for they knew that hee was† Christ.
speake: for they knew that he was

♣Or, say that they knew him to be Christ
"Or, to say that they knew him to be Christ

42 *And when it was day, hee departed, and went into a desert place: and the people

unto stayed
*sought him, and came †to† him, and †kept† him, that hee should not depart

*from them.

43 *And he said unto them, I must preach the kingdome of God to other cities also:

*For therefore am I sent.

preached
44 *And hee †was preaching† in the Synagogues of Galilee.

The v. Chapter.

And as
1 * It came to passe, that †when† the people preassed upon him, to heare the word

stood
*of God, he †was standing† by the lake of Genezareth.

[Delete] standing by the lake
2 *And †hee† sawe two shippes †stand by the lakes side:† but the fishermen

*were gone out of them, and were washing their nettes.

was Simons
hee pertained to Simon
3 *And †when hee was† entred into one of the ships which †pertained to Simon,†
was Simons

put
and thrust
*†he† prayed him that hee would †thrust† out a little from the land: and he

*sate downe, and taught the people out of the shippe.

[Delete]
Now Lanch out
4 * When he had left speaking, hee saide unto Simon, †Lanch out†

downe for a draught
*into the deepe, and let †slippe† your nets †to catch.†

toyled all the
toyled all the
5 *And Simon answering, saide unto him, Master, wee have †laboured all†

word
*night, and have taken nothing: neverthelesse, at thy †commandement†

let downe
*I will †loose forth† the net.

6 *And when they had this done, they inclosed a great multitude of fishes,

*†but† their net brake:
and

7 *And they beckened unto their partners, which were in the other shippe, that

*they should come and helpe them. And they came, and filled both the ships that
so

[Delete]
*they †sunke† †againe.†
began to sinke

it
8 *When Simon Peter sawe †this,† hee fell downe at Jesus knees, saying,

Depart
*†Go out† from me, for I am a sinfull man, O Lord.

astonished draught
9 *For hee was †utterly astonied,† and all that were with him, at the †taking†

made
taken
*of the fishes, which they had †caught together.†

10 *And so was also James and John the sonnes of Zebedee, which were partners with

*Simon. And Jesus saide unto Simon, Feare not, from henceforth thou shalt catch men.

[Delete] shippes to land
11 *And when they had brought †up† their †boates to the shore,† they forsooke

*all, and followed him.

[Delete]
12 *And it came to passe, †that† when hee was in a certaine citie, beholde,

[Delete] Whoe seeing
*†there was† a man full of leprosie: †and† †when hee had spied† Jesus,

fell
*†hee fell flat† on his face, and besought him, saying, Lord, if thou wilt, thou
*canst make mee cleane.

hee put and
13 *And †when hee had stretched† foorth his hand, †hee† touched him, saying, I
*will: bee thou cleane. And immediatly, the leprosie departed from him.

[Delete]
14 *And hee charged him to tell no man: but, Goe †saith he,† and shew thy
*selfe to the Priest, and offer for thy clensing, according as Moses commanded,

testimonie
*for a †witnesse† unto them.

greate multitudes
15 *But so much the more went there a fame abroad of him, and †much people†

by of
*came together to heare, and to bee healed †of† him †from† their infirmities.

withdrewe him self into
16 *And hee †kept himselfe apart in† the wildernesse, and prayed.

and the
17 *And it came to passe on a certaine day, as hee was teaching, †that there were†
that there were

every towne
*Pharisees, and doctours of the Law sitting by, which were come out of †all the townes†
*of Galilee, and †Jurie,† and Hierusalem: and the power of the Lord was
Judea

present
present
*†present,† to heale them.
present

[Delete]
And
[Delete]
18 *†And† beholde, men brought in a bedde a man which was taken with a palsie:
And

*and they sought meanes to bring him in, and to lay him before him.

by what way
19 *And when they coulde not finde †on what side† they might bring him in, because

up to
multitude upon
*of the †prease,† they went †upon the top of† the house , and let him down through
top

[Delete]
*the tyling with his couch, †even† into the middest before Jesus.

And
20 * When he saw their faith, he said unto him, Man, thy sinnes are forgiven

*thee.

reason Whoe
21 *And the Scribes and the Pharsees began to †“thinke,† saying, †what fellow†

alone
*is this which speaketh blasphemies? Who can forgive sinnes, but God †onely?†

“Or, reason

22 *But when Jesus perceived their thoughts, he answering, said unto them,

reason
*What †thinke† yee in your hearts?

23 *Whether is easier to say, Thy sinnes be forgiven thee: or to say, Rise up and

*walke?

upon earth to forgive sinnes
24 *But that yee may know that the sonne of man hath power †to forgive sinnes on earth†

*(he said unto the sicke of the palsie,) I say unto thee, Arise, and

take and
*†when thou hast taken† up thy couch, goe into thine house.

took up
25 *And immediatly hee rose up before them, and †when hee had taken up†

that and [Delete]
*†this couch,† whereon he lay, †he† departed to his †owne† house,
own

*glorifying God.

glorifyed
26 *And they were all amazed, and they †gave the glorie unto† God, and were filled

[Delete]
*with feare, saying, †Doubtlesse† wee have seene strange things to day.

And
27 *†An† after these things he went forth, and sawe a Publicane, named Levi,

*sitting at the receite of custome: and hee sayd unto him, Follow me.

hee [Delete]
28 *And †when hee had† left all, †he† rose up, and followed him.

29 *And Levi made him a great feast in his owne house: and there was a great

downe
*companie of Publicanes, and of †other† that sate †at meate† with them.
others

theyr Scribes and Pharisees
30 *But †they that were Scribes and Pharisees among them,† murmured against his

*disciples, saying, Why doe ye eate and drinke with Publicanes and sinners?

31 *And Jesus answering, sayde unto them, They that are whole neede not a Phisition:

*but they that are sicke.

32 *I came not to call the righteous: but sinners to repentance.

33 *And they said unto him, Why do the disciples of John fast often, and make

*prayers, and likewise the disciples of the Pharisees: but thine eate and drinke.

And bride
34 * Hee sayd unto them, Can yee make the children of the †wedding† chamber

*fast, while the Bridegrome is with them?

35 *But the dayes will come: †and† when the Bridegrome shalbe taken away from
[Delete]

*them, then shall they fast in those dayes.
and

And a parable unto them a
36 * Hee spake also †unto them a similitude,† No man putteth a piece of new

upon an old garment els
*garment †into an old vesture:† †for then† the new †renteth the old,†
upon an old if otherwise, then both maketh a rent

[Delete]
*and the piece †that was taken† out of the new, agreeth not with the old.
that was taken

putteth bottles els
37 *And no man †powreth† new wine into olde †vessels:† †for if he doe,†

bottles it will runne out
*the new wine wil burst the †vessels,† and †runne out it selfe,† and the
bee spilled

bottles
*†vessels† shall perish.

bottles
38 *But new wine must be put into new †vessels,† and both are preserved.

straightway desireth
straightwayes desireth
39 *No man also having drunke olde wine, †will straightway have† new: for he
straightway desireth

*saith, The olde is better.

The vi. Chapter.

1 *And it came to passe on the Second Sabboth after the first, that he went thorowe

[Delete]
*the corne fieldes: and his disciples plucked the eares of corne and did eate †,†
,

*rubbing them in their hands.

2 *And certain of the Pharisees said unto them, Why doe ye that which is not

*lawfull to doe on the Sabboth dayes?

what
3 *And Jesus answering them, said, Have yee not read so much as this †that†

[Delete]
*David did, when †he† himselfe was an hungred, and they which were with him:

4 *How hee went into the house of God, and did take and eate the Shew bread,

it
*and gave also to them that were with him, which is not lawfull to eate but for

alone
*the Priests †onely?†

5 *And he said unto them, That the Sonne of man is Lord also of the

[Delete]
*Sabboth †day.†

on
6 *And it came to passe also †in† another Sabboth, that hee entred into the

*Synagogue, and taught: and there was a man whose right hand was

withered
*†dried up.†

7 *And the Scribes and Pharisees watched him, whether hee would heale on the

an accusation against him
*Sabboth day: that they might finde †how to accuse him.†

8 *But he knewe their thoughts, and said to the man which had the withered hand,

*Rise up, and stand foorth in the middes. And he arose, and stood foorth.

one thing
9 *Then saide Jesus unto them, I will aske you †a question, Whether† is it lawfull

[Delete]
*on the Sabboth dayes to do good, or to do evil? to save †ones†

[Delete]
life
*†life,† or destroy it?
to

looking about upon them all
looking round about upon them all
10 *And †when he had beheld them all in compasse,† he saide unto the man, Stretch

*foorth thy hand. And he did so: and his hand was restored

[Delete]
*†againe as† whole as the other.

one with another
11 *And they were filled with madnesse, and communed †together among themselves†

*what they might do to Jesus.

12 *And it came to passe in those dayes, that he went out into a mountaine to

[Delete]
*pray, and continued all night †there† in prayer to God.

unto him
13 *And when it was day, hee called his disciples: and of them hee

named
*chose twelve, whom also he †called† Apostles:

[Delete] (whom he also named Peter)
14 *†(† Simon, †whom he also named Peter,† and Andrew his brother: James and

*John, Philip, and Bartholomew,

the sonne [Delete]
15 *Matthew, and Thomas, James †the sonne† of Alpheus, and Simon, †which is†

*called Zelotes,

the brother of James
16 *And Judas, †James brother,† and Judas Iscariot, which also was the

[Delete]
*traitour. †)†

[Delete] and
17 *And †when† he came downe with them, †he† stood in the plaine

[Delete]
*†field,† and the company of his disciples, and a great multitude of people,

coast
*out of all †Jurie† and Hierusalem, and from the sea †coast† of Tyre and Sidon,
Judea

*which came to heare him, and to be healed of their diseases,

uncleane
18 *And they that were vexed with †foule† spirits: and they were healed.

the whole multitude sought
19 *And †all the people preassed† to touch him: for there went vertue out of him,

*and healed them all.

hee on and
20 *And †when hee had† lifted up his eyes †upon† his disciples, †hee† saide,

*Blessed be ye poore: for yours is the kingdome of God.

filled
21 *Blessed are ye that hunger nowe: for ye shalbe †satisfied.† Blessed are ye

*that weepe now, for ye shall laugh.

22 *Blessed are ye when men shall hate you, and when they shall separate you

company
*from their †company,† and shall †raile on† you, and †put† out your name as evil,
reproch cast

*for the Sonne of mans sake.

[Delete]
23 *Rejoyce ye in that day, and leape †ye† for joy: for beholde, your reward

*is great in heaven, for in the like maner did their fathers unto the Prophets.

receaved
24 *But woe unto you that are rich: for yee have your consolation.

25 *Woe unto you that are full: for yee shall hunger. Woe unto you that

laugh now weepe
*†now laugh:† for yee shall mourne and †waile.†

all speake well of
26 *Woe unto you when men shall †praise† you: for so did their fathers

*to the false prophets.

27 *But I say unto you which heare, Love your enemies, doe good to them which hate

*you,

28 *Blesse them that curse you, and pray for them which

offer you violence
dispitefully use you
*†wrongfully trouble you.†

[Delete] one
29 *†And† unto him that smiteth thee on the †one† cheeke, offer also the other:
And

*and him that taketh away thy cloake, forbid not to take thy coat also.

30 *Give to every man that asketh of thee, and of him that taketh away thy goods,

*aske them not againe.

even so doe yee unto them
doe ye also to them likewise
31 *And as yee would that men should doe to you, †doe ye also to them likewise.†

And
32 *†For† if yee love them which love you, what thanke have ye? for sinners also
For

those that love them
*love †their lovers.†

to to
33 *And if ye doe good †for† them which do good †for† you, what thanke have yee?

*for sinners also do even the same.

34 *And if yee lende to them of whom yee hope to receive, what thanke have yee?

as much
*for sinners also lend to sinners, to receive †such like† againe.

hoping
35 *But love ye your enemies, and doe good, and lend, †looking† for nothing

*againe: and your reward shalbe great, and yee shalbe the children of the

unthankfull
*Highest: for he is kinde unto the †unkinde,† and to the evill.

36 *Bee ye therefore mercifull, as your father also is mercifull.

[Delete]
37 *Judge not, and yee shall not be judged †at all:† condemne not, and yee

[Delete]
*shall not be condemned †at all:† forgive, and ye shalbe forgiven.

and
38 *Give, and it shalbe given unto you, good measure, preassed downe, shaken

bosome
*together, and running over, shal men give into your †bosomes:† for with the same

*measure that ye mete withal, it shalbe measured to you againe.

spake a parable
39 *And he †put foorth a similitude† unto them, Can the blinde leade the blinde?

*Shall they not both fall into the ditch?

40 *The disciple is not above his master: but

every one shall be perfected according
every one shall be perfected
*†whosoever will be a perfect disciple, shall be† as his master †is.†
every one “that is perfect shall be [Delete]

“Or, shalbe perfected as his master

beholdest
41 *And why †seest† thou the mote that is in thy brothers eye, but

perceivest
*†considerest† not the beame that is in thine owne eye?

42 *Either how canst thou say to thy brother, Brother, let me pul out the mote that

beholdest
*is in thine eye: when thou thy selfe †seest† not the beame that is in thine

pul first the beame out of thine owne eye
*owne eye? Thou hypocrite, †cast† out †the beame out of thine owne eye first,†
cast

clearly
*and then shalt thou see †perfectly† to pull out the mote that is in thy brothers eye.

♣evill
corrupt
43 *For †it is not a good tree that bringeth† forth †evill† fruit:
a good tree bringeth not

is that an ♣evil tree that bringeth
is that a corrupt tree that bringeth
*neither †is that an evil tree that bringeth† foorth good fruit.
doeth a corrupt tree bring

♣Or, rotten [Cancelled]

44 *For every tree is knowen by his owne fruit: for of thornes †do not men†
men doe not

*gather figs, nor of a bramble bush gather they grapes.

45 *A good man out of the good treasure of his heart, bringeth forth that which

*is good: and an evill man out of the evill treasure of his heart, bringeth foorth

*that which is evil: For of the abundance of the heart, his mouth speaketh.

And the things which I say
46 * Why call ye me Lord, Lord, and do not †as I bid you?†

47 *Whosoever commeth to me, and heareth my sayings, and doth †the same,†
them

*I wil shew you to whom he is like.

48 *He is like a man which built an house, and digged deepe, and layd the foundation

a flood streame
*on †the† rocke. And when the †waters† arose, the †flood† beat vehemently upon

shake founded a
*that house, and could not †moove† it: for it was †grounded† upon †the† rocke.

[Delete]
49 *But he that heareth, and doeth †it† not, is like a man that without
a

streame
*foundation built an house upon the earth: against which the †flood† did beat

immediatly it fell ruine
*vehemently, and †it fel immediatly,† and the †fall† of that house was great.

The vii. Chapter.

1 * When he had ended all his sayings in the audience of the people, he
Now

*entred into Capernaum.

whoe
2 *And a certaine Centurions servant, †which† was deare unto him,

was sick & ready to dye
*†being sicke, was in peril of death.†

3 *And when he heard of Jesus, he sent unto him the Elders of the Jewes, beseeching

*him that he would come and heale his servant.

that he is
that he was
4 *And when they came to Jesus, they besought him instantly, saying, †He is†

for whom hee should do this
*worthy †that thou shouldest do this for him.†

he
hee
5 *For he loveth our nation, and hath built us a Synagogue.

6 *Then Jesus went with them. And when he was now not farre from the house,
*the Centurion sent friendes to him, saying unto him, Lord, trouble not thy selfe:
*for I am not worthy that thou shouldest enter under my roofe.

neither thought I
7 *Wherefore, †I thought not† my selfe worthy to come unto thee: but say
in a healed
*†thou the† word, and my servant shalbe †whole.†

subject to
set under authority
8 *For I also am a man †set under† †power,† having under mee souldiers: and I
*say unto one, Go, and he goeth: and to another, Come, and he commeth: and to
*my servant, Doe this, and hee doeth it.

9 *When Jesus heard these things, hee marveiled at him, and turned him about, &
*said unto the people that followed him, I say unto you, I have not found so great faith,
*no, not in Israel.

when were returned to the house they
[Delete] returning to the house [Delete]
10 *And they that were sent, †when they were returned home,†
*found the servant whole that had bene sicke.

the day
11 *And it came to passe †<u>the</u> <u>day</u>† after, that hee went into a city called
Nain
Naim
*†Naim:† and many of his disciples went with him, and much people.

Now
12 * When he came nigh to the gate of the city, beholde, there was a dead man
[Delete]
*caryed out, †<u>which</u> <u>was</u>† the onely sonne of his mother, and shee was
*a widowe: and much people of the city was with her.

13 *And when the Lord saw her, he had compassion on her, and said unto her,
*Weepe not.

he drew nigh and
14 *And †when he was come nigh,† †he† touched the beere (and they that bare him,
he came "beere
*stood stil.) And he said, Yong man, I say unto thee, Arise.

"Or, coffin

he
15 *And he that was dead, sate up, and began to speake: and †he† delivered him
*to his mother.

[Delete] glorifyed
16 *And there came a feare on †them† all, and they †gave the glory unto†
[Delete] [Delete]
*God, saying †that† a great Prophet is risen up among us, and †verily†
that that
*God hath visited his people.

17 *And this rumour of him went foorth throughout all †Jury,† and throughout all
Judea
region [Delete]
*the †regions† †which lie† round about.

18 *And the disciples of John shewed him of all these things.

calling [Delete]
19 *And John, †when hee had called† unto him two of his disciples, †he† sent
should come
*them to Jesus, saying, Art thou he that †commeth,† or looke we for another?

20 *When the men were come unto him, they said, John Baptist hath sent us unto thee,
should come
*saying, Art thou he that †commeth,† or looke wee for another?

21 *And in that same houre he cured many of their infirmities & plagues, and of
*evill spirits, and unto many that were blinde, he gave sight.

tell
22 *Then Jesus answering, said unto them, Go your way, and †bring word againe to†

[Delete]
*John, what things ye have seene and heard, how that the blinde see †againe,†

lame walke are raised
*the †halt goe,† the lepers are clensed, the deafe heare, the dead †rise,†

*to the poore †is the Gospel preached.†
the Gospel is preached

♣at me
blessed in me
23 *And †happy† is hee whosoever shall not be offended †at me.†

♣Or, in me

24 *And when the messengers of John were departed, he beganne to speake unto the

*people concerning John: What went yee out into the wildernesse for to see? A

*reede shaken with the winde?

25 *But what went yee out for to see? A man clothed in soft raiment? Behold,

*they which are gorgeously apparelled, and live delicately, are in Kings courts.

26 *But what went yee †foorth† to see? A Prophet? Yea, I say unto you, and
out for much

*more then a Prophet.

27 *This is hee of whom it is written, Behold, I send my messenger before thy face

*which shall prepare thy way before thee.

there is
28 *For I say unto you, among †womens children† †is there† not a
those that are borne of women

the
*greater Prophet then John Baptist: †neverthelesse,† hee that is least in the
but

*kingdome of God, is greater then he.

29 *And all the people that heard him, and the Publicanes,

justifyed God being baptized with the baptisme of John
*†being baptized with the baptisme of John, justified God.†

rejected
30 *But the Pharisees and Lawyers †despised† the counsell of God against themselves,
"rejected "against themselves

*being not baptized of him.

"Or, frustrated
"Or, within themselves

then
31 *And the Lord saide, Whereunto shall I liken the men of this generation?

whereunto
*and †to what thing† are they like?
to what

calling
32 *They are like unto children sitting in the market place, and †crying† one to

*another, and saying, We have piped unto you, and ye have not daunced: we have mourned

*to you, and ye have not wept.

the
33 *For John Baptist came, neither eating bread, nor drinking wine, and ye say,

*He hath a devill.

34 *The sonne of man is come, eating and drinking, and ye say, Behold a gluttonous

*man, and a wine bibber, a friend of Publicanes and sinners.

35 *†And† wisedome is justified of all her children.
But

36 *And one of the Pharisees desired him that hee would eate with him. And hee

*went into the Pharisees house, and sate downe to meate.

the
37 *And behold, a woman in †that† city, which was a sinner, when she knew that

[Delete]
*Jesus sate at meate in the Pharisees house, †shee† brought an Alabaster

*boxe of oyntment:

38 *And stood at his feet behind him, weeping, and began to wash his feete with

[Delete]
*teares, and did wipe them †cleane† with the haires of her head, and

[Delete]
*†all to† kissed his feete, and annoynted them with the oyntment.

Now
39 * When the Pharisee which had bidden him, sawe it, hee spake within himselfe,

This man if he would have knowen
*saying, †If this man† were a Prophet, †hee would surely know† who, and what

*manner of woman this is that toucheth him: for she is a sinner.

40 *And Jesus answering, said unto him, Simon, I have somewhat to say unto thee. And

*he sayth, Master, say on.

41 *There was a certaine †lender,† which had two debters: the one ought five
creditor

*hundred pence, and the other fiftie.

And
42 * When they had nothing to pay, he forgave them both. Tell me
frankely

*therefore, which of them will love him most?

43 *Simon answered, and sayde, I suppose, that he to whome he forgave most. And he

rightly
*sayd unto him, Thou hast †truely† judged.

44 *And hee turned to the woman, and sayde unto Simon, Seest thou this woman?

*I entred into thine house, thou gavest me no water for my feet: but shee hath washed

cleane
[Delete]
*my feete with teares, and wiped them with the hayres of her head.

45 *Thou gavest me no kisse: but this woman, since the time I came in, hath not

*ceased to kisse my feet.

46 *Mine head with oyle thou diddest not annoynt: but this woman hath anoynted my

*feet with oyntment.

her sinnes which are many are forgiven
47 *Wherefore, I say unto thee, †many sinnes are forgiven her,† for she

but
*loved much: to whome little is forgiven, the same loveth little.

[Delete]
48 *And he sayd unto her, Thy sinnes are forgiven †thee.†

49 *And they that sate at meate with him, began to say within themselves, Who is this
*that forgiveth sinnes also?

50 *And he said to the woman, Thy faith hath saved thee, goe in peace.

The viii. Chapter.

[Delete]
1 *And it came to passe afterward, that hee †himselfe† went throughout every
*city and village preaching, and shewing the glad tydings of the kingdome of God:

[Delete]
*and the twelve †were† with him,
were

[Delete]
2 *And †also† certaine women which had bene healed of evill spirites and

[Delete]
*infirmities, Mary †which is† called Magdalene, out of whome went seven devils,

3 *And Joanna the wife of Chuza, Herodes steward, and Susanna, and many †other,†
others

ministred
*which †ministreh† unto him of their substance.

And
4 * When much people were gathered together, and were come to him out of

every citie parable
*†all cities,† hee spake by a †similitude.†

A
5 *†The† Sower went out to sowe his seede: and as hee sowed, some fell by the

heaven
the aire
*†way† side, and it was troden downe, and the fowles of †the aire† devoured it †up.†
wayes [Delete]

6 *And some fell †on stones,† and as soone as it was sprung up, it withered
upon a rocke

*away, because it lacked †moistnesse.†
moisture

7 *And some fell among thornes, and the thornes sprang up with it, and choked it.

other
8 *And †some† fell on good ground, and sprang up, and bare fruite an hundred

*folde. And †as† hee sayd these things, he cryed, He that hath eares to heare,
when

*let him heare.

might this parable bee
9 *And his disciples asked him, saying, What †manner of similitude is this?†

[Delete] misteryes
10 *And hee sayd †unto them,† Unto you it is given to know the †secrets†

in seeing
*of the kingdom of God: but to †other† †by† parables, that †when they see,†
others

might hearing might
*they †should† not see, and †when they heare,† they †should† not understand.

Now
11 * The parable is this, The seed is the word of God.

by side
12 *Those †that are beside† the way , are they that heare: then commeth the devil,

*and taketh away the worde out of their hearts, least they should beleeve, and be

*saved.

are they
13 *They on the †stones,† †are they,† which when they heare, receive the word with
rocke

roote
*joy: and these have no †roots,† which for a while beleeve, and in time of

fall
*temptation †goe† away.

14 *And that which fell among thornes, are they, which when they have heard, go

pleasures of <u>this</u> life
*forth, and are choked with cares and riches, and †voluptuous living,†

no fruict to perfection
no fruit to perfection
*and bring †forth no fruit.†

[Delete] in an honest
15 *But that †<u>which</u> <u>fell</u>† on the good ground, are they, which †with a pure†

having heard [Delete]
*& good heart †heare† the word, †and† keepe it, and bring foorth

in
*fruite †through† patience.
with

he hath lighted
hath lighted
16 *No man when hee †lighteth† a candle, covereth it with a vessell, or

*putteth it under a bed: but setteth it on a candlesticke, that they which

*enter in, may see the light.

17 *For nothing is secrete, that shall not be made manifest: neither any thing

abroad
*hid, that shall not be knowen, and come †to light.†

18 *Take heede therefore how ye heare: for whosoever hath, to him shall be given:

*& whosoever hath not, from him shall be taken, even that †same† which
[Delete]

it seemeth he hath
he seemeth to have
*†he supposeth that he hath.†
he “seemeth to have

“Or, <u>thinketh</u> <u>that</u> <u>he</u> <u>hath</u>

19 *Then came to him his mother and his brethren, and could not come at him,

the
*for prease.

20 *And it was told him <u>by</u> <u>certaine</u> which said, Thy mother and thy brethren stand

desiring
*without, †willing† to see thee.

And
21 * Hee answered and sayde unto them, My mother and my brethren are these which

*heare the word of God, and doe it.

Now
22 *†And† it came to passe on a certaine day, that he went into a ship, †and†
with

[Delete]
*his disciples †also:† and he sayde unto them, Let us goe over unto the other

*side of the lake. And they lanched forth.

23 *But as they sailed, he fell asleepe, and there came downe a storme of wind on

*the lake, & they were filled with water, and were in jeopardie.

perish
24 *And they came to him, and awoke him, saying, Master, master, we †are lost.†

arose raging of the
*Then he †rose,† and rebuked the winde, and the †tempest of† water: and they
rose

there was a
*ceased, and †it waxed† calme.

25 *And hee sayde unto them, Where is your faith? And they †feared,†
being afraid

What maner of man
*†and† wondred, saying one to another, †Who† is this? For
[Delete]

the
*he commaundeth †both† the winds and water, and they obey him.
even [Delete]

Gadarens
26 *And they †sayled unto† the †region† of the †Gadarenites,† which is over
arrived at countrey

*against Galilee.

27 *And when he went †out† to land, there met him out of the city a certaine man
foorth

*which had devils long time, and ware no clothes, neither abode in any house,

the tombes
*but in †graves.†

he cryed out, and
28 *When he saw Jesus, †and had cryed aloud, he† fell downe before him, and with a
*loud voyce sayd, What have I to doe with thee Jesus, thou sonne of God

highe
*most †highest?† I beseech thee torment me not.

had uncleane
29 *(For he commaunded the †fowle† spirite to come out of the man: For oftentimes

it in
*†hee† had caught him, and hee was †bound with chaines, and kept† †with† fetters:
kept bound with chaines, and

driven devill
*and hee brake the bands, and was †caried† of the †fiend† into the wildernes.)
30 *And Jesus asked him, saying, What is thy name? And hee sayd, Legion: because
*many devils were entred into him.
31 *And they besought him that he would not commaund them to goe out into the deepe.

the mountaine
32 *And there was there an heard of many swine feeding on †an hill:† and they
*besought him that hee would suffer them to enter into them: and he suffered them.
33 *Then went the devils out of the man, & entred into the swine: and the heard

rushed violently from a steepe place
*†ran headlong with violence† into the lake, & were choked.
ranne violently downe a steepe place

they that fed them
34 *When †the heardmen† saw what was done, they fledde: and

departing Countrye
*†when they were departed, they† told it in the city, and in the †villages.†
went, and

Then went
35 *†Therefore† they †came† out to see what was done, and came to Jesus, and found
*the man, out of whome the devils were departed, sitting at the feete of Jesus,
*cloathed, and in his right mind: and they were afraid.

36 *They also which sawe it, tolde them by what meanes hee that was possessed of

*the devils, was healed.

of the Gadarens round about
37 *Then the whole multitude of the countrey †about the Gadarenites,† besought

to
*him †that he would† depart from them, for they were taken with great feare:

went
*and hee †gate him† up into the shippe, and returned backe againe.

Now
38 *†Then† the man, out of whome the devils were departed, besought him that he might

*be with him: but Jesus sent him away, saying,

Returne how greate ♣things
39 *†Goe home againe† to thine owne house, and shewe †what "things soever† God
how great things

unto published the
*hath done †for† thee. And hee went his way, and †preached† throughout †all

for
whole how greate things unto
*the† citie, †what things soever† Jesus had done †unto† him.

♣Or, what great things God hath done unto thee
"Or, what great things God hath done unto thee

returned
40 *And it came to passe, that when Jesus was †come againe,† the people

welcomed
gladly received
*†received† him: for they were all waiting for him.

of
41 *And beholde, there came a man, named Jairus, and he was a ruler †in† the

beseeching
& besought
*Synagogue, and hee fell downe at Jesus feete, †praying† him that he would come

*into his house.

an onely daughter about
42 *For he had †but one daughter onely,† †upon a† twelve yeres of age, and she lay
one onely daughter

*a dying. (But as he went, the people thronged him.

43 *And a woman, having an issue of blood twelve yeres, which had spent all her

living healed
*†substance† upon Physicians, neither could be †holpen† of any,

garment
44 *Came behind him, and touched the †hemme† of his †raiment:† & immediatly her
border

*issue of blood stanched.

[Delete] every one
45 *And Jesus said, Who †is it that† touched me? When †every man† denyed,
all

multitude
*Peter and they that were with him, sayd, Master, the †people†

throng preasse
*†thrust† thee, and †vexe† thee, and sayest thou, Who touched me?

46 *And Jesus sayd, Some body hath touched mee: for I perceive that vertue is gone

*out of me.

And
47 * When the woman sawe that she was not hidde, shee came trembling, and

falling downe to him declared unto
*†fell at his feete,† †and told† him before all the people, for what
falling downe before him she declared unto

*cause she had touched him, and how shee was healed immediatly.

48 *And he sayde unto her, Daughter, be of good comfort, thy faith hath

made thee whole
*†saved thee,† goe in peace.)

49 *While he yet spake, there commeth one from the ruler of the Synagogues

house trouble
*†house,† saying to him, Thy daughter is dead, †disease† not the master.

it saying
50 *But when Jesus heard †that word,† hee answered him, †saying,† Feare not,

*beleeve only, and she shalbe made whole.

[Delete]
51 *And when he came into the house, he suffered no man to go in †with him,†

*save Peter, and James, and John, and the father and the mother of the maiden.

And all bewayled shee
52 *†Every body† wept, and †sorowed for† her: †and† he sayd, Weepe not, †the damosell†
but

*is not dead, but sleepeth.

53 *And they laughed him to scorne, knowing that she was dead.

called
54 *And he †thrust† them all out, and tooke her by the hand, and †cryed,†
put

*saying, Maid, arise.

55 *And her spirit came againe, and shee arose straightway: and hee commaunded

*to give her meate.

astonished charged
56 *And her parents were †astonied:† but hee †warned† them that they should tel no

*man what was done.

The ix. Chapter.

Then he called his twelve Disciples together, and
1 *†Jesus when hee had called the twelve together,† gave them power and authority

*over all devils, and to †heale† diseases.
cure

2 *And he sent them to preach the kingdome of God, and to heale the sicke.

for
3 *And he sayd unto them, Take nothing †to† your journey, neither

rods
staves
*†rod,† nor scrippe, neither bread, neither money, neither have two coates apiece.

4 *And whatsoever house ye enter into, there abide, and thence depart.

5 *And whosoever will not receive you, when yee goe out of that city, shake off

*the verie dust from your feete, for a testimonie against them.

6 *And they departed, and went thorow the townes, preaching the Gospel,
*and healing every where.

Now
7 *†And† Herode the Tetrarch heard of all that was done by him: and he
was perplexed
*†doubted,† because that it was sayde of some, that John was risen from
the deade
*†death:†

others
8 *And of some, that Elias had appeared: and of †some,† that one of the old
againe
*Prophets was risen .

I John have beheaded
I have beheaded
9 *And Herode sayd, †John have I beheaded:† but who is this of whome I heare such
John have I beheaded
*things? And he desired to see him.

were
10 *And the Apostles when they returned, told him all that they had done.
belonging to
privately desert of
*And he tooke them, and went aside into a †solitary† place, †nigh unto†
belonging to
*the city called Bethsaida.

And the people when they knewe, it he
11 *†Which when the people knewe, they† followed him: and †when he had† received
and
*them, †he† spake unto them of the kingdome of God, and healed them that had
*need †to be healed.†
of healing

[Delete]
weare
12 *And when the day began to †weare† away, then came the twelve, and sayd
multitude townes
*unto him, Send the †people† away, that they may goe into the †villages†

cuntrye
*and †fieldes† round about, and lodge, and get †meate:† for we are here
victuals

desert place
*in a †place of wildernesse.†

13 *But he sayd unto them, Give ye them to eate. And they sayd, Wee have no more

*but five loaves and two fishes, except we should goe and buy meat for all this

*people.

For
14 *†And† they were about five thousand men. And hee sayd to his disciples,

make them
*†Cause them to† sit downe by fifties in a company.

caused them all to
made them all
15 *And they did so, and †made them all to† sit downe.

Then he tooke looking
16 *†And when hee had taken† the five loaves and the two fishes, and †looked†

[Delete]
*up to heaven, hee blessed them, and brake †them,† and gave to the

multitude
*disciples to set before the †people.†

filled
17 *And they did †all† eate, and were †satisfied.† And there was
[Delete] all

the overplus of their broken peeces, twelve baskets
*taken up †of that remained to them, twelve baskets full of broken meat.†
of fragments that remained to them, twelve baskets

18 *And it came to passe, as hee was alone praying, his disciples were with him:

*and hee asked them, saying, Whome say the people that I am?

others
19 *They answering, sayd, John the Baptist: some say, Elias: and †some†
but

againe
*say, that one of the old Prophets is risen .

And
20 * Hee sayde unto them, But whome say yee that I am? Peter answering,
[Delete]

The
*sayd, †Thou art that† Christ, of God.

warned them
charged them [Delete]
21 *And he †warned† and commanded †them† to tell no man that
straitly them

*thing:

[Delete]
22 *Saying, †That† the Sonne of man must suffer many things, and

rejected [Delete]
*be †reprooved† of the Elders, and †of the† †high† Priests and
chiefe

be raised
*Scribes, and be slaine, and †rise† the third day.

23 *And he said to them all, If any man will come after me, let him deny himselfe,

*and take up his crosse daily, and follow me.

24 *For whosoever will save his life, shall lose it: but whosoever will lose his

*life, for my sake, the same shall save it.

gaine
25 *For what †avantageth it a man,† if hee †winne† the whole world, and
is a man advantaged

runne into damage of himselfe
[Delete] indamage himselfe
*lose †himselfe,† or †runne in danger of himselfe?†
himselfe be cast away

26 *For whosoever shall be ashamed of mee, and of my words, of him shall the

*sonne of man be ashamed when hee shall come in †the glorie of himselfe,†
his owne glory

*and †of his Father,† and of the holy angels.
in his Fathers

But
27 * I tell you of a trueth, there be some standing here, which shall

*†in no wise† taste of death, till they see the kingdome of God.
not

28 *And it came to passe, about an eight daies after these sayings, hee tooke Peter,
"sayings

*and John, and James, and went up into a mountaine to pray.

"Or, things

[Delete]
29 *And †it came to passe† as he prayed, the fashion of his countenance

altered raiment was glistring white
*was †changed,† and his †garment† †shining very white.†
was white and glistering

30 *And beholde, there talked with him two men, which were Moses and Elias,

Who decease
31 *†That† appeared in glory, and spake of his †departing,† which he should

accomplish
*†end† at Hierusalem.

32 *But Peter, and they that were with him, were heavie with sleepe: and when

*they †awoke,† they sawe his glory, and the two men †standing†
were awake that stood

*with him.

33 *And it came to passe, as they departed from him, Peter sayd unto Jesus,

for us to be here
*Master, it is good †being here for us,† and let us make three tabernacles, one for

*thee, and one for Moses, and one for Elias: not knowing what he sayd.

34 *While hee thus spake, there came a cloud and overshadowed them, and they

as they entred
*feared, †when they were come† into the cloud.

beloved
35 *And there came a voice out of the cloud, saying, This is my †deare† sonne,

*heare him.

36 *And †as soone as† the voice was past, Jesus was found alone: and they kept it
when

*close, and told no man in those daies any of those things which they had seene.

37 *And it came to passe, that on the next day, when they were come downe from the

*hill, much people met him.

38 *And behold, a man of the company cryed out, saying, Master, I beseech thee

looke upon mine only childe
*†behold† my sonne, for he is †all that I have:†

suddenly it cryeth out
Loe suddenly cryeth out
39 *And †see,† a spirit taketh him, and †suddenly he cryeth,† & teareth him
he suddenly crieth out it

hardly departeth from him, when he bruiseth him
bruising him hardly departeth from him
*that he fometh againe, and †with much paine departeth from him, when he renteth him.†

it
40 *And I besought thy disciples to cast †him† out, and they could not.
him

And crooked generation
41 * Jesus answering, sayde, O faithlesse and †perverse† †nation,†
perverse

indure
*how long shall I be with you, and †shall suffer† you? bring thy sonne hither.
suffer

And devill
42 * As hee was yet a comming, the †fiend† †rent him,† and tare him:
threw him downe

*and Jesus rebuked the uncleane spirit, and healed the child, and delivered him

*againe to his father.

mighty power
43 *And they were all amazed at the †majestie† of God: But while they wondred

*every one at all things which Jesus did, he sayd unto his disciples,

♣Put theise sayings diligently
Marke theise sayings diligently
Receive these sayings into
Receive these sayings [Delete]
44 *†Let these sayings sinke downe† into your eares: for †it will come to passe,
Let these sayings sinke downe

*that† the sonne of man shall be delivered into the hands of men.

♣Or, <u>marke them diligently</u>

And they understood this saying
45 *†But they wist† not †what that word ment,† and it was hid from them,
But they understood

should not perceive it
*that they †should not understand it:† and they feared to aske him of that saying.
perceived it not

reasoning
46 *Then there arose a †disputation† among them, which of them should be

*†the† greatest.
[Delete]

And Jesus perceiving [Delete]
47 *†When Jesus perceived† the thought of their heart, †he† tooke a child,

[Delete]
*and set him †hard† by him,

48 *And sayd unto them, Whosoever shall receive this child in my name, receiveth

*me: and whosoever shall receive me, receiveth him that sent me: For hee that is

*least among you all, the same shalbe great.

answered and
49 *And John †answering,† sayd, Master, we saw one casting out devils in thy name,

[Delete]
*and we forbade him, because hee followeth not †<u>thee</u>† with us.

[Delete] him
50 *And Jesus sayde unto him, Forbidde †yee† †<u>him</u>† not: for hee that is not

for
*against us, is †with† us.

51 *And it came to passe, when the time was come that he should be received up,

*hee stedfastly set his face to goe to Hierusalem,

52 *And sent messengers before his face, and they went and entred into a village

*of the Samaritanes to make ready for him.

if
53 *And they did not receive him, because his face was as †though† he would go
though

*to Hierusalem.

And
54 * When his disciples, James and John saw this, they sayd, Lorde, wilt thou

*that wee command fire to come downe from heaven, and consume them, even as Elias

*did?

But hee and sayd
55 * †Jesus† †turning about,† rebuked them, †saying,† Yee †wote† not what manner
turned, and know

*spirit yee are of.

56 *For the sonne of man is not come to destroy mens lives, but to save them.

*And they went to another village.

57 *And it came to passe, that as they went †walking† in the way, a
[Delete]

*certaine man sayd unto him, †I will followe thee, Lorde,† whithersoever
Lord, I will follow thee

*thou goest.

58 *And Jesus sayde unto him, Foxes have holes, and birds of the

heaven
ayre
*†ayre† have nestes: but the sonne of man hath not where to lay his head.

But he
59 *And he sayd unto another, Follow me: †And the same† said, Lord, suffer me first

*to go and bury my father.

60 *Jesus sayd unto him, Let the dead burie their dead: but goe thou and preach

*the kingdome of God.

also
61 *And another sayd, Lorde, I will followe thee: but let me first goe bidde

*them farewell which are at home at my house.

And
62 * Jesus said unto him, No man having put his hand to the plough, and looking

fitt for
*backe, is †apt to† the kingdome of God.

The x. Chapter.

1 *After these things, the Lorde appoynted other seventie also, and sent them two

*and two before his face, into every city & place, whither hee himselfe woulde come.

truely
2 *Therefore sayd hee unto them, The harvest is great, but the labourers

that he would thrust forth
*are few: pray ye therefore the Lord of the harvest, †to† †send "forth†
send foorth

*labourers into his harvest.

"Or, thrust forth

3 *Goe your wayes: Beholde, I send you forth as lambes among wolves.

Cary neither purse nor
4 *†Beare no wallet, neither† scrip, nor shoes, and salute no man by the way.

And
5 * Into whatsoever house ye enter, first say, Peace be to this house.

6 *And if the sonne of peace be there, your peace shall rest upon †him:†
it

*if not, it shall turne to you againe.

remaine
7 *And in the same house †tary still,† eating and drinking such things as they

have
give hire
*†have:† For the labourer is worthy of his †reward.† Goe not from house to house.

8 *And into whatsoever citie ye enter, and they receive you, eate such things as

*are set before you:

9 *And heale the sicke that are therein, and say unto them, The kingdome of God is

unto
*come nigh †upon† you.

10 *But into whatsoever city yee enter, and they receive you not, goe your wayes

*out into the streets of the same, and say,

11 *Even the very dust of your city which cleaveth on us, we doe wipe off against

*you: notwithstanding, be yee sure of this, that the kingdome of God †was†
is

unto
*come nigh †upon† you.

But more tolerable
12 * I say unto you, That it shall be †easier† in that day for Sodome, then

*for that citie.

13 *Woe unto thee Chorazin, woe unto thee Bethsaida: For if the mightie workes had

*bene done in Tyre and Sidon, which have bene done in you, they had a great while

*agoe repented, sitting in sackcloth and ashes.

more tolerable
14 *†Therefore† it shalbe †easier† for Tyre and Sidon at the judgement,
But

*then for you.

15 *And thou Capernaum, which art exalted to heaven, shalt be thrust downe to hell.

rejecteth rejecteth
16 *He that heareth you, heareth me: and he that †despiseth† you, †despiseth†
despiseth despiseth

rejecteth rejecteth
*me: and he that †despiseth† me, †despiseth† him that sent me.
despiseth despiseth

returned [Delete]
17 *And the seventie †turned† againe with joy, saying, Lorde, even the †very†

*devils are †subdued† unto us through thy name.
subject

beheld
18 *And hee sayde unto them, I †sawe† Satan

as, fall downe from heaven as it were lightning
as lightning, fall downe from heaven
*†as it had beene lightning, falling downe from heaven.†
as lightening fall from heaven

19 *Behold, I give unto you power to tread on serpents and scorpions, and over all

manner force
the power wronge
*†manner power† of the enemie: and nothing shall by any meanes †hurt† you.
hurt

Notwithstanding
20 *†But† in this rejoyce not, that the spirits are †subdued†
subject

*unto you: but rather rejoyce, because your names are written in †the heavens.†
heaven

In that very [Delete]
21 *†The same† houre Jesus rejoyced in †the† spirit, and sayd, I
In that

thanck O
*†confesse unto† thee, father, Lorde of heaven and earth, that thou hast hidde these

reveiled
*things from the wise and prudent, and hast †opened† them unto babes: even so

seemed good in thy sight
*father, for so it †pleased thee.†

♣All and
22 *All things are †given† me of my father: no man knoweth who the sonne is,
"All delivered to

*but the father: and who the father is but the sonne, and hee to whome the sonne

*will reveale him.

♣Some [Cancelled]
many ancient Copyes adde theise words: And turning to his Disciples, he said
"Many ancient copies adde these words, And turning to his disciples, he said

privately Blessed
23 *And he turned unto his disciples, and sayd †secretly,† †Happy† are the
him

*eyes which see the things that ye see.

24 *For I tell you, that many Prophets and kings have desired to see those things

*which yee see, and have not seene them: and to heare those things which ye heare,

*and have not heard them.

25 *And beholde, a certaine Lawyer stood up, and tempted him, saying, Master,

*what shall I doe to inherite eternall life? He sayd unto him,

26 *What is written in the law? how readest thou?

27 *And he answering, sayd, Thou shalt love the Lord thy God with all thy heart, and

*with all thy soule, and with all thy strength, and with all thy minde, and thy

*neighbour as thy selfe.

28 *And he sayd unto him, Thou hast answered right: this doe, and thou shalt live.

29 *But he willing to justifie himselfe, said unto Jesus, And who is my neighbour?

went downe

30 *And Jesus answering, sayd, A certaine man †descended† from Hierusalem to

stripped

*Jericho, and fell among theeves, which †robbed† him of his raiment, and wounded

*him, and departed leaving him halfe dead.

[Delete]

31 *And †it befell that† there came downe a certaine priest that †same†

by chance

*way, and when hee sawe him, he passed by on the other side.

was at

32 *And likewise a Levite, when he †came nigh to† the place, came and looked on

*him, and passed by on the other side.

33 *But a certaine Samaritane as hee journeyed, came †by him:† and when he

where hee was

*saw him, hee had compassion on him,

34 *And went to him, & bound up his wounds, powring in oile and wine, and set him on

a common

an tooke care

*his owne beast, & brought him to †a <u>common</u>† Inne, and †made provision† †for† him.

of

35 *And on the morow when he departed, hee tooke out two pence, and gave them to the

care
*host, and sayd unto him, Take †cure† of him, and whatsoever thou spendest more,

repay it
*when I come againe I will †recompense† thee.
repay

36 *Which now of these three, thinkest thou, was neighbour unto him that fell among

*the theeves?

37 *And he said, He that shewed mercie on him. Then sayd Jesus unto him, Goe, and

*doe thou likewise.

38 *Now it came to passe as they went, that he entred into a certaine village:

*and a certaine woman, named Martha, received him into her house.

shee
39 *And †this woman† had a sister called Marie, which also sate at Jesus feete,

*and heard his word:

40 *But Martha was cumbred about much serving, and came to him, and sayde,

*Lord, doest thou not care that my sister hath left me to serve alone? Bid her

*therefore that she helpe me.

41 *And Jesus answered, and sayd unto her, Martha, Martha, thou art carefull, and

*troubled about many things:

But and
42 *†Verely† one is needefull, Marie hath chosen †the† good part,
thing that

*which shall not be taken away from her.

The xi. Chapter.

it came to passe
1 *And †so it was,† that as hee was praying in a certain place, when he ceased,

*one of his disciples said unto him, Lord, teach us to pray, as John also taught

*his disciples.

[Delete]
2 *And he said unto them, When ye pray, say, †O† our Father which art in
*heaven, Halowed be thy name, Thy kingdome come, Thy will bee done,

as in heaven so also in earth
in earth as it is in heaven
*†even in earth as it is in heaven.†
as in heaven, so in earth

Give us day by day Our dayly bread
Give us Our dayly bread day by day
3 *†Our dayly bread give us this day.†
Give us "day by day our daily bread

"Or, <u>for the day</u>

wee also one
4 *And forgive us our sinnes: for †even wee† forgive every †man†
is indebted to
*that †trespasseth† us. And leade us not into temptation, but deliver us from
[Delete]
*†the† evill.

5 *And hee sayd unto them, Which of you shall have a friend, and shall go unto
*him at midnight, and say unto him, Friend, lend mee three loaves:

in his journey is come
6 *For a friend of mine †is come out of the way† to me, and I have nothing
"in his journey is come
*to set before him.

"Or, <u>out of his way</u>

7 *And he from within shal answere, and say, Trouble me not, the doore is now
*shut, and my children are with me in bed: I cannot rise and give thee.

8 *I say unto you, Though hee will not rise, and give him, because hee is his
*friend: yet because of his importunitie, he will rise, and give him as many as
*he needeth.

9 *And I say unto you, Aske, and it shall be given you: seeke, and ye shall finde:
*knocke, and it shall be opened unto you.

10 *For every one that asketh, receiveth: and hee that seeketh, findeth: and to
*him that knocketh, it shall be opened.

a
11 *If †the† sonne shal aske bread of any of you that is a father, will he give
a a
*him a stone? Or if he aske fish, will he for fish give him a serpent?

give
12 *Or if he shall aske an egge, will hee †offer† him a scorpion?
offer

know how
13 *If ye then, being evill, †have knowledge† to give good gifts unto your children:
heavenly father
*how much more shall your †father of heaven† give the holy spirit to them that
aske
*†desire it of† him?

it
14 *And hee was casting out a devill, and †the same† was dumbe. And it came to passe,
*when the devill was gone out, the dumbe spake: and the people wondred.
15 *But some of them said, He casteth out devils, through Beelzebub the chiefe
*of the devils.

sought
16 *And other tempting him, †required† of him a signe from heaven.
17 *But he knowing their thoughts, sayd unto them, Everie kingdome divided against
made desolate
brought to desolation
*it selfe, is †desolate:† and a house divided against a house, falleth.

stande
18 *If Satan also be divided against himselfe, how shall his kingdome †endure?†
*Because ye say that I cast out devils through Beelzebub.

And sonnes
19 * If I by Beelzebub cast out devils, by whom do your †children† cast them out?
*therefore shall they be your judges.

20 *But if I with the finger of God cast out devils, no doubt the kingdome of God is
*come upon you.

a
21 *When †the† strong man armed, keepeth his palace, his goods are in peace.
22 *But when a stronger then hee shall come upon him, and overcome him, hee taketh

armour
*from him all his †harnesse† wherein hee trusted, and divideth his spoiles.
23 *He that is not with me, is against me: and he that gathereth not with me,
*scattereth.
24 *When the uncleane spirit is gone out of a man, he walketh thorow drie places,
*seeking rest: and finding none, hee sayth, I will returne unto my house, whence
*I came out.
25 *And when he commeth, he findeth it swept, and garnished.

more wicked
26 *Then goeth hee, and taketh to him seven other spirits †worse† then himselfe,
*and they enter in, and dwell there, and the last state of that man is worse
*then the first.

multitude
companie
27 *And it came to passe as hee spake these things, a certaine woman of the †companie†

Blessed
*lift up her voyce, and saide unto him, †Happy† is the wombe that bare thee, and
*the pappes which thou hast sucked.

blessed
28 *But he sayd, Yea, rather †happy† are they that heare the word of God, and
*keepe it.

And
29 * When the people were gathered thick together, he began to say, This is an

generation after
*evill †nation:† they seeke a signe, and there shall no signe bee
[Delete]

it
*given †them,† but the signe of Jonas the Prophet.

30 *For as Jonas was a signe unto the †Nivivites,† so shall also the sonne of man bee
Ninevites

generation
*to this †nation.†

up the
31 *The Queene of the South shall rise in judgement with the men of this

generation
*†nation,† & condemne them: for she came from the utmost parts of the earth, to

more
*heare the wisedom of Solomon: and beholde, †a greater† then Solomon is here.
a greater

up the generation
32 *The men of Ninive shal rise in judgement with this †nation,† and shall

it
*condemne †them:† for they repented at the preaching of Jonas, and beholde,

more
*†a greater† then Jonas is here.
a greater

hidden place
vaulte
cave
33 *No man when he hath lighted a candle, putteth it in a †privie place,†
secret place

*neither under a bushell: but on a candlesticke, that they which come in, may

*see the light.

light
34 *The †[a]candle† of the body is the eye: therefore when thine eye is single,

[Delete]
thy whole full of when is wicked
*†all thy† body also is †full of† light, but †if† thine eye †be evill,†
is evill

[Delete]
[Delete] full of
*†all† thy body also is †full of† darkenesse.

[a]That is, the light

35 *Take heede therefore, that the light which is in thee, be not darkenesse.

light
thy whole full of light
36 *If †all thy† bodie therefore bee †cleere,† having no part darke:

[Delete]
all
the whole shall full of [Delete]
*†then shall it all† be †full of† light, †even† as when

a light lightneth thee with shining
*†a candle doth light thee with brightnesse.†
the bright shining of a candle doeth give thee light

37 *And as hee spake, a certaine Pharisee besought him to dine with him: And

hee
*†Jesus† went in, and sate downe to meate.

And
38 * When the Pharisee saw it, hee marveiled that he had not first washed before

*dinner.

39 *And the Lord said unto him, Now do ye Pharisees make cleene the outside of the

*cuppe and the platter: but your inward part is full of ravening and wickednesse.

40 *Yee fooles, did not hee that made that which is without, make that which is

*within also?

such as you have
41 *But rather give almes of †those† things †which are within:† and behold, all
"as you have

*things are cleane unto you.

"Or, as you are able

42 *But woe unto you Pharisees: for ye tithe mint, and rue, and all maner herbs,
of

*and passe over judgement, and the love of God: These ought ye to have done, and

[Delete]
*†yet† not to leave the other undone.

43 *Woe unto you Pharises: for ye love the uppermost seates in the synagogues, and

*greetings in the markets.

44 *Woe unto you Scribes and Pharisees hypocrites: for yee are as graves which appeare

aware
*not, and the men that walke over them, are not †ware† of them.

45 *Then answered one of the lawyers, and said unto him, Master, thus saying,

reprochest us
*thou †puttest us to rebuke† also.

46 *And hee sayd, Wo unto you also ye lawyers: for yee lade men with burdens grievous

*to bee borne, and yee your selves touch not the burdens with one of your fingers.

47 *Woe unto you, for ye builde the sepulchres of the Prophets, and your fathers

*killed them.

48 *Truely ye beare witnesse that ye alow the deedes of your fathers: for they

inddeede
* killed them, and ye build their sepulchres.

49 *Therefore sayde the wisedome of God, I will send them Prophets and
also

*Apostles, and <u>some</u> of them they shall slay and persecute:

50 *That the blood of all the Prophets, which was shed from the foundation of the

*world, may be required of this generation,

Zacharyas
51 *From the blood of Abel unto the blood of †Zachary,† which perished betweene

*the altar and the temple: Verily I say unto you, it shall be required of

generation
*this †nation.†

52 *Woe unto you lawyers, for ye have taken away the key of knowledge: yee entred

would goe
*not in your selves, and them that †came† in, ye †forbade.†
were entring "hindered

"Or, <u>forbade</u>

And as he sayd these things Scribes
53 *†When hee thus spake† unto them, the †lawyers† and the Pharisees beganne

*to urge him vehemently, and to provoke him to speake many things:
of

54 *Laying waite for him, and seeking to catch something out of his mouth, †wherby†
that

*they might accuse him.

The xii. Chapter.

1 *In the meane time, when there were gathered together an innumerable multitude of

upon one another
insomuch one upon another
*people, †insomuch† that they trode †one another,† hee began to say unto his

[Delete] yee
*disciples first †of all,† Beware of the leaven of the Pharises, which is
of all

*hypocrisie.

But revealed
2 *†For† there is nothing covered, that shall not be †uncovered,† neither hid,
For

*that shall not bee knowen.

3 *Therefore, whatsoever ye have spoken in darkenesse, shall be heard in the light:

in closets
*and that which ye have spoken in the eare, †even in secret places,† shall

proclamed upon
*be †preached on the top of† the †houses.†
house tops

4 *And I say unto you my friends, Be not afraide of them that kill the body, and

*after that, have no more that they can do.

5 *But I will forewarne you whom you shal feare: Feare him, which after he hath

*killed, hath power to cast into hel, yea, I say unto you, Feare him.

6 *Are not five sparrowes solde for two farthings, and not one of them is

*forgotten before God?

all
7 *But, even the very haires of your head are numbred: Feare not therefore, yee are

better of
of more
*†more of† value then many sparrowes.

8 *Also I say unto you, Whosoever shal confesse me before men, him shall the

also confesse
*sonne of man †knowledge also† before the Angels of God.

denieth
9 *But hee that †shall denie† me before men, shall be denied before the angels

*of God.

10 *And whosoever shall speake a word against the sonne of man, it shall be forgiven

against [Delete]
*him: but unto him that blasphemeth the holy Ghost, †it† it

*shall not be forgiven.

magistrates
11 *And when they bring you unto the Synagogues, and unto †the rulers† and

powers [Delete]
*†officers,† †take† take ye no thought how or what thing yee shall answere,

ye shall speake
ye shall say
*or what †shall ye speake:†

12 *For the holy Ghost shall teach you in the same houre, what ye ought to say.

And
13 * One of the company said unto him, Master, speake to my brother, that he

*divide the inheritance with me.

14 *And he said unto him, Man, who made me a judge, or a devider over you?

15 *And he said unto them, Take heed, and beware of covetousnesse: for

a mans life consisteth not
*†no mans life standeth† in the abundance of the things which hee possesseth.

spake parable
16 *And he †put foorth† a †similitude† unto them, saying, The ground of a

plentifully
*certaine rich man brought forth †plentifull fruits.†

17 *And he thought within himselfe, saying, What shal I do, because I have no roume

*where to bestow my fruits?

18 *And he said, This will I doe, I will pull downe my barnes, and build greater,

there bestow
*and †therin† will I †gather† all my fruits and my goods.

[Delete]
19 *And I will say to my soule, Soule, thou hast much goods laid up †in store†

*for many yeeres, take thine ease, eate, drinke, and be merie.

20 *But God said unto him, Thou foole, this night †do they require thy soule again from†
"thy soule shalbe required of

*thee: then whose shal those things be which thou hast provided?

"Gr. doe they require thy soule

layeth up threasure for
21 *So is he that †gathereth riches to† himself, and is not rich towards God.

sayd
22 *And he †spake† unto his disciples, Therefore I say unto you, Take no thought for

*your life what ye shall eate, neither for the body what yee shall put on.

23 *The life is more then meate, and the body is more then raiment.

24 *Consider the ravens, for they neither sowe nor reape, which neither have

[Delete]
*storehouse nor barne, & †notwithstanding† God feedeth them: How much more

*are ye better then the foules?

And
25 * Which of you with taking thought can adde to his stature one cubite?

26 *If yee then bee not able to doe that thing which is least, why take ye thought

rest
*for the †remnant?†

toyle
27 *Consider the Lilies how they growe, they †labour† not, they spinne not: and

glory arayed
*yet I say unto you, that Solomon in all his †royalty,† was not †clothed†

*like one of these.

then
28 *If God so clothe the grasse, which is to day in the field, and to morow

oven
*is cast into the †fornace:† how much more will he clothe you, O ye of little faith?

seeke
29 *And †aske† not ye what ye shall eate, or what ye shal drinke, neither be
"neither bee

*ye of doubtfull mind.
ye of doubtfull mind

"Or, live not in carefull suspence

these nations after
30 *For all †such† things doe the †people† of the world seeke †for:†

But
and
*†and† your father knoweth that ye have neede of these things.

[Delete]
But [Delete]
31 *†But† rather seeke ye †after† the kingdome of God, and all these

*things shalbe added unto you.

[Delete]
32 *Feare not †O† little flocke, for it is your fathers good pleasure to

*give you †a† kingdome.
the

provide your selves
33 *Sell that ye have, and give almes: †and prepare you† bagges which waxe not

[Delete]
*olde, †even† a treasure †that faileth not in the heavens,† where no theefe
in the heavens that faileth not

*approcheth, neither moth corrupteth.

34 *For where your treasure is, there wil your heart be also.

[Delete]
35 *Let your loynes be girded about, and †your† lights burning,
your

[Delete]
36 *And ye your selves †bee† like unto men that waite for their Lord, when he

commeth & knocketh
*will returne from the wedding, that when he †shal come and knock,† they may open

*unto him immediatly.

Blessed
37 *†Happy† are those servants, whom the Lord when he commeth, shall finde

watching
*†waking:† Verily I say unto you, That hee shall girde himselfe, and make them to

serve
*sit downe to meate, and wil come forth, and †minister unto† them.

and if he shall
38 *And if he shall come in the second watch, †yea, if he shall† come
or

blessed
*in the third watch, and finde them so, †happie† are those servants.

And this know
39 *†This understand ye,† that if the good man of the house had knowen what houre the

[Delete]
*theefe would come, he would †surely† have watched, and not have suffred his

digged
broken
*house to be †broken† thorow.

40 *Be ye therefore ready also: for the sonne of man commeth at an houre when ye

*thinke not.

Lord speakest parable
41 *Then Peter said unto him, †Master,† †tellest† thou this †similitude† unto us,

*or to all?
even

42 *And the Lord sayd, Who †is a† faithfull and wise steward, whom his Lorde
then is that

sett
make ruler
*shall †make ruler† over his houshold, to give them their portion of meate in

*due season?

Blessed
43 *†Happie† is that servaunt, whom his Lorde when he commeth, shall finde so doing.

sett him
make him ruler
44 *Of a trueth, I say unto you, that hee will †make him ruler† over

that he hath
*all †his substance.†

45 *But and if that servaunt say in his heart, My Lorde delayeth his comming: and

beate the men
*shall beginne to †smite the† servants and maidens, and to eate and drinke,

*and to be drunken,

46 *The lord of that servant wil come in a day when hee looketh not for him, and at

cutt him in pieces
*an houre when hee is not ware, and will †hewe him in pieces,† and will
"cut him in sunder

appoynt
*†set† him his portion with the unbeleevers.

"Or, cut him off

that which Lords himself
47 *And †the† servant †that† knewe his †masters† will, & prepared not †himselfe,†

stripes
*neither did according to his wil, shalbe beaten with many †stripes.†

48 *But he that knew not, and did commit things worthie of stripes, shall be beaten

stripes
*with fewe †stripes.† For unto whomsoever much is given, of him shalbe much required:

*and to whom men have committed much, of him they will aske the more.

cast
send will I more
49 *I am come to †send† fire on the earth, and what †is my desire,†
will I

*if it be alreadie kindled?

But have a baptisme to be baptized with
50 *†Notwithstanding,† I †must bee baptized with a baptisme,† and how am I

streightned accomplished
*†payned† till it be †ended?†
"straitned

"Or, pained

give
51 *Suppose ye that I am come to †send† peace on earth? I tell you, Nay, but rather

*division.

52 *For from henceforth there shall bee five in one house devided, three against

*two, and two against three.

53 *The father shall bee divided against the sonne, and the sonne against the father:

*the mother against the daughter, and the daughter against the mother: the mother

*in law against her daughter in law, & the daughter in law against her mother in law.

And
54 * He said also to the people, When yee see a cloude rise out of the West,

*straightway yee say, There commeth a showre: and so it is.

There will be heate
55 *And when ye see the South winde blow, ye say, †It will be hot,† and it

[Delete]
*commeth †so† to passe.

56 *Ye hypocrites, yee can discerne the face of the skie, and of the earth: but howe

*is it that ye doe not discerne this time?

57 *Yea, and why †judge yee not of your selves† what is right?
even of your selves judge ye not

magistrate
58 *When thou goest with thine adversarie to the †ruler:† as thou art in the way,

haile the
haile
*give diligence that thou mayest be delivered from him, least he †draw† thee

[Delete]
*†violently† to the judge, and the judge deliver thee to the †sergeant,†
officer

*and the †sergeant† cast thee into prison.
officer

payd
59 *I tell thee, Thou shalt not depart thence, till thou hast †made good†

even the uttermost
even the very last
the very last
*†the uttermost† mite.

The xiii. Chapter.

that
1 *There were present at †the same† season, †certaine men that shewed† him of
some that told

whose sacrifices
*the Galileans, †who† blood Pilat had mingled with their †owne sacrifice.†

2 *And Jesus answering, saide unto them, Suppose ye that these Galileans were

sinners above all the
*†greater sinners then all the other† Galileans, because they suffered such

things
*†punishment?†

3 *I tell you, Nay: but except ye repent, ye shall all likewise perish.

Siloam [Cancelled]
whom [Delete]
4 *Or those eighteene, upon †which† the tower in †[b]Siloe† fell,
Siloe

♣sinners [Delete]
*and slew them, thinke ye that they were sinners above all †men†
"sinners men

*that dwelt in Hierusalem?

[b]Which tower stood by the fish poole or river Siloam in Hierusalem
♣Or, debters
"Or, debters

5 *I tell you, Nay: but except ye repent, ye shall all likewise perish.

spake parable
6 *He †told† also this †similitude,† A certaine man had a figge tree planted in

*his vineyard, and he came and sought fruit thereon, and found none.

7 *Then said he unto the dresser of his vineyard, Behold, †this† three yeeres
these

*I come seeking fruit †in† this figge tree, & find none: cut it downe, why
on

*cumbreth it the ground?

8 *And he answering, said unto him, Lord, let it alone this yeere also, til I shal

[Delete]
*digge †round† about it, and dung it:

well [Delete]
9 *And if it beare fruit, †thou maiest let it alone:† and if †it beare† not,

*then after that thou shalt cut it downe.

Sabothes
the Sabboth dayes
10 *And he was teaching in one of †their† Synagogues on the †Sabboth dayes.†
Sabbath

11 *And behold, there was a woman which had a spirit of infirmitie eighteene yeeres,

her selfe
*and was bowed together, and could in no wise lift up †her selfe.†

And
12 * When Jesus saw her, he called her to him, and said unto her, Woman, thou

infirmity
*art loosed from thy †disease.†

13 *And he laid his hands on her, and immediatly she was made straight, and glorified

*God.

14 *And the ruler of the Synagogue answered with indignation, because that Jesus

*had healed on the Sabboth day, and said unto the people, There are sixe daies in

and
*which men ought to worke: in them therefore come †that ye may† be healed,

*and not on the Sabboth day.

[Delete] therefore
15 *†But† the Lord answered him, and sayde, Thou hypocrite, doth
then

[Delete]
*not ech one of you on the Sabboth †day† loose his oxe or his asse from the

away
*stall, and leade him to †the water?†
watering

16 *And ought not this daughter of Abraham, whom Satan hath bound
woman beeing a

*loe eighteene yeeres, be loosed from this bond on the Sabboth day?
these

17 *And when he said these things, all his adversaries were ashamed: and all the
had

glorious things
*people rejoyced for all the †excellent deedes† that were done by him.

hee Unto and whereunto
18 *Then said †Jesus,† What is the kindgome of God like? †or whereto†

resemble
*shall I †compare† it?

cast into
19 *It is like a graine of mustard seed which a man tooke, and †sowed in†

*his garden, and it grew, and waxed a great tree: and the foules of

heaven
the aire lodged
*†the aire† †made nests† in the branches of it.

20 *And againe he said, Whereunto shall I liken the kingdome of God?

21 *It is like leaven, which a woman tooke and hid in three †peckes†
measures

the whole
*of meale, till †all† was leavened.

the cittyes
22 *And he went thorowe †all† †townes† and villages, teaching, and journeying
[Delete]

*towardes Hierusalem.

23 *Then said one unto him, Lord, are there few that be saved? and he said unto

*them,

24 *Strive to enter in at the straite gate: for many I say unto you, will seeke to

*enter in, and shall not be able.

25 *When †the good man† of the house is risen up, and hath shut to the doore,
once the master

*and ye beginne to stand without, and to knock at the doore, saying, Lord, Lord,

*open unto us, and he shall answere, and say unto you, I knowe you not whence you

*are:

26 *Then shall ye begin to say, We have eaten and †drunken† in thy presence, & thou
drunke

*hast taught in our streetes.

27 *†And† he shall say, I tell you, I know you not whence †ye† are, depart from me
But you

workers of
*all yee †that worke† iniquitie.

28 *There shall be weeping and gnashing of teeth, when ye shall see Abraham, and

*Isahac, and Jacob, and al the Prophets in the kingdom of God, and †ye your selves†
you <u>your</u> <u>selves</u>

*thrust out.

29 *And they shall come from the East, and from the West, and from the North, and

*from the South, and shall sit downe in the kingdome of God.

30 *And behold, there are last, which shall be first, and there are first, which

*shall be last.

there came
31 *The same day †came there† certaine of the Pharisees, saying unto him, Get thee
*out, and depart hence, for Herode will kill thee.
32 *And he sayd unto them, Goe ye and tell that foxe, Behold, I cast out devils, and
♣shalbe perfected
shalbe perfected
*I doe cures to day and to morrow, and the third day I shalbe perfected.
♣Or, make an end [cancelled]
33 *Neverthelesse, I must walke to day and to morow, and the day following, for it
*cannot be that a Prophet perish out of Hierusalem.
34 *O Hiersualem, Hierusalem, which killest the Prophets, and stonest them that are sent
*unto thee, how often would I have gathered thy children together, as a henne doeth
broode
brood
*gather her †yong† under her wings, and ye would not?
And
35 *Behold, your house is left unto you desolate. Verily I say unto you, ye shal
when
*not see me, untill the time come †that† ye shall say, Blessed is he that commeth
*in the name of the Lord.

The xiiii. Chapter.

watched
1 *And it came to passe, as he went into the house of one of the chiefe Pharisees
*to eate bread on the Sabboth day, they †were watching† him.
that
2 *And behold, there was a certaine man before him which had the dropsie.
3 *And Jesus answering, spake unto the lawyers and Pharisees, saying, Is it
*lawfull to heale on the Sabboth day?
4 *And they helde their peace. And he tooke him, and healed him, and let him goe,

†6†*And answered them, saying, Which of you shall have an asse or an oxe fallen
5

*into a pit, and will not straightway pull him out on the Sabboth day?

6 *And they could not answere him againe to these things.

And [Delete] parable those which were bidden
7 * He put forth †also† a †similitude† to †the ghests,†

*when he marked how they chose out the chiefe roomes, saying unto them,

8 *When thou art bidden of any man to a wedding, sit not downe in the highest

*roome: least a more honourable man then thou be bidden of him,

9 *And he that bade thee and him come, and say to thee, Give this man †roome:†
place

*and thou †then† begin with shame to take the lowest roome.
[Delete]

downe
10 *But when thou art bidden, goe and sit in the lowest roome, that when he

*that bade thee commeth, he may say unto thee, Friend, †sit† up higher: then shalt
goe

*thou have worship in the presence of them that sit at meate with thee.

abased abaseth
11 *For whosoever exalteth himselfe, shalbe †brought lowe:† and he that †humbleth†
humbleth

*himselfe, shalbe exalted.

[Delete]
12 *Then sayd hee also to him that bade him †to meate,† When thou makest a

*dinner or a supper, call not thy friends, nor thy brethren, neither thy kinsmen,

*nor thy rich neighbours: least they also bid thee againe, and a recompence bee

*made thee.

13 *But when thou makest a feast, call the poore, the maimed, the lame, and

*the blind,

blessed
14 *And thou shalt be †happie,† for they cannot recompence thee: For thou shalt be

[Delete]
*recompenced at the resurrection of the just †men.†

And with him
15 * When one of them that sate at meate †also† heard these things, he said

Blessed
*unto him, †Happie† is he that shall eate bread in the kingdome of God.

made
16 *Then said he unto him, A certaine man †ordeined† a great supper, and bade many:

17 *And sent his servant at supper time, to say to them that were bidden, Come, for

*all things are now readie.

with one consent
18 *And they al †at once† began to make excuse: The first said unto him, I

farme
*have bought a †piece of ground,† and I must needes goe and see it: I pray thee have
piece of ground

*me excused.

19 *And another said, I have bought five yoke of oxen, and I goe to proove them:

*I pray thee have me excused.

20 *And another said, I have married a wife: and therefore I cannot come.

So that came Lord
21 *†And the† servant †returned,† and shewed his †master† these things. Then

*the †goodman† of the house being angry, said to his servant, Goe out quickly
master

[Delete]
*into the †broad† streetes and lanes of the citie, and bring in hither the

*poore, and the maimed, and the halt, and the blind.

22 *And the servant said, Lord, it is done as thou hast commanded, and yet there

*is roome.

23 *And the Lord said unto the servant, Goe out into the high wayes and hedges,

*and compell them to come in, that my house may be filled.

24 *For I say unto you, that none of those men which were bidden, shall taste

*of my supper.

And great multitudes turned
25 * There went †a great companie† with him: and he †returned,† and said unto them,

26 *If any man come to me, and hate not his father, and mother, and wife, and children,

*and brethren, and sisters, yea, and his owne life also, he cannot be my disciple.

27 *And whosoever doth not beare his crosse, and come after me, cannot be

*my disciple.

intending first
28 *For which of you †disposed† to builde a tower, sitteth not downe †before,†

*and counteth the cost, whether hee have sufficient to †performe† it?
finish

happily
29 *Least †at any time† after he hath laide the foundation, and is not able to

finish
*†performe† it, all that behold it, begin to mocke him,

finish
30 *Saying, This man began to build, and was not able to †make an end.†

warre
31 *Or what king going to make †battel† against another king, sitteth not downe

consulteth
*first, and †casteth in his minde† whether he be able with ten thousand, to meete

*him that commeth against him with twenty thousand?

32 *Or els, while the other is yet a great way off, he sendeth an ambassage, and

*desireth conditions of peace.

33 *So likewise, whosoever he be of you, that forsaketh not all that he hath, he

*cannot be my disciple.

become savourlesse
become unsavoury
become savourlesse wherewith
34 *Salt is good: but if the salt †have lost the saltnesse,† †wherein†
have lost his savour

*shall it be seasoned?

is fitt but
35 *It †it† neither †good† for the land, nor yet for the dunghill: †but† men
but

[Delete]
*cast it out †at the doores.† He that hath eares to heare, let him heare.

The xv. Chapter.

drew neare
1 *Then †resorted† unto him al the Publicanes and sinners, for to heare him.

This man
2 *And the Pharisees & Scribes murmured, saying, †He† receiveth sinners, and

*eateth with them.

And he spake
3 *†But he put foorth† this parable unto them, saying,

4 *What man of you, having an hundred sheep, if he lose one of them, doth not

the
*leave ninetie and nine in the wildernesse, and go after that which is lost,

*untill he find it?

5 *And when he hath found it, he laieth it on his shoulders, rejoycing.

6 *And when he commeth home, hee calleth together his friendes and neighbours,

*saying unto them, Rejoyce with me: for I have found my sheepe which was lost.

7 *I say unto you, that likewise joy shalbe in heaven over one sinner that repenteth,

*more then over ninetie and nine just persons, which neede no repentance.

♣ten pieces of silver
8 *Either what woman having [a]ten pieces of silver, if she lose one piece, doth
tenne "pieces of silver

*not light a candle, and sweep the house, and seeke diligently til she find †it?†
it

♣One piece of this money is the eighth part of an ounce of silver
[a]One piece of this money, is somewhat more then five pence: of olde sterling money
"Drachma here translated a piece of silver is the eight part of an ounce, which commeth to seven pence halfe penie, and is equall to the Romane penie, Matth. 18.28

9 *And when she hath found it, shee calleth her friends and her neighbours together,
*saying, Rejoyce with me, for I have found the piece which I had lost.
10 *Likewise I say unto you, there is joy in the presence of the angels of God
*over one sinner that repenteth.
11 *And he sayde, A certaine man had two sonnes:
mee
12 *And the younger of them saide to his father, Father, give †mee† the portion
goods falleth to me
*of †the substance† that †to me belongeth.† And he devided unto them his living.
[Delete] [Delete]
13 *And not many dayes after, †when† the younger sonne †had† gathered
[Delete] and
*all †that he had† together, †he† tooke his journey into a farre countrey,
*and there wasted his substance with riotous living.
mighty famin
14 *And when he had spent all, there arose a †great dearth† in that land, and hee
*beganne to †lacke.†
be in want
he went and
15 *And †going, he† joyned himselfe to a citizen of that countrey: and he
*sent him into his fields to feede swine.
16 *And he would faine have filled his belly with the †cods† that the swine did
huskes
*eate: and no man gave unto him.
17 *And when he came to himselfe, he saide, Howe many hired servants of my fathers
to
*have bread ynough and spare, and I perish with hunger?
18 *I will arise and goe to my father, and will say unto him, Father, I have sinned
*against heaven, and before thee,
19 *And am no more worthy to be called thy sonne: make me as one of thy hired

*servants.

20 *And he arose and came to his father. But when he was yet a great way off, his

*father saw him, and had compassion, and ran, and fell on his necke, and

[Delete]
*†all to† kissed him.

21 *And the sonne said unto him, Father, I have sinned against heaven, and in thy

*sight, and am no more worthy to be called thy sonne.

22 *But the father sayde to his servaunts, Bring foorth the best †garment,† and put
robe

*it on him, and put a ring on his hand, and shoes on his feete,

hither the fatted
23 *And bring †hither† †that fat† calfe, and kill it, and let us eate, and be merie.

24 *For this my sonne was dead, and is alive againe: he was lost, and is found. And

*they began to be merie.

Now his elder sonne as
25 * †The elder brother† was in the field: & †when† he came and drew nigh to the

musick
*house, hee heard †minstrelsie† and dauncing,

hee the
26 *And called one of †his† servants, and asked what these things meant.

27 *And he said unto him, Thy brother is come, and thy father hath killed

fatted
*the †fat† calfe, because he hath received him safe and sound.

he
28 *And †he† was angrie, and would not goe in: therefore came his father out, and

*intreated him.

And he
And
29 * He answering, said to his father, Lo, these many yeeres do I serve thee,

transgressed
*neither †brake† I at any time thy commandement, and yet thou never gavest

*me a kidde, that I might make merie with my friends:

30 *But as soone as this thy sonne was come, which hath devoured thy living with

killed for him the fatted calfe
*harlots, thou hast †for his pleasure killed† †that fat† †Calfe.†

31 *And he saide unto him, Sonne, thou art ever with me, and all that I have is thine.

32 *It was meete that wee should make merrie, and be glad: for this thy brother was

*dead, and is alive againe: and was lost, and is found.

The xvi. Chapter.

also
1 *And he saide unto his Disciples, There was a certaine rich man which had

*a Stewarde, and the same was accused unto him that he had wasted his goods.

he and
2 *And †when he had† called him, †he† said unto him, How is it that I heare this

an accompt
*of thee? Give †accompts† of thy stewardship: for thou mayest be no longer steward.

Then Lord
3 * The Steward said within himselfe, What shall I doe, for my †master† taketh

[Delete]
*away from me the stewardship? I cannot digge, †and† to begge I am ashamed.

I will
4 *I †wote† what †to† doe, that when I am put out of the stewardship,
am resolved to

*they may receive me into their houses.

hee every one of his Lords unto him and
5 *So †when hee had† called †all his masters† detters †together,† †he†

thou Lord
*said unto the first, Howe much owest unto my †master?†

6 *And he said, An hundred measures of oile. And he said unto him, Take thy bill,

*& sit downe quickly, and write fiftie.

And
7 *Then said he to another, How much owest thou? And he saide, An hundred

And
*measures of wheate. He said unto him, Take thy bill, and write fourescore.

8 *And the Lord commended the unjust steward, because he had done wisely: for

generation
*the children of this world are in their †nation† wiser then the children of

*light.

to your selves unjust ♣Mammon
9 *And I say unto you, Make †you† friends of the †[c]unrighteous Mammon,†
"Mammon of unrighteousnes

fayle [Delete]
*that when yee †shall have neede,† they may receive you into †the†

*everlasting habitations.

♣Or, riches
[c]Not that riches are evill of themselves, but that for the most part they be occasions of evill
"Or, riches

10 *He that is faithfull in that which is least, is faithfull also in much: and he

unjust unjust
*that is †unrighteous† in the least, is †unrighteous† also in much.

If therefore unjust
11 *†So then, if† ye have not bene faithfull in the †unrighteous† Mammon, who
unrighteous "Mammon

will comitt to your trust
*†shall trust you in† the true †treasure?†
riches

"Or, riches

12 *And if ye have not bene faithfull in that which is another mans, who shall

*give you that which is your owne?

will
13 *No servant can serve two masters, for either he †shall† hate the one, and love

will sticke
*the other: or els he †shal leane† to the one, and despise the other: ye cannot
will hold

*serve God and Mammon.

And the Pharisees also whoe were covetous heard all these things
14 * †All these things heard the Pharisees also which were covetous:†

mocked him
*and they †mocked him greatly.†
derided him

15 *And he said unto them, Ye are they which justifie your selves before men, but

high with
*God knoweth your hearts: for that which is †highly esteemed among† men, is
highly esteemed amongst

*abomination in the sight of God.

were [Delete]
16 *The law and the Prophets †reigned† until John, †and† since that time

[Delete]
*†the glad tidings of† the kingdome of God is preached, and every

preasseth into it
*man †striveth to goe in.†

And it is easier [Delete]
17 *†Easier it is† for heaven and earth to passe †away,† then one title

fall
faile
*of the law to †faile.†

putteth away
18 *Whosoever †forsaketh† his wife, and marrieth another, committeth adultery:

whosoever putt away
*and †he that† marrieth her that is †divorced† from her husband, committeth

[Delete]
*adulterie †also.†

linnen
19 *There was a certaine rich man, which was clothed in purple and fine †white,†

made merry
fared sumptuously
*and †fared very deliciously† every day.

20 *And there was a certaine beggar named Lazarus, which was layd at his gate

*full of sores:

fedde
21 *And desiring to bee †refreshed† with the crummes which fell from the rich mans

table [Delete] moreover
*†board,† †and no man gave unto him:† †but† the dogs came and licked

*his sores.

hee
hee
[Delete]
22 *And it came to passe that the begger died, and was caried by the

*Angels into Abrahams bosome: the rich man also died, and was buried.

in hell lifting up his eyes being in torments, he
in hell he lift up his eyes being in torments, and
23 *And †being in hell in torments, when he had lifted up his eyes, he† seeth

*Abraham afarre off, and Lazarus in his bosome:

24 *And he cryed, and saide, Father Abraham, have mercie on mee, and send Lazarus,

*that he may dip the tip of his finger in water, and coole my tongue, for I am

*tormented in this flame.

25 *But Abraham saide, Sonne, remember that thou in thy life time receivedst thy

good things evill things
*†pleasure,† and likewise Lazarus †paines,† but now hee is comforted, and thou

*art tormented.

And
26 * Besides all this, betweene us and you there is a great gulfe

settled
fixed passe
*†stedfastly set,† so that they which would †goe† from hence to you, can not,

can they passe through
can they passe
*neither †have they passage† to us that would come from thence.

27 *Then he saide, I pray thee therefore father, that thou wouldest send him to my

*fathers house:

testifye
28 *For I have five brethren, that he may †witnesse† unto them, least they also come

*into this place of torment.

29 *Abraham saith unto him, They have Moses and the Prophets, let them heare them.

went
30 *And he said, Nay, father, Abraham: but if one †come† unto them from the dead,

*they will repent.

And
31 * He said unto him, If they heare not Moses and the Prophets, neither wil

be perswaded the deade
*they †beleeve† though one rose from †death.†

The xvii. Chapter.

Then said he is impossible but that
1 *†He said† unto the disciples, It †cannot be but† offences will come,

but
*†neverthelesse,† woe unto him through whom they come.

2 *It were better for him that a milstone were hanged about his necke, and he cast

*into the sea, then that he should offend one of these litle ones.

And
3 *Take heede to your selves: If thy brother trespasse against thee, rebuke
[Delete]

*him, and if he repent, forgive him.

if trespasse
4 *And †though† he †sinne† against thee seven times in a day, and seven times

*in a day turne againe to thee, saying, I repent, thou shalt forgive him.

5 *And the Apostles said unto the Lord, Increase our faith.

as much faith as is
6 *And the Lord said, If ye had †faith as much as† a graine of mustard seede,
faith as

*ye †should† say unto this Sycamine tree, Be thou plucked up by the roote, & be thou
might

*planted in the sea, and it should obey you.

7 *But which of you having a servant plowing, or feeding cattell, will say unto

is Come
*him by and by when he †were† come from the field, †Goe and† sit downe
Goe and

to meate
*†at the table?†

8 *And will not rather say unto him, †Dresse† wherewith I may sup, and
Make ready

[Delete]
*gird †up† thy selfe, and serve me, till I have eaten and drunken: and afterward

*thou shalt eate and drinke?

9 *Doeth he thanke that servant because he did the things that were commanded

[Delete]
*†unto† him? I trow not.

10 *So likewise ye, when yee shall have done all those things which are commanded

*you, say, We are unprofitable servants: wee have done that which was our duetie

*to doe.

it came to passe
11 *And †so it was,† as he went to Hierusalem, that he passed thorow the

*middes of Samaria and Galilee.

12 *And as he entred into a certaine village, there met him ten men that were

*lepers, which stood afarre off,

lifted up
13 *And they †put foorth† their voices, and said, Jesu master, have mercie on us.

And them
14 * When he sawe †them,† he saide unto them, Goe shew your selves unto the

*Priests. And it came to passe, that as they went, they were cleansed.

[Delete]
15 *And one of them when he saw that he was healed, turned backe †againe†

* with a loude voice, †glorifying† God,
and glorified

hee
16 *And fell downe on his face at his feete, giving him thankes: and †the same†

*was a Samaritane.

Were
17 *And Jesus answering, said, †Are† there not ten cleansed, but where are

the
*†those† nine?

[Delete]
18 *There are not found that returned †againe† to give glory to God, save

[Delete]
*†onely† this stranger.

19 *And he said unto him, Arise, goe thy way, thy faith hath made thee whole.

And
20 * When he was demanded of the Pharisees when the kingdom of God

should come he answered them and
*†commeth, he answering them,† said, The kingdome of God commeth not

♣observation
*with observation.
"observation

♣Or, with outward shew
"Or, with outward shew

or
21 *Neither shall they say, Lo here, lo there: for behold, the kingdome of God

*is [d]within you.
"within you

[d]It cannot be discerned by any outward shew
"Or, among you

ye
22 *And he said unto the Disciples, The daies will come when †he† shall desire to

one one of the dayes
one of the dayes
*see †one day† of the sonne of man, and ye shall not see it.

or
23 *And they shall say to you, See here, see there: goe not after them, nor follow

*them.

[Delete]
24 *For as the lightening that lighteneth out of the †one† part †that is†
one

other [Delete]
*under heaven, shineth unto the †other† part †which is† under heaven: so

*shall also the sonne of man be in his day.

rejected generation
25 *But first must he suffer many things, and be †disallowed† of this †nation.†

26 *And as it was in the daies of Noe: so shal it be also in the dayes of the

*sonne of man.

they dranke they were given in mariage untill the
27 *They did eat †& drinke,† they maried wives, †and were maried, even unto the same†

*day that Noe †went† into the arke: and the flood came, and destroyed them all.
entred

28 *Likewise also as it was in the dayes of Lot, they did eat, they dranke, they

*bought, they sold, they planted, they builded:

[Delete]
29 *But †even† the same day that Lot went out of Sodome, it rained fire and

*brimstone from heaven, and destroyed them all:

30 *Even thus shall it be in the day when the sonne of man is revealed.

In upon house
31 *†At† that day he which shal be †on† the †house top,† & his stuffe in the house,
house top

away he
*let him not come downe to take it †out:† and †let not him† that is in the fielde,

let him likewise not returne backe.
*†turne backe againe likewise to the things that he left behinde.†

32 *Remember Lots wife.

shall seeke
33 *Whosoever †wil go about† to save his life, shall lose it, and whosoever shall

*lose his life, shal †quicken† it.
preserve

men
34 *I tell you, in that night there shalbe two in one bed, the one shalbe

taken [Delete]
*†received,† the other shal be left †alone.†

woemen taken
35 *Two †women† shall bee grinding together: the one shall be †received,†

[Delete]
*and the other left †alone.†

♣36 men
36 *Two †men† shalbe in the field: the one shall be †received,† and the
"Two taken

*other †forsaken.†
left

♣The 36 verse is wanting here in the most of the Greeke copyes
"This 36. verse is wanting in most of the Greeke copies

answered, and And
37 *And they †answering,† sayde unto him, Where, Lord? He said unto them,

is [Delete]
*Wheresoever the body †shalbe,† thither will †also† the Egles

resort
*†be gathered together.†
be gathered together

The xviii. Chapter.

spake
1 *And he †put foorth† a parable unto them, to this end, that men ought alwayes to

faynt
be wearie
*pray, and not to †be wearie:†
faint

2 *Saying, there was in a †certaine† citie a †certaine† Judge, which
[Delete] [Delete]

stood in awe of
reverenced
regarded
*feared not God, neither †regarded† man.

[Delete] that
3 *And there was a †certaine† widow in †the same† citie, and she came unto
*him, saying, Avenge me of mine adversarie:
4 *And he would not for a while. But afterward he sayd within himselfe, Though I
stand in awe of
regard
*feare not God, nor †care for† man,
[Delete]
5 *Yet because this widow †much† troubleth me, I will avenge her,
at the last she come and wearie me out
*least †she come at the last,† †and make me wearie.†
by her continuall comming she weary me
unjust
6 *And the Lord sayd, Heare what the †unrighteous† Judge saith.
owne
7 *And shall not God avenge his elect, which cry day and night unto him,
[Delete] his anger long concerning
*†yea,† though he †deferre †them?
beare long with
speedily
8 *I tell you that he will avenge them, †and that quickly.† Neverthelesse, when
*the sonne of man commeth, shall he find faith on the earth?
spake also
spake
9 *And he †tolde† this parable unto certaine which trusted in themselves
set all others at naught
despised others
*that they were righteous, and †despised other.†
"that they were righteous despised other
"Or, as being righteous
10 *Two men went up into the Temple to pray, the one a Pharisee, and the other
*a Publicane.
11 *The Pharisee stood and prayed thus with himselfe, God, I thanke thee, that I
*am not as other men are, extortioners, unjust, adulterers, or

even
* as this Publicane.

12 *I fast twise in the weeke, I give †tithe† of all that I possesse.
tithes

so much as
13 *And the Publicane standing afarre off, would not lift up his

unto
*eyes †to† heaven: but smote upon his breast, saying, God be mercifull to me

*a sinner.

went downe
14 *I tell you, this man †departed <u>home</u>† to his house justified rather then the

abased
*other: For every one that exalteth himselfe, shalbe †brought low:† and he that

abaseth
*†humbleth† himselfe, shalbe exalted.
humbleth

And but
15 * They brought unto him also infants, that he †should† touch them: when
would

it
*his disciples saw , they rebuked them.

[Delete] and
16 *But Jesus, †when he had† called them unto him, said, Suffer litle children

for of such is
of such is
*to come unto me, and forbid them not: for †unto such belongeth† the kingdome of God.

17 *Verily I say unto you, Whosoever shall not receive the kingdom of God as

*a litle child, shall in no wise enter therein.

shall I
18 *And a certaine ruler asked him, saying, Good master, what †ought I to† doe

inherit
*to †possesse† eternall life?

And
19 * Jesus said unto him, Why callest thou me good? None is good save

one <u>even</u> God
one <u>that</u> <u>is</u> God
*†God onely.†

20 *Thou knowest the commandements, Do not commit adulterie, Doe not kill, Doe not
*steale, Doe not beare false witnesse, Honour thy father and thy mother.

[Delete]
up
21 *And he said, All these have I kept from my youth †up.†

Now these things
22 * When Jesus heard †that,† hee sayd unto him, Yet lackest thou one
*thing: Sell all that thou hast, and distribute unto the poore, and thou shalt
*have treasure in heaven, and come, follow me.

sorrowfull
And very sory
23 * When he heard this, he was †very sory:† for he was very rich.
very sorrowfull

sorrowfull
And very sory
24 * When Jesus sawe that he was †very sory,† he said, How hardly shall they
very sorrowfull

riches
*that have †money† enter into the kingdome of God?

25 *For it is easier for a Camel to goe thorow a needles eye, then for a rich man
*to enter into the kingdome of God?

it <u>then</u>
26 *And they that heard †<u>it</u>,† said, †And† who †then† can be saved?
[Delete] then

27 *And he said, The things which are unpossible with men, are possible with God.

left
28 *Then Peter said, Loe, we have †forsaken† all, and followed thee.

And
29 * He said unto them, Verily I say unto you, there is no man that hath

left or or
*†forsaken† house, †either† parents, †either† brethren, or wife, or children, for

*the kingdome of Gods sake,

Whoe time
30 *†Which† shall not receive manifold more in this †world,† and in the world
present

*to come life everlasting.

Then hee
31 *†Jesus† tooke unto him the twelve, and said unto them, Behold, we goe up to

shall be accomplished that are written by the prophets
shall be accomplished to the sonne of man that are written
*Hierusalem, and all things †shall be fulfilled to the sonne of man that are written
that are written by the Prophets concerning the sonne of

touching the sonne of man
by the prophets
*by the prophets.†
man shall be accomplished

32 *For he shalbe delivered unto the Gentiles, and shall be mocked, and

reprochfully used spitte
*†spitefully entreated,† and †spitted† on:
spitefully intreated spitted

they shall scourge and
33 *And †when they have scourged† him, †they will† put him to death, and the third

againe
*day he shall rise .

[Delete]
34 *And they understoode none of †all† these things: and this saying

neither perceived they
*was hid from them, †so that they perceived not† the things which were spoken.
neither knewe they

35 *And it came to passe, that as he was come nigh unto Jericho, a certaine blind

*man sate by the †wayes† side, begging.
way

multitude
36 *And †when he heard† the †people† passe by, he asked what it meant.
hearing

told
37 *And they †said unto† him, that Jesus of Nazareth passeth by.

38 *And he cryed, saying, Jesu thou sonne of David, have mercie on me.

39 *And they which went before, rebuked him, that he should hold his peace: but hee
*cryed so much the more, Thou sonne of David have mercie on me.

stood and
40 *And Jesus †staying,† commanded him to be brought unto him: & when he was come
*neere, he asked him,

41 *Saying, What wilt thou that I shall doe unto thee? And he said, Lord, that I
*may receive my sight.

42 *And Jesus saide unto him, Receive thy sight, thy faith hath saved thee.

43 *And immediatly he received his sight, and followed him, glorifying God: and all
*the people when they saw †it,† gave praise unto God.
it

The xix. Chapter.

[Delete] passed
1 *And Jesus entred †in,† and †went† thorow Jericho.

who was a ruler
which was the chiefe
2 *And beholde, there was a man named Zacheus, †which was the chiefe† among the
hee [Delete]
*Publicanes, and was rich †also:†

which was Jesus
[Delete] Jesus whoe he was
3 *And he sought †meanes† to see †Jesus what he should be,† and could not
*for the prease, because he was litle of stature.

sycomore
4 *And he ranne before, and climed up into a †wilde figge† tree, to see him:
passe
*for he was to †come† that way.

5 *And when Jesus came to the place, he looked up, and saw him, and said
Zacheus make haste, and [Delete]
*unto him, †Zache,† come downe †at once:† for to day I must

*abide at thy house.

made haste, & [Delete]
6 *And he came downe †hastily,† and received him joyfully.

[Delete] all
7 *And when they †all† saw it, they murmured, saying, that he was gone

lodge
♣abide
abide
♣abide
*†in† to †tary† with a man that is a sinner.
[Delete] bee guest

♣as a guest
♣as a guest

Zacheus [Delete]
8 *And †Zache† stood †foorth,† and said unto the Lord, Behold, Lord, the half of my

any thing false
*goods I give to the poore, and if I have taken from any man by †forged

accusation
*"cavillation,† I restore him foure fold.

"Or, false accusation

And
9 * Jesus said unto him, This day is salvation come to this house:

forsomuch as also is the sonne
*†because that† he †is also the childe† of Abraham.

10 *For the sonne of man is come to seeke and to save that which was lost.

11 *And as they heard these things, he added, and spake a parable, because he was

*nigh to Hierusalem, & because they thought that the kingdome of God

immediatly
*should †shortly† appeare.

12 *He said therefore, A certaine noble man went into a farre countrey, to receive

returne
*for himselfe a kingdome, and to †come againe.†

he and
13 *And †when he had† called his ten servants, †he† delivered them ten

pounds & said Traffick
*†"pieces of money,† †saying† unto them, †Occupie† till I come.
Occupie

"Or, pounds

14 *But his citizens hated him, and sent a message after him, saying, We wil
*not have this man to reigne over us.

was having received
15 *And it came to passe, that when he †had† returned, †receiving†
the
*†this† kingdome, then he commanded these servants to be called unto him, to whom
*he had given the money, that he might knowe how much every man had
in trafficking
*gained †in occupying.†
by trading

pound pounds
16 *Then came the first, saying, Lord, thy †piece† hath gained ten †pieces.†
17 *And he said unto him, Well, thou good servant: because thou hast bene faithfull
the leaste
*in †a very litle thing,† have thou authoritie over ten cities.
a very little

pound gained pounds
18 *And the second came, saying, Lorde, thy †piece† hath †increased† five †pieces.†

he said to him also
he said to him
he said to him also. And [Delete]
19 *And †to the same he said,† Be thou also †ruler† over
he said likewise to him
*five cities.

pound
20 *And another came, saying, Lord, behold, here is thy †piece,† which I
kept
*have laid up in a napkin:

a severe
21 *For I feared thee, because thou art †a strait† man: thou takest up that
an austere

*thou laiedst not down, and reapest that thou diddest not sow.

And Out
22 *†Then† he saieth unto him, Of thine owne mouth will I judge thee, thou

wicked Thou knewest was a severe
*†evill† servant: †Knewest thou† that I †am† †a straite† man, taking up that I layd
an austere

*not downe, and reaping that I did not sow †?†

Wherefore then that
23 *†And wherefore† gavest not thou my money into the banke, †and† at my comming

usurie
*I might have required mine owne with †vantage?†

the pound
24 *And he said unto them that stood by, Take from him †that piece,† and give it

pounds
*to him that hath ten †pieces.†

pounds
25 *And they said unto him, Lord, he hath ten †pieces.†

26 *For I say unto you, That unto every one which hath, shalbe given: & from him

even that he hath shalbe taken away from him
*that hath not, †shalbe taken away even that he hath.†

27 *†Moreover,† those mine enemies which would not that I should reigne over them,
But

*bring hither, and slay them before me.

before
28 *And when he had thus spoken, he went †forward,† ascending up to Hierusalem.

29 *And it came to passe, when he was come nigh to Bethphage and Bethanie,

to
at called the mount of Olives
*†besides† the mount †which is called Olivet,† hee sent two of his disciples,

village [Delete]
30 *Saying, Goe ye into the †towne† †which is† over against you, in the which

*at your entring ye shall find a Colt tied, whereon yet never man sate: loose him, *and bring him hither.

31 *And if any man aske you, Why do ye loose him? Thus shall ye say unto him,

[Delete]
*†Because† the Lord hath neede of him.
Because

And
32 * They that were sent, went their way, and found even as he had said

*unto them.

[Delete]
33 *And as they were †a† loosing the Colt, the owners thereof said unto

*them, Why loose yee the Colt?

[Delete]
34 *And they sayd, †For† the Lord hath neede of him.

they cast their garments upon and
35 *And they brought him to Jesus: and †their garments being cast on† the Colt,

*they set Jesus thereon.

36 *And as he went, they spread their clothes in the way.

of Olives
37 *And when he was †nowe come nigh to the going downe† of the mount †Olivet,†
come nigh, even now at the descent

to rejoyce and
*the whole multitude of the disciples beganne †rejoycing to† praise God with a

mighty workes
*loud voice, for al the †miracles† that they had seene,

38 *Saying, Blessed be the king that commeth in the name of the Lord, peace in

*heaven, and glory in the highest.

from among multitude
39 *And some of the Pharisees †of† the †company† said unto him, Master,

*rebuke thy disciples.

And answered and should
40 * He †answering,† said unto them, I tell you, that if these †would† holde

the stones would immediatly cry out
*their peace, †then shall the stones cry immediatly.†

over .
41 *And when he was come neere, he beheld the citie, and wept †on† it †,†
,

even thou; at this least day of thine
O even thou; at least in this day of thine
42 *Saying, If thou hadst knowen †those things which belong unto thy peace,
[Delete] even thou, at least in this thy day,

the things which belong unto thy peace:
the things which belong unto thy peace! they are
*even in this thy day:† but nowe †are they† hid from thine eyes.
the things which belong unto thy peace!

[Delete]
43 *For the dayes shall come upon thee, that thine enemies †also† shall cast

trenche streighten thee
*a †banke† about thee, and compasse thee round, and †keepe thee in† on every side,
keepe thee in

shall lay thee, to the ground
shall dashe thee, to the ground
shall beate thee, flatt to the ground within
44 *And †make† †thee even with the ground,† and thy children †which are in†
shall lay thee even with the ground

even with the ground
even with the ground
[Delete]
*thee : and they shall not leave in thee one stone

*upon another, because thou †knowest† not the time of thy visitation.
knewest

45 *And he went into the temple, and began to cast out them that sold therein,

*and them that bought,

46 *Saying unto them, It is written, My house is the house of praier: but ye have

*made it a den of theeves.

Chiefe
47 *And he taught dayly in the Temple. But the †high† Priests and the Scribes, and

sought
*the chiefe of the people †went about† to destroy him,

they might
48 *And could not find what †to† doe: for all the people

were ♣very attentive to heare him
*†did hang of him, when they heard him.†
were “very attentive to heare him

♣Or, hanged on him
“Or, hanged on him

The xx. Chapter.

1 *And it came to passe, that on one of those dayes, as hee taught the people in

*the Temple, and preached the Gospel, the †hight† Priests and the Scribes came
chiefe

*upon him, with the Elders,

2 *And spake unto him, saying, Tell us, by what authoritie doest thou these

Or
*things? †Either† who is he that gave thee this authoritie?

And he answered, and thing
3 * †He answering,† said unto them, I wil also aske you one †word,†

*and answere me.

4 *The baptisme of John, was it from heaven, or of men?

5 *And they reasoned with themselves, saying, If we shall say, From heaven, he will

*say, Why then beleeved ye him not?

6 *But and if we say, Of men, all the people will stone us: For they be

was
*perswaded that John †is† a Prophet.

7 *And they answered, that they could not tell whence it was.

8 *And Jesus said unto them, Neither tell I you by what authoritie I doe these things.

speake
9 *Then beganne he to †put foorth† to the people this parable: A certaine man

[Delete]
*planted a vineyard, and let it foorth to husbandmen, and went †himself†

long time
*into a †strange† countrey for a †great season.†
farre

at the season
10 *And †when† †the time was come,† he sent a servant to the husbandmen, that they

the husbandmen beate him, and
*should give him of the fruit of the vineyard, but †they, when they had beaten him,†

*sent him away emptie.

hee [Delete] and they beate
11 *And againe, †hee† sent †yet† another servant: †but they, when they

and
*had beaten† him also, and entreated him shamefully, sent him away emptie.

And they
12 * Againe, he sent the third, and †when they had† wounded him also,

and
*†they† cast him out.

beloved
13 *Then said the lord of the vineyard, What shall I doe? I will send my †deare†

*sonne: it may be they will reverence him when they see him.

among
14 *But when the husbandmen saw him, they reasoned †within† themselves, saying, This

*is the heire, come, let us kill him, that the inheritance may be ours.

So they and
15 *†And† †when they had† cast him out of the vineyard, †they† killed him.

*What †then† shall the lord of the vineyard doe unto them?
therefore

theise give the
16 *He shall come and destroy †those† husbandmen, and shall †let out his†

others And it
*vineyard to †other.† When they heard †this,† they said, God forbid.

17 *And he beheld them, and saide, What is this then that is written, The

which rejected
*stone †that† the builders †disallowed,† the same is become the head of the corner?

fall to pieces
18 *Whosoever shall †stumble† upon that stone, shalbe broken :
[Delete]

*but on whomsoever it shall fall, it will grinde him to powder.

sought
19 *And the †high† Priests and the Scribes the same houre †went about† to lay
chiefe

*hands on him, & they feared the people: for they perceived that he had spoken

parable
*this †similitude† against them.

20 *And they watched him, and sent foorth spies, which should faine themselves

just catch him in
*†righteous† men, that they might †take hold of† his wordes, †to†
take hold of that so they might

governour
*deliver him unto the power and authoritie of the †deputie.†

21 *And they asked him, saying, Master, we know that thou saiest and teachest

rightly acceptest person any
*†right,† neither †considerest† thou the †outward appearance† of †any man,†
of

*but teachest the way of God truely:
"truely

"Or, of a trueth

22 *Is it lawfull for us to give tribute unto Cesar, or no?

But he and
23 *†When he had† percceived their craftinesse, †he† said unto them, Why tempt ye me?

answered, and
24 *Shew me a penie: whose image & superscription hath it? They †answering,†

*said, Cesars.

Give therefore
Render therfore
25 *And he said unto them, †Give then† unto Cesar the things which

be Cesars which be Gods
*†belong unto Cesar:† and †to† God, the things †that pertaine unto God.†
unto

catch him in his talk
26 *And they could not †reprove† †this sayings† before the people:
take hold of his words

*and they marveiled at his answere, and held their peace.

27 *Then came to him certaine of the Saduces (which denie that there is any

*resurrection) and they asked him,

28 *Saying, Master, Moses wrote unto us, If any mans brother die, having a wife,

[Delete]
*and he die without children, that †then† his brother should take his wife,

*and raise up seede unto his brother.

tooke
29 *There were therefore seven brethren, and the first, †when he had taken†

and
*a wife, died without children.

30 *And the second tooke her to wife, and he died childlesse.

maner also.
31 *And the third tooke her, and in like †wise the residue of† the seven ,

And they [Delete]
*†and† left no children †behinde them,† and died.

32 *Last of all, the woman died also.

Therefore
33 *†Now† in the resurrection, whose wife of them is she? for seven had her to

*wife.

And
34 * Jesus answering, sayd unto them, The children of this world marrie

[Delete] given in marriage
*†wives,† and are †married:†

accounted
35 *But they which shalbe †counted† worthy to †enjoy† that world, and the
obtaine

neither [Delete] nor
*resurrection from the dead, †doe not† marrie †wives,† †neither†

given in marriage
*are †maried:†

[Delete]
36 *†For† neither can they die any more, for they are equall unto the

children being
*Angels, and are the †sonnes† of God, †in as much as they are† the children

*of the resurrection.

at
37 *†And† that the dead †be† raised, †Moses also† shewed †besides†
Now are even Moses

[Delete]
*the †bramble† bush, when he calleth the Lord, the God of Abraham, and the

*God of Isahac, and the God of Jacob.

the the
38 *For he is not a God of dead, but of living: for all live unto him.

Scribes
39 *Then certaine of the †Pharisees† answering, said, Master, thou hast well said.

they durst
40 *And after that, †durst they† not aske him any question at all.

41 *And he said unto them, How say they that Christ is Davids sonne,

[Delete]
42 *And David himselfe saith in the booke of †the† Psalmes, The Lord said

*to my Lord, Sit thou on my right hand,

43 *Till I make thine enemies thy footestoole?

[Delete]
44 *David therefore calleth him Lorde, †and† how is he then his sonne?

45 *Then in the audience of all the people, he said unto his disciples,

desire to walke
46 *Beware of the Scribes, which †will goe† in long robes, & love greetings

*in the markets, and the highest seates in the Synagogues, and the chiefe roumes *at feasts,

and for a shew make
47 *Which devoure widowes houses, †under colour of† long prayers: the same shall

*receive greater damnation.

The xxi. Chapter.

And and casting
1 *†As† he looked up, †he† saw the rich men, †which cast† their gifts into the treasurie.

And
2 * Hee sawe also a certaine poore widow, casting in thither two mites.

cast
3 *And he said, Of a trueth, I say unto you, that this poore widowe hath †put†

*in more then they all.

4 *For all these have of their †superfluitie† cast in unto the offerings of God,
abundance

*but she of her penurie hath cast in all the living that she had.

as some
5 *And †unto some that† spake of the Temple, how it was †garnished† with goodly
adorned

consecrated
*stones and gifts, he said,
[Delete]

these
6 *<u>As for</u> †those† things which ye behold, the dayes will come, in the which there

*shall not be left one stone upon another, that shall not be throwen downe.

But
7 *And they asked him, saying, Master, when shall these things be? and what

*signe will there be, when these things shall come to passe?

8 *And he said, Take heede that ye be not deceived: for many shall come in my name,

*saying, I am <u>Christ</u>, and the time draweth neere: goe ye not therefore after them.

commotions terrefyed
9 *But when ye shall heare of warres and †seditions,† be not †afraid:† for these

is
*things must first come to passe, but the ende †followeth† not by and by.

10 *Then said he unto them, Nation shall rise against nation, and kingdome against

*kingdome:

famines
11 *And great earthquakes shall be in divers places, and †hungers,† and

: sights,
*pestilences †,† and fearefull †things:† and great signes shall there be from heaven.
sights

their
their
12 *But before all these, they shall lay †their† hands on you, and persecute you,

to be brought
being brought
*delivering you up to the Synagogues, and into prisons, †and shall bring you†

before
*†unto† kings, and rulers, for my names sake.

testimonie
13 *And it shal turne to you for a †testimoniall.†

Settle it meditate
14 *†Be at a sure point† therfore in your harts, not to †studie† before what ye shall

*answere.

which
15 *For I wil give you a mouth and wisdom, †whereagainst† all your adversaries

gainsay
*shall not be able to †speake,† nor resist.

And both by
16 *†Yea,† ye shall be betrayed †also of your† parents, and brethren, and kinsfolks,

some cause to be
*and friends, and †some† of you shall they put to death,

yee shall be hated
17 *And †hated shall yee be† of all men for my names sake.

But not a
18 *†And† there shall †in no case one† haire of your head perish.

In your patience Possesse yee your soules.
19 *†Possesse yee your soules by your patience.†

compassed with armies know
20 *And when ye shall see Hierusalem †besieged with an hoste,† then †be sure†

therof
*that the desolation †of the same† is nigh.

21 *Then let them which are in †Jurie,† flee to the mountaines, and let them which
Judea

*are in the mids of it, depart out, and let not them that are in

the cuntrie therinto
*†other countreys,† enter †therein.†
the countreys

22 *For these bee the dayes of vengeance, that all things which are written may be

*fulfilled.

23 *But woe unto them that are with childe, and to them that give sucke in those

*dayes, for there shalbe great distresse in the land, and wrath †over†
upon

*this people.

by
24 *And they shall fall †through† the edge of the sword, and shall be led away captive

*into all nations, and Hierusalem shall be troden downe of the Gentiles, untill

times
*the †time† of the Gentiles be fulfilled.

25 *And there shall be signes in the Sunne, and in the Moone, and in the Starres,

distresse of
*and upon the earth †trouble among the† nations, with perplexitie, the sea and the

*†water† roaring,
waves

[Delete]
26 *†And† mens hearts failing them for feare, and for looking after those

earth
*things which are comming on the †world:† For the powers of heaven shall be shaken.

27 *And then shall they see the sonne of man comming in a cloude, with power and
*great glorie.
28 *And when these things begin to come to passe, then looke up, and lift up your
*heads, for your redemption draweth nigh.
spake to them a parable
29 *And he †shewed them a similitude,† Behold the figge tree, and all the trees,
now [Delete] see, and
30 *When they shoot foorth †their buds,† yee †beholding,† know of your
now
*owne selves that sommer is †then† nigh at hand.
know yee
31 *So likewise ye, when ye see these things come to passe, †be yee sure†
at hand
*that the kingdome of God is nigh
not passe away
32 *Verily I say unto you, this generation shall †in no wise passe,† till all
*be fulfilled.
away not passe away
33 *Heaven & earth shall passe , but my words shall †in no wise passe.†
And overcharged
34 * Take heede to your selves, least at any time your hearts be †overcome†
*with surfetting, and drunkennesse, and cares of this life, and so that day come
*upon you unawares.
35 *For as a snare shal it come on al them that dwell on the face of the whole earth.
and pray alwayes
36 *Watch ye therefore, †at all times praying,† that ye may be accompted worthy
to passe to
*to escape all these things that shall come , and †that yee may†
*stand before the sonne of man.
And
37 * In the day time hee was teaching in the temple, and at night he went out,

the mount of Olives
*and abode in the mount that is called †Olivet.†

38 *And all the people came earely in the morning to him in the temple, for to

*heare him.

The xxii. Chapter.

Now unlevened
1 * The feast of †sweete† bread drew nigh, which is called the Passeover.

2 *And the †high† Priestes and Scribes sought howe they might kill him, for they
chiefe

*feared the people.

surnamed
3 *Then entred Satan into Judas, †whose sirname was† Iscariot, being of the number

*of the twelve.

4 *And hee went his way, and communed with the †high† priests & captaines, how
chiefe

*he might betray him unto them.

covenanted
5 *And they were glad, and †promised† to give him money.

promised
6 *And hee †consented,† and sought opportunitie to betray him unto them

in the absence of the multitude
*†without tumult.†
"in the absence of the multitude

"Or, without tumult

unlevened [Delete]
7 *Then came the day of †sweet† bread, when †of necessitie† the Passeover

*must be killed.

8 *And hee sent Peter and John, saying, Goe and prepare us the Passeover, that

*we may eate.

And [Delete]
9 * They said unto him, Where wilt thou that we †should†

[Delete]
*prepare †it?†

10 *And he said unto them, Behold, when ye are entred into the citie, there shall

follow him [Delete]
*a man meete you, bearing a pitcher of water, †him follow† into the †same†

where
*house †that† he entreth in.

11 *And ye shall say unto the good man of the house, The master saith unto thee,

*Where is the ghest chamber, where I shall eate the Passeover with my disciples?

large roome furnished
12 *And he shal shew you a †great† upper †chamber† †prepared,† there make readie.

13 *And they went, and found as hee had said unto them, and they made readie the

*Passeover.

14 *And when the houre was come, he sate downe, and the twelve Apostles with him.

♣With desire
15 *And he said unto them, †With hearty desire,† I have desired to eate this Passeover
"With desire

[Delete]
*with you before †that† I suffer.

♣Or, I have hartily desired
"Or, I have heartely desired

[Delete] any more eate thereof
16 *For I say unto you, †Hencefoorth† I will not †in any wise eate of it any more,†

*untill it be fulfilled in the kingdome of God.

he tooke gave and
17 *And †when he had taken† the cup, and †given† thankes, †he† said, Take this, and

your selves
*divide it among †you.†

[Delete]
18 For I say unto you, I will not †in any wise† drinke of the fruit of the

*vine, until the kingdom of God shall come.

he tooke gave and
19 *And †when he had taken† bread, and †given† thanks, †he† brake it, and gave unto

*them, saying, This is my body which is given for you, this do

[Delete]
*in †the† remembrance of me.

the cup after supper,
20 *Likewise also †when he had supped, hee tooke the cup,† saying, This cup is

*the new Testament in my blood, which is shed for you.

But
21 *†Yet† behold, the hand of him that betrayeth me, is with me on the table.

22 *And truely the sonne of man goeth as it †is appointed,† but woe unto that man
was determined

*by whom he is betrayed.

23 *And they began to enquire among themselves, which of them it was that should

*doe this thing.

also be accompted
24 *And there was a strife among them, which of them should †seeme to be†

*the greatest.

the Gentles exercise lordship
25 *And hee sayd unto them, The kings of †nations† †be lords† over them,

exercise bountifull
*and they that †have† authoritie upon them, are called †benefactours.†
benefactors

let him
26 *But ye shall not be so: but he that is greatest among you, †shall† be

[Delete] serve
*as the younger, and he that is chiefe, †shalbe† as he that doth †minister.†

27 *For whether is greater, he that sitteth at meate, or he that serveth? Is not

serveth
*he that sitteth at meate? But I am among you as he that †ministreth.†

continued
28 *Ye are they which have †continually bidden† with me in my temptations.

29 *And I appoint unto you a kingdome, as my father hath appointed unto me,

thrones
30 *That ye may eate and drinke at my table in my kingdome, and sit on †seates,†

*judging the twelve tribes of Israel.

demanded to have you
desired to have you
31 *And the Lord said, Simon, Simon, behold, Satan hath †earnestly desired†

*†to† sift you, as †it were† wheate:
that he may [Delete]

faile not
32 *But I have prayed for thee, that thy faith †should not faile,† and

thou once
*†when thou art† converted, strengthen thy brethren.
when thou art

33 *And hee sayde unto him, Lorde, I am readie to goe with thee both into prison,

*and to death.

not
34 *And he said, I tell thee Peter, the Cocke shall †in no wise† crow this day,

*before that thou shalt thrise denie that thou knowest me.

purse
35 *And he said unto them, When I sent you without †wallet,† and scrip, and shoes,

Nothing
*lacked ye any thing? And they said, †No.†

purse
36 *Then said he unto them, But now he that hath a †wallet,† let him take it

[Delete] no sword
*†up,† and likewise his scrip: and he that hath †none,† let him sell his

garment one
*†coate,† and buy †a sword.†

this that
37 *For I say unto you, that †yet† †the same which† is written must be
[Delete] yet

accomplished And he was reputed among the wicked
*†perfourmed† in mee, †which is, Even among the wicked was he reputed:†
And hee was reckoned among the transgressors

the concerning
*For †those† things †which are written of† me, have an end.

38 *And they said, Lord, beholde, here are two swords. And he said unto them,

*It is ynough.

the mount of Olives
39 *And hee came out, and went as hee was wont to †mount Olivet,† and his

also
*disciples followed him.

was at that ye enter not
40 *And when hee †came to† the place, he sayd unto them, Pray, †least ye fall†

*into temptation.

withdrawen
41 *And he was †pulled away† from them about a stones cast, and kneeled downe,

*and prayed,

be willing to
42 *Saying, Father, if thou †wilt,† remove this cup from mee, neverthelesse,
be willing

*not my will, but thine be done.

strengthning
43 *And there appeared an Angel unto him from heaven, †comforting† him.

being [Delete]
44 *And †he was† in an agonie, †and† he prayed more earnestly, and his

as it were greate falling
*sweate was †like† droppes of blood, †trickling† downe to the ground.

45 *And when he rose up from prayer, and was come to his disciples, he found them

sorrowe
*sleeping for †heavinesse,†

enter
46 *And said unto them, Why sleepe ye? Rise, and pray, least ye †fall†

*into temptation.

And a multitude
47 * While hee yet spake, behold, †there came a company,† and he that was called

drew neare
*Judas, one of the twelve, went before them, and †preassed nigh† unto Jesus,

*to kisse him.

48 *But Jesus said unto him, Judas, betrayest thou the sonne of man with a kisse?

49 *When they which were about him, sawe what would follow, they said unto him, Lorde,

*shall we smite with the sword?

cut of
50 *And one of them smote the servant of the high Priest, and †tooke away†

*his right eare.

And [Delete] [Delete]
51 * Jesus answered, and sayd, Suffer ye thus farre †foorth.† And †when†

and
*he touched his eare, †he† healed him.

Chiefe captaines
52 *Then Jesus said unto the †high† priests and †“rulers† of the temple, and the

against
*elders which were come to him, Bee yee come out as †unto† a thiefe, with swords

*and staves?

“Or, captaines

53 *When I was dayly with you in the temple, ye stretched forth no hands against me:

[Delete] [Delete]
*but this is †even† your †very† houre, and the power of darkenesse.

into
54 *Then tooke they him, and led him, and brought him †to† the high Priests house,

*and Peter followed afarre off.

55 *And when they had kindled a fire in the midst of the hall, and were set downe

[Delete]
*together, Peter †also† sate downe among them.

[Delete] maide
56 *But †when† a certain †wench† beheld him as hee sate by the fire, &

and man
*earnestly looked upon him, †she† said, This †same fellow† was also with him.

57 *And hee denied him saying, Woman, I know him not.

litle
58 *And after a while another sawe him, and sayd, Thou art also of them.

*And Peter sayde, Man, I am not.

one confidently
59 *And about the space of †an† houre after, another affirmed, saying,

Of a truth also was with him a Galilean
*†Verely† this fellow †was with him also:† for he is †of Galilee.†

know
60 *And Peter sayd, Man, I †wote† not what thou sayest. And immediatly while he

*yet spake, the Cocke crew.

[Delete]
61 *And the Lord turned †backe,† and looked upon Peter: and Peter remembred

*the word of the Lord, how hee had sayd unto him, Before the Cocke crowe, thou

*shalt denie me thrise.

62 *And Peter went out and wept bitterly.

63 *And the men that helde Jesus, mocked him, and smote him.

64 *And when they had blindfolded him, they strooke him on the face, and asked

Prophesye
*him, saying, †Areade,† who is it that smote thee?

65 *And many other things blasphemously spake they against him.

chiefe
66 *And assoone as it was day, the elders of the people, and the †high† priests,

*and the Scribes came together, and led him into their councell, saying,

the
67 *Art thou †very† Christ? Tell us. And he said unto them, If I tell you,

[Delete]
*you will not beleeve †in any wise.†

also [Delete]
68 *And if I aske you, you wil not †in any wise† answere me, nor let me goe.

69 *†Hereafrer† shall the sonne of man sit on the right hand of the power of God.
Hereafter

And he sayd unto them
70 *Then said they al, Art thou then the sonne of God? †He sayd,†

*Ye say that I am.

71 *And they said, What neede we any further witnesse? For we our selves have heard

*of his owne mouth.

The xxiii. Chapter.

1 *And the whole multitude of them arose, and led him unto Pilate.

2 *And they began to accuse him, saying, Wee found this felow perverting the

nation himself
*†people,† and forbidding to give tribute to Cesar, saying that hee is

*Christ a king.

3 *And Pilate asked him, saying, Art thou the King of the Jewes?

And
* Hee answered him, and sayd, Thou sayest it.

Chiefe
4 *Then sayd Pilate to the †hight† Priests, and to the people, I finde no fault

*in this man.

stirreth up
5 *And they were the more fierce, saying, He †moveth† the people, teaching

beginning from [Delete]
*thorowout all Jurie, †and began† †at† Galilee, †even† to this place.

[Delete]
6 *When Pilate heard †mention† of Galilee, he asked whether the man were

a Galilean
*†of Galilee.†

7 *And assoone as he knew that he belonged unto Herods jurisdiction, he sent him

who him self also was
*to Herode, †which† †was also† at Hierusalem at that time.

8 *And when Herod saw Jesus, hee was exceeding glad, for he was desirous to see

hoped
*him of a long season, because hee had heard many things of him, and hee †trusted†

*to have seene some miracle done by him.

in
9 *Then he questioned with him many words, but he answered him nothing.

And chiefe [Delete]
10 * The †high† priests and Scribes stood †forth,† and

*†accused him straitly.†
vehemently accused him

set him at naught [Delete]
11 *And Herod with his men of warre †despised him,† and †when he had†

and a gorgeous robe
*mocked him, †he† arayed him in †white clothing,† and sent him againe to Pilate.

12 *And the same day Pilate and Herod were made friends together, for before they

enmitie
*were at †variance† betweene themselves.

chiefe
13 *And Pilate, when hee had called together the †high† Priestes, and the rulers,

*and the people,

14 *Sayd unto them, Yee have brought this man unto me, as one that perverteth the

*people, and behold, I having examined him before you, have found no fault in this

touching
*man, †of† those things whereof ye accuse him,

15 *No, nor yet Herod: for I sent you to him, and loe, nothing worthie of death is

*done †to† him.
unto

chastize release him
16 *I will therefore †chasten† him, and †let him loose.†

release one
17 *For of necessitie he must †have let one loose† unto them at the feast.

they out all at once this man
18 *And †all the people† cried †aloude,† saying, Away with †him,† and

release unto
*†deliver† †to† us Barabbas,

Who sedition
19 *†Which† for a certaine †insurrection† made in the citie, and for murder was cast

*in prison.

spake againe to them, willing to release Jesus
20 *Pilate therfore †spake againe to them, willing to let Jesus loose.†
willing to release Jesus, spake againe to them

21 *But they cryed, saying, Crucifie him, crucifie him.

And But
22 * He sayd unto them the third time, What evil hath he done? I have found
Why

chastize
*no cause of death in him, I will therefore †chasten† him, and let him goe.

23 *And they were instant with loud voices, requiring that hee might bee crucified,

chiefe
*and the voices of them, and of the †thigh† Priestes, prevailed.

24 And Pilate gave sentence that it should be as they required.
"gave sentence

"Or, assented

released sedition
25 *And hee †let loose† unto them, him that for †insurrection† and murder was cast

*into prison, whom they had desired, †and† he delivered Jesus to their will.
but

layed hold upon a Cyrenian
26 *And as they led him away, they †caught† one Simon †of Cyrene,†

[Delete]
cuntry and
*comming out of the †field,† †and† on him they layd the crosse, that hee

*might beare it after Jesus.

27 *And there followed him a great companie of people, and of women, which also
*bewailed and lamented him.

[Delete] [Delete]
28 *But Jesus turning †backe† unto them, sayd, †Yee† daughters of Hierusalem,
*weepe not for me, but weepe for your selves, and for your children.

Blessed
29 *For behold, the dayes are comming, in the which they shall say, †Happie†
*are the barren, and the wombes that never bare, & the paps which never gave sucke.
30 *Then shall they beginne to say to the mountaines, Fall on us, and to the hilles,
*Cover us.

♣moist
31 *For if they doe these things in a †moist† tree, what shall be done in the drie?
greene

♣Or, greene

also two other malefactors
32 *And there were †other two evill doers† led with him, to be put to death.

when ♣Calvarie
33 *And †after that† they were come to the place which is called Calvarie,
"Calvarie

malefactors
*there they crucified him, and the †evill doers,† one on the right hand, and the
*other on the left.

♣Or, the place of a skull
"Or, the place of a skull

know
34 *Then sayd Jesus, Father, forgive them, for they †wote† not what they doe:
*And they parted his raiment, and cast lots.

also
35 *And the people stoode beholding, and the rulers †mocked him with them,†
with them derided him

others [Delete]
*saying, He saved †other men,† let him save himselfe, if hee be †verie†

*Christ, the chosen of God.

And skoffed
36 * The souldiers also †mocked† him, comming to him, and offering him vineger,
mocked

37 *And saying, If thou bee the king of the Jewes, save thy selfe.

also in
38 *And a superscription was written over him †with† letters of Greeke, and

*Latin, and Hebrewe, THIS IS THE KING OF THE JEWES.

malefactors
39 *And one of the †evill doers,† which were hanged, railed on him, saying, If thou

*be Christ, save thy selfe and us.

doest thou not feare
40 *But the other answering, rebuked him, saying, †Fearest thou not† God,
Dost not thou feare

condemnation
*seeing thou art in the same †damnation?†

justly the due reward of
41 *And we †truely† †are righteously punished,† for we receive †according to†
indeed

*our deeds, but this man hath done nothing amisse.

42 *And he sayd unto Jesus, Lord, remember me when thou commest into thy kingdome.

43 *And Jesus said unto him, Verely I say unto thee, to day shalt thou be with

*me in paradise.

♣earth
44 *And it was about the sixt houre, and there was a darkenesse over all the earth,
“earth

*untill the ninth houre.

♣Or, Land
“Or, land

in
45 *And the Sunne was darkened, and the vaile of the temple was rent, †even thorow†

*the middes.

greate
46 *And when Jesus had cried with a †loude† voice, hee sayd, Father, into thy hands
loud

[Delete] having said thus
*I †will† commend my spirit: And †when he thus had said,† he gave up the ghost.

Now Certainly
47 * When the Centurion saw what was done, he glorified God, saying, †Verely†

*this was a righteous man.

beholding
48 *And all the people that came together to that sight, †when they sawe† the things

*which were done, smote their breasts, and returned.

49 *And all his aquaintance, and the women that followed him from Galilee, stood

*afarre off, beholding these things.

50 *And beholde, there was a man named Joseph, a counseller, and hee was a good

*man, and a just,

hee
51 *(The same had not consented to the counsell and deed of them) †which† was of

who also himself
*Arimathea, a citie of the Jewes, †which same also† waited for the kingdome of God.

52 *†He† went unto Pilate, and begged the body of Jesus.
This man

he tooke and fine linnen
53 *And †when he had taken† it downe, †he† wrapped it in †a linnen cloth,†
linnen

*and layd it in a sepulchre that was hewen in stone, wherein never man before was layd.

Preparation
54 *And that day was the †preparing of the Sabboth,† and the Sabboth drew on.

And also which came with him from Galilee followed after and
55 * The women †that followed after, which had come with him from Galilee,†

*beheld the sepulchre, and how his body was layd.

spices and
56 *And they returned, and prepared †sweete odours† and ointments, †but† rested the

*Sabboth day, according to the commandement.

The xxiiii. Chapter.

Now weeke
1 *†But† [a]upon the first day of the †Sabboths,† very early in the morning, they came

spices
*unto the sepulchre, bringing the †sweete odours,† which they had prepared, and

certaine others
*†other women† with them.

[a]That is, the first day of the weeke

2 *And they found the stone rolled away from the sepulchre.

entred and Jesus
3 *And they †went† in, †but† found not the bodie of the Lord †Jesu.†

musing thereupon
4 *And it came to passe, as they were †amazed thereat,† beholde, two men
much perplexed thereabout

*stood by them in shining garments.

5 *And as they were afraid, and bowed down their faces to the earth, they sayde

the ♣living
*unto them, Why seeke ye the living among the dead?
"the living

♣Or, him that liveth
"Or, him that liveth

6 *He is not here, but is risen: Remember how he spake unto you when he was yet

*in Galilee,

7 *Saying, The Sonne of man must bee delivered into the hands of sinful men, and

againe
*be crucified, and the third day rise .

8 *And they remembred his words,

the
9 *And returned from the sepulchre, and told all these things unto †those†

rest
*eleven, and to all the †remnant.†

the mother of James woemen
10 *It was Marie Magdalene, and Joanna, & Marie †Jacobi,† & other

*that were with them, which told these things unto the Apostles.

as idle tales, and they beleeved them not
11 *And their wordes seemed to them †fayned things, neither beleeved they them.†

stooping downe
12 *Then arose Peter, and ranne unto the sepulchre, and †when he had looked in,†

beheld
*hee †sawe† the linnen clothes layd by themselves, and departed, wondring in

*himselfe at that which was come to passe.

13 *And behold, two of them went that same day to a village called Emaus, which was

*from Hierusalem about threescore furlongs.

which had happened
14 *And they talked together of all these things †that had come to passe.†

15 *And it came to passe, that while they communed together, and reasoned, Jesus

*himselfe drew neere, and went with them.

held
16 *But their eyes were †holden,† that they should not know him.
holden

17 *And he sayd unto them, What manner of communications are these that yee have

*one to another as ye walke, and are sad?

18 *And the one of them, whose name was Cleophas, answering, sayd unto him, Art thou

*onely a stranger in Hierusalem, and hast not knowen the thinges which are come

*to passe there in these dayes?

And Concerning
19 * He saide unto them, What things? And they said unto him, †Of† Jesus

*of Nazareth, which was a Prophet, mightie in deede & word before God and all

*the people,

Chiefe
20 *And how the †high† Priests and our rulers delivered him to bee condemned to

*death, and have crucified him.

21 *But we trusted that it had bene he which should have redeemed Israel: and

beside all this [Delete]
*†as touching all these things,† to day is †even† the third day since

these things
*†they† were done.

astonished
22 *Yea, and certaine women also of our companie made us †astonied,† which

were early at
*†came early unto† the sepulchre,

23 *And when they found not his body, they came, saying that they had seene
also

saide
*a vision of Angels, which †say† that he was alive.

24 *And certaine of them which were with us, went to the sepulchre, and found it even

woemen
women
*so as the †woman† had sayde, but him they saw not.

25 *†And† he saide unto them, O fooles, and slow of heart, to beleeve all that
Then

*the Prophets have spoken:

26 *Ought not Christ to have suffered these things, and to enter into his glory?

beginning hee expounded
27 *And †he began† at Moses, and all the Prophets, †and throughly interpreted†

the concerning
*unto them in all the Scriptures, †those† things †which were written of† himselfe.

whether they went
28 *And they drewe nigh unto the village, †which they went unto,† and he made as

*though he would have gone further.

is
29 *†And† they constrained him, saying, Abide with us, for it †draweth†
But

towards evening spent
*†toward night,† and the day is farre †passed:† And he went in to tarie with them.

30 *And it came to passe, as he sate at meate with them, he tooke bread, and blessed
*it, and brake, and gave to them.

♣vanished
31 *And their eyes were opened, & they knew him, and he vanished out of their sight.
"vanished

♣Or, ceassed to be seene of them
"Or, ceased to be seene of them

heart
32 *And they said one unto another, Did not our †hearts† burne within us, while
while he
*hee talked with us by the way, and opened to us the Scriptures?

[Delete]
33 *And they rose up the same houre, and returned †againe† to Hierusalem, and
*found the eleven gathered together, and them that were with them,

34 *Saying, The Lord is risen in deede, and hath appeared to Simon.

35 *And they tolde what things were done in the way, and how he was knowen of them
[Delete] [Delete]
*in †the† breaking of †the† bread.

36 *And as they thus spake, Jesus himselfe stood in the mids of them, and saith
*unto them, Peace be unto you.

terrifyed afrighted
37 *But they were †abashed† and †afraide,† and supposed that they had seene a spirit.

38 *And hee sayde unto them, Why are yee troubled, and why doe thoughts arise in
*your heartes?

[Delete]
39 *Behold my hands and my feete, that it is †even† I my selfe: handle me
*and see, for a spirit hath not flesh and bones, as ye see me have.

40 *And when he had thus spoken, he shewed them his hands and his feete.

41 *And while they yet beleeved not for joy, and wondered, he said unto them,

yee
*Have †he† here any meate?

gave
42 *And they †offered† him a piece of broyled fish, and of an hony combe.

43 *And he tooke it, and did eate before them.

44 *And he saide unto them, These are the wordes which I spake unto you, while I

thinges [Delete]
*was yet with you, that all must †needes† be fulfilled which were

[Delete]
*written †of me† in the law of Moses, and in the Prophets, and in

concerning me
*the Psalmes .

understanding
45 *Then opened he their †wits,† that they might understand the Scriptures,

46 *And said unto them, Thus it is written, and thus it behoved Christ to suffer,

the dead
*and to rise from †death† the third day:

47 *And that repentance and remission of sins should be preached in his Name

beginning
*among all nations, †and must begin† at Hierusalem.

48 *And ye are witnesses of these things.

[Delete]
49 *And beholde, I †will† send the promise of my father upon you: But tarie ye

clothed
*in the citie of Hierusalem, untill yee be †endued† with power from on high.
indued

as farre as to hee
50 *And he led them out †into† Bethanie, and lift up his hands, and

*blessed them.

while
51 *And it came to passe, †as† he blessed them, he †departed† from them, and
was parted

*†was† caried up into heaven.
[Delete]

they and
52 *And †when they had† worshipped him, †they† returned to Hierusalem, with great

*joy:

blessing
53 *And were continually in the Temple, praising and †lauding† God. Amen.

Bishops' Bible

The Gospel by Saint John

Authorized Version

The Gospel according to S. John

The xvii. Chapter.

1 *These words spake Jesus, and lift up his eyes to heaven, and said, Father, the
*houre is come, glorifie thy sonne, that thy sonne also may glorifie thee:
2 *As thou hast given him power over all flesh, that he should give eternall life
*to as many as thou hast given him.

And
3 * This is †the† life eternall, that they might know thee the onely
[Delete]
*true God, and Jesus Christ whom thou hast sent.
4 *I have glorified thee on the earth: I have finished the worke which thou gavest
*me to doe.

o father glorifie thou me
5 *And now †glorifie thou me, O father,† with thine owne selfe, with the glory

before
*which I had with thee †yer† the world was.

manifested
6 *I have †declared† thy Name unto the men which thou gavest me out of the

*world: thine they were, and thou gavest them mee, and they have kept thy word.

7 *Now they have knowen that all things whatsoever thou hast given me, are of thee:

8 *For I have given unto them the words which thou gavest mee, and they have

*received them, and have knowen surely that I came out from thee, & they have beleeved

*that thou didst send me.

9 *I pray for them, I pray not for the world: but for them which thou hast given

*me, for they are thine.

10 *And all mine are thine, & thine are mine: and I am glorified in them.

I am no more but these
11 *And now †am I not† in the world, †and† †they† are in the world, and I come

those whom
*to thee. Holy Father, keepe through thine owne Name, †them † †which† thou hast

[Delete]
*given me, that they may †also† be one, as we are.

12 *While I was with them in the world, I kept them in thy Name: those that thou

the son of perdition
*gavest me, †have I kept,† and none of them is lost, but †that lost childe:†
I have kept

*that the Scripture might be fulfilled.

And things
13 * Now come I to thee, & these †words† †speake I† in the world, that they
I speak

*might have my joy fulfilled in themselves.

14 *I have given them thy word, and the world hath hated them, because they are

[Delete]
*not of the world, even as I †also† am not of the world.

15 *I pray not that thou shouldest take them out of the world, but that thou

*shouldest keepe them from the evill.

even as I
16 *They are not of the world, †as I also† am not of the world.

[Delete]
17 *Sanctifie them through thy trueth: thy word is †the† trueth.

hast sent
18 *As thou †didst send† me into the world: even so have I also sent them into the world.

19 *And for their sakes †sanctifie I† my selfe, that they also might be sanctified
I sanctifie "sanctified

*through the trueth.

"Or, <u>truely</u> <u>sanctified</u>

Neither pray I for these
20 *†<u>Neverthelesse</u>, I pray not for them† alone: but for them also which shall

word
*beleeve on mee through their †preaching:†

[Delete]
21 *That they all may be one, as thou Father art in me, and I in thee, †and†

*that they also may be one in us: that the world may beleeve that thou hast sent me.

[Delete]
22 *And the glory which thou gavest mee, I have given them: that they †also†

even as we
*may be one, †as we also† are one,

23 *I in them, and thou in me, that they may be made perfect in one, and that the

*world may know that thou hast sent me, & hast loved them, as thou hast loved me.

also whom
24 *Father, I will that they †which† thou hast given me, be with me where I am,

behold
*that they may †see† my glory which thou hast given me: for thou lovedst mee

*before the foundation of the world.

[Delete]
25 *O righteous Father, the world †also† hath not knowen thee: but I have

*knowen thee, and these have knowen that thou hast sent me.

26 *And I have declared unto them thy name, and wil declare it: that the love

*wherewith thou hast loved me, may be in them, and I in them.

The xviii. Chapter.

1 *When Jesus had spoken these words, he went foorth with his disciples over the

*brooke Cedron, where was a garden, into the which hee entred and his disciples.

And
2 * Judas also which betrayed him, knew the place: for Jesus oft times resorted

*thither with his disciples.

having from
3 *Judas then, †after he had† received a band of men, and officers †of† the

chief
*†high† Priests and Pharises, commeth thither with lanternes and torches, and weapons.

Jesus therefore uppon
4 *†And Jesus† knowing all things that should come †on† him, went foorth,

*and sayd unto them, Whom seeke ye?

hee
5 *They answered him, Jesus of Nazareth. Jesus sayeth unto them, I am †hee.†

And
* Judas also which betrayed him, stood with them.

6 *Assoone then as he had sayd unto them, I am he, they went backward, & fell to

*the ground.

And
7 *Then asked he them againe, Whom seeke ye? They sayd, Jesus of Nazareth.

he therefore ye seeke me
8 *Jesus answered, I have tolde you that I am †he:† If †ye seeke me therefore,†

*let these goe their way.

9 *That the saying might be fulfilled which he spake, Of them which thou gavest

lost none
*me, have I †not lost one.†

10 *Then Simon Peter having a sword, drew it, and smote the high Priests

*servant, and cut off his right eare: The servants name was Malchus.

Then
11 *†Therefore† sayd Jesus unto Peter, Put up thy sword into the sheath:

the cup which my father hath given me shall I not drinke it
*†Shall I not drinke of the cup which my father hath given me?†

band
12 *Then the †company,† and the captaine, and officers of the Jewes, tooke Jesus,

*and bound him,

13 *And led him away to Annas first, (for he was father in law to Caiaphas) which

yere♣ [Delete]
*was the high Priest that same yere. †And Annas sent Christ bound unto Caiaphas
yeere"

*the high Priest.†

♣And Annas sent Christ bound unto Caiaphas the high priest. ver 24
"And Annas sent Christ bound unto Caiaphas the high priest, ver. 24

Now
14 * Caiaphas was he which gave counsel to the Jewes, that it was expedient

*that one man should die for the people.

the other
another And
15 *And Simon Peter followed Jesus, and so did †another† Disciple:
[Delete]

*That Disciple was knowen unto the high Priest, and went in with Jesus into the

*palace of the high Priest.

16 *But Peter stood at the doore without. Then went out that other disciple, which

her
*was knowen unto the high Priest, and spake unto †the damosell† that kept the doore,

*and brought in Peter.

17 *Then sayeth the damosell that kept the doore unto Peter, Art not thou also one

*of this mans disciples? He sayth, I am not.

And who
18 * The servants & officers stood there, †which† had made a fire of coales

And stood
*(for it was colde) and they warmed themselves: Peter †also was standing†

with and warmed himself.
*†among† them, †warming him.†

19 *The high Priest then asked Jesus of his disciples, and of his doctrine.

20 *Jesus answered him, I spake openly to the world, I ever taught in the synagogue,

*and in the temple, whither †all the Jews† resort, and in secret have I sayd nothing:
the Jewes alwayes

21 *Why askest thou me? Aske them which heard me what I have sayd unto them:

know
*behold, they †can tell† what I sayd.

And
22 * When he had thus spoken, one of the officers which stood by, †smote†
stroke

with a rod
*Jesus †with a rod,† saying, Answerest thou the high Priest so?
"with the palme of his hand

"Or, with a rod

spoken evill
23 *Jesus answered him, If I have †evill spoken,† beare witnesse of the evill:

well
*but if †I have well spoken,† why smitest thou me?

24 *Now Annas had sent him bound unto Caiaphas the high Priest.

And stood and warmed And they sayd
25 * Simon Peter †was standing & warming† himselfe: †Then sayd they†
They sayd therefore

*unto him, Art not thou also one of his disciples? He denied it, and sayd, I am not.

being his kinsman
26 *One of the servants of the high Priests (†his cousin† whose eare

cut [Delete]
*Peter †smote† off) sayeth †unto him,† Did not I see thee in the garden with him?

then
27 *Peter †therefore† denied againe, and immediatly the cocke crew.

And
28 *Then ledde they Jesus from Caiaphas, †into† the hall of judgement: It
unto "the hall of Judgement

earely
*was †in the morning,† and they themselves went not into the judgement hall,

*lest they should be defiled: but that they might eat the Passeover.

"Or, Pilats house

29 *Pilate then went out unto them, and said, What accusation bring you against

*this man?

a malefactor
30 *They answered and sayd unto him, If he were not †an evill doer,† we would not

*have delivered him unto thee.
up

according to your
31 *Then sayd Pilate unto them, Take yee him, and judge him †after your owne† law.

put any man to death
*The Jewes therefore sayd unto him, It is not lawfull for us to †kill any man.†

saying
32 *That the †words† of Jesus might be fulfilled, which he spake, signifying what

*death hee should die.

33 *Then Pilate entred into the judgement hall againe, and called Jesus, and said

*unto him, Art thou the King of the Jewes?

others
34 *Jesus answered him, Sayest thou this thing of thy selfe? or did †other†

*tell it thee of me?

the Chiefe
35 *Pilate answered, Am I a Jew? Thine owne nation and †high† Priests have

*delivered thee unto me: what hast thou done?

36 *Jesus answered, My kingdome is not of this world: if my kingdome were of this

have striven
*world, then would my servants †surely fight,† that I should not be delivered
fight

*to the Jewes: but nowe is my kingdome not from hence.

37 *Pilate therefore sayd unto him, Art thou a king then? Jesus answered, Thou

was
am
To this end was
*sayest that I am a king: †For this cause† †am† I borne, and for this cause came

every one that is
*I into the world, that I should beare witnesse unto the trueth: †and all that are†

heareth
*of the trueth †heare† my voice.

38 *Pilate sayth unto him, What is trueth? And when he had sayd this, he went out

*againe unto the Jewes, and sayth unto them, I finde in him no fault at all.

Now
But release unto [Delete]
39 * Ye have a custome that I should †deliver† you one †loose†

therefore release
*at the Passeover: will yee that I †loose† unto you the king of the Jewes?

this man Now
40 *Then cried they all againe, saying, Not †him,† but Barabbas. †This†

*Barabbas was a robber.

The xix. Chapter.

therefore tooke Jesus
1 *Then Pilate †tooke Jesus therefore,† and scourged him.

[Delete] and
2 *And the souldiers, †when they had† †wound† a crowne of thornes, †they did†
platted

put on
*put it on his head, & they †did cast about† him a purple †garment,†
robe

they smote
3 *And sayd, Haile king of the Jewes: and †strooke† him with †rods.†
their hands

therefore saith
4 *Pilate went foorth againe, and †sayd† unto them, Beholde, I bring him

*forth to you, that ye may know that I finde no fault in him.

thornes purple garment
5 *Then came Jesus foorth, wearing the crowne of †thorne,† and the †robe of purple:†
purple robe

*and Pilate sayth unto them, Beholde the man.

chiefe out
6 *When the †hight† Priests therefore and officers saw him, they cried , saying,

*Crucifie him, crucifie him. Pilate sayth unto them, Take ye him, and crucifie

*him: for I find no fault in him.

7 *The Jewes answered him, Wee have a law, and by our law he ought to die: because

*he made himselfe the sonne of God.

therefore
8 *When Pilate heard that saying, he was the more afrayd,

9 *And went again into the judgement hall, and sayth unto Jesus, Whence art thou?

*But Jesus gave him no answere.

10 *Then sayeth Pilate unto him, Speakest thou not unto mee? Knowest thou not that

release
*I have power to crucifie thee, and have power to †loose† thee?

11 *Jesus answered, Thou couldest have no power at all against mee, except it were

greater
*given thee from above: therefore he that delivered me unto thee, hath the †more†

*sinne.

Pilate sought release
12 *And from thenceforth †sought Pilate means† to †loose† him: but the Jewes

out this man
*cried , saying, If thou let †him† go, thou art not Cesars friend:

[Delete]
*†For† whosoever maketh himselfe a king, speaketh against Cesar.

therefore brought
13 *When Pilate heard that saying, he †broght† Jesus forth, and

[Delete] on
*†he† sat downe †in† the judgement seat, in a place that is called the pavement,
in

[Delete]
*but in the Hebrew †tongue,† Gabbatha.

And preparation
14 * It was the †preparing† of the Passeover, and about the sixt houre: and he

*sayth unto the Jewes, Behold your king.

But out
15 * They cried , Away with him, away with him, crucifie him. Pilate saith

chiefe
*unto them, Shal I crucifie your king? The †high† Priests answered, We have no

*king but Cesar,

16 *Then delivered hee him therefore unto them to be crucified: and they tooke

*Jesus, and led him away.

he [Delete]
17 *And †he† bearing his crosse, went foorth into a place †which is†

and which is called
which is called
*called the place of a skull, †but† in the Hebrew, Golgotha:

18 *Where they crucified him, and two other with him, on either side one, and

middest
*Jesus in the †middes.†

And
19 *And Pilate wrote a title, and put it on the crosse. The writing was,

*JESUS OF NAZARETH, THE KING OF THE JEWES.

then
20 *This title read many of the Jewes: for the place where Jesus was crucified,

*was nigh to the citie: and it was written in Hebrew, and Greeke, and Latine.

Chiefe
21 *Then sayd the †hie† Priests of the Jewes to Pilate, Write not, The king of the

*Jewes: but that he sayd, I am king of the Jewes.

I have
22 *Pilate answered, What I have written, †that have I† written.

23 *Then the souldiers, when they had crucified Jesus, tooke his garments, (and made

Now
*foure parts, to every souldier a part) and also his coat: the coat was without

♣woven
*seame, woven from the top thorowout.
"woven

♣Or, wrought
"Or, wrought

not us rent
24 *They sayd therefore among themselves, Let †us not† †divide† it, but cast lots

which sayeth
*for it, whose it shall be: that the Scripture might be fulfilled, †saying,†

vesture they did
*They parted my raiment among them, and for my †coat† †did they† cast lots.

And the souldiers indeed did these things
These things therefore the souldiers did
*†And the souldiers did such things in deed.†

And
Now
25 * There stood by the crosse of Jesus, his mother, and his mothers sister,

♣Cleophas
*Mary the wife of Cleophas, and Mary Magdalene.
"Cleophas

♣Or, Clopas
"Or, Clopas

26 *When Jesus therfore saw his mother and the disciple standing by, whom he loved,

*he saith unto his mother, Woman, beholde thy sonne.

that
27 *Then sayth he to the disciple, Beholde thy mother. And from that houre †the†

home
*disciple tooke her unto his owne †house.†

this accomplished
28 *After †these things,† Jesus knowing that all things were now †performed,†

[Delete]
*that the scripture might be fulfilled, †he† sayth, I thirst.

Now there was set a vessell And they
29 *†So there stood a vessell by,† full of vineger: †Therefore when they had†
hyssope and put
*filled a spunge with vineger, and put it upon †hysope,† †they offered†
*it to his mouth.
30 *When Jesus therefore had received the vineger, he said, It is finished,
he and
*and †when he had† bowed his head, †he† gave up the ghost.
Preparation
31 *The Jewes therefore, because it was the †preparing of the Sabboth,† that the bodies
*should not remaine upon the Crosse on the Sabboth day (for that Sabboth day was an
*high day) besought Pilate that their legs might be broken, and that they might
away
*be taken †downe.†
32 *Then came the souldiers, and brake the legs of the first, and of the other
*which was crucified with him.
33 *But when they came to Jesus, & saw that he was dead already, they brake not
*his legs.
pierced his
34 *But one of the souldiers with a speare †thrust him into the† side, & forthwith
*came thereout blood and water.
35 *And he that saw it, bare record, and his record is true, and he knoweth that
[Delete]
*he sayth true, that ye might beleeve †also.†
36 *For these things were done that the scripture should be fulfilled, A bone of
*him shall not be broken.
37 *And again another scripture saith, They shall looke on him whom they pearsed.
And
38 * After this, Joseph of Arimathea (being a Disciple of Jesus, but secretly

away
*for feare of the Jewes) besought Pilate that hee might take †downe† the body of

leave
*Jesus, and Pilate gave him †licence:† he came therefore, and tooke the body of

*Jesus.

first
39 *And there came also Nicodemus, which at the †beginning† came to Jesus by night,

a mixture of myrrhe and aloes
*and brought †of myrrhe and aloes mingled together,† about an hundred pound weight.

40 *Then tooke they the body of Jesus, and wound it in linnen clothes, with the

spices
*†odours,† as the maner of the Jewes is to bury.

41 *†And† in the place where hee was crucified, there was a garden, and in the
Now

*garden a new sepulchre, wherein was never man yet layd.

Jewes preparation day
42 *There layd they Jesus therefore, because of the †preparing of the Sabboth

*of the Jewes,† for the sepulchre was nigh at hand.

The xx. Chapter.

weeke
1 *The first day of the † [a]Sabboths,† commeth Marie Magdalene earely when it was yet

sepulcher
*darke, unto the sepulchre, and seeth the stone taken away from the †grave.†

[a]That is, of the weeke

2 *Then shee runneth, and commeth to Simon Peter, and to the other disciple whom

sepulcher
*Jesus loved, and sayth unto them, They have taken away the Lord out of the †grave,†

know not
*and we †can not tell† where they have layd him.

3
†4† *Peter therefore went forth, and that other disciple, and came to the sepulchre.

So
4 * They ranne both together, and the other disciple did outrun Peter, and came
*first to the sepulchre.

he and
5 *And †when he had† †stouped† downe, †he† saw the linnen clothes lying,
stouping and looking in
*yet went he not in.

6 *Then commeth Simon Peter following him, and went into the sepulchre, and seeth
*the linnen clothes lie,

7 *And the napkin that was about his head, not lying with the linnen clothes, but
*wrapped together in a place by it selfe.

8 *Then went in also that other disciple which came first to the sepulchre, and hee
*saw, and beleeved.

must rise againe from the dead
9 *For as yet they knew not the Scripture, that he †should rise from death.†

home
10 *Then the disciples went away againe unto their owne †house.†

But and
11 * Marie stood without at the sepulchre, weeping: †so† as she wept, she
stooped downe
*†bowed herselfe† into the sepulchre,
and looked

[Delete]
12 *And seeth two angels †clothed† in white, sitting, the one at the head, and
had laine
*the other at the feet, where the body of Jesus †was layd.†

And Because
13 * They say unto her, Woman, why weepest thou? She sayth unto them, †For†
know
*they have taken away my Lord, and I †wote† not where they have layd him.

And
14 * When she had thus sayd, she turned herselfe backe, and saw Jesus standing,

*and knew not that it was Jesus.

15 *Jesus sayth unto her, Woman, why weepest thou? Whom seekest thou? She supposing

him to bee
*†that it had beene† the gardiner, sayeth unto him, Sir, if thou have borne him hence,

take him away.
*tel me where thou hast layd him, and I will †fetch him.†

sayth
16 *Jesus sayth unto her, Mary. She turned herselfe, and †sayd† unto him, Rabboni,

*which is to say, Master.

17 *Jesus sayth unto her, Touch me not: for I am not yet ascended to my Father,

*but goe to my brethren, and say unto them, I ascend unto my Father, and your

*Father, and to my God, and your God.

18 *Mary Magdalene †commeth,† †bringing tidings to† the disciples that she had
came and told

*seene the Lord, and that he had spoken †such† things unto her.
these

Then evening, beeing weeke
19 * The same day at †night, which was† the first day of the †"Sabbboths,†

[Delete]
*when the doores were shut, where the Disciples were assembled †together†

*for feare of the Jewes, came Jesus, and stood in the mids, and sayth unto them,

*Peace be unto you.

"Or, weeke

20 *And when he had so sayd, he shewed unto them his hands and his side. Then were

*the disciples glad, when they saw the Lord.

21 *Then sayd Jesus to them againe, Peace be unto you: As my father hath sent me,

[Delete]
*even so send I you †also.†

this
22 *And when hee had sayd †those words,† hee breathed on them, and sayth unto them,

*Receive ye the holy Ghost.

If ye remit the sinnes of any
Whosoevers sinnes ye remit
23 *†Whosoevers sinnes ye remit,† they are remitted unto them, and
Whose soever sinnes ye remit

if ye retaine the sinnes of any
whosoevers sinnes ye retaine
*†whosoevers sinnes ye retaine,† they are retained.
whose soever sinnes ye retaine

[Delete]
24 *But Thomas, one of the twelve, †which is† called Didymus, was not with
*them when Jesus came.

25 *The other Disciples therefore sayd unto him, We have seene the Lord. But he
*sayd unto them, Except I shall see in his hands the print of the nailes, and put my
*finger into the print of the nailes, and thrust my hand into his side, I
not
*will †in no wise† beleeve.

26 *And after eight dayes, againe his disciples were within, and Thomas with
Then
*them: †Then† came Jesus, the doores being shut, and stood in the mids, and sayd,
*Peace be unto you.

Then reach hither thy finger beholde
27 *†After that,† saith he to Thomas, †Bring thy finger hither,† and †see†
*my hands, and reach hither thy hand, and thrust it into my side, and be not
faithfull
*faithlesse, but †beleeving.†
beleeving

And
28 * Thomas answered, and sayde unto him, My Lord, and my God.

29 *Jesus sayth unto him, Thomas, because thou hast seene me, thou hast beleeved, blessed
*are they that have not seene, and yet have beleeved.

in the presence
30 *And many other signes truely did Jesus †before the eyes† of his Disciples,

*which are not written in this booke.

But is the Christ
31 * These are written, that ye might beleeve that Jesus †Christ is† the sonne

[Delete]
*of God, and that †in† beleeving, yee might have life through his Name.

The xxi. Chapter.

After these things Jesus shewed the
1 *†Afterward did Jesus shew† himselfe againe to †his† Disciples at the

*sea of Tiberias, and on this wise shewed he himselfe.

[Delete]
2 *There were together, Simon Peter, & Thomas, †which is† called Didymus,

*and Nathanael of Cana in Galilee, and the sonnes of Zebedee, & two other of his

*disciples.

3 *Simon Peter sayeth unto them, I goe a fishing. They say unto him,

will
will
[Delete] foorth
*Wee also goe with thee. They went †their way,† and entred into a shippe

they caught
*immediatly, and that night †caught they† nothing.

but
4 *But when the morning was now come, Jesus stood on the shore: †neverthelesse,†

*the disciples knew not that it was Jesus.

Then
5 * Jesus sayth unto them, "Children, have ye any meat? They answered him, No.
"Children

"Or, <u>Sirs</u>
"Or, <u>Sirs</u>

sayd [Delete]
6 *And he †sayth† unto them, Cast †out† the net on the right side of the

[Delete] now
*ship, & ye shall finde. They cast †out† therefore, and †anon† they were

at all
[Delete]
*not able to draw it for the multitude of fishes.

Therefore that disciple whom Jesus loved sayeth
7 *†Then† †said the disciple whom Jesus loved,† unto Peter, It is the Lord.

Now fishers
* When Simon Peter heard that it was the Lord, he girt his coat unto

*him (for hee was naked) and did cast himselfe into the sea.

And
8 * The other disciples came in a little shippe, (for they were not far from land,

dragging
*but as it were two hundred cubits) †drawing† the net with fishes.

a fire of coales there
9 *Assoone then as they were come to land, they saw †hote coales,†

*and fish layd thereon, and bread.

10 *Jesus sayth unto them, Bring of the fish, which ye have now caught.

11 *Simon Peter went up, and drew the net to land full of great fishes, an hundred

*and fiftie and three, and for all there were so many, yet was not the net broken.

12 *Jesus sayth unto them, Come, and dine. And none of the Disciples durst

*aske him, Who art thou? knowing that it was the Lord.

13 *Jesus then commeth, and taketh bread, and giveth them, and fish likewise.

shewed him self
14 *This is nowe the third time that Jesus †appeared† to his disciples, after

the dead
*that he was risen from †death.†

sonne of Jonas
15 *So when they had dined, Jesus sayth to Simon Peter, Simon †"Joanna,†

doe
*lovest thou me more then these [Delete] ? He sayeth unto him, Yea Lord, thou knowest

*that I love thee. He sayth unto him, Feed my lambs.

"Or, sonne of Jona

sonne of Jonas
16 *Hee sayth to him againe the second time, Simon †Joanna,† lovest thou me?
*He sayth unto him, Yea Lord, thou knowest that I love thee. He sayth unto him,
*Feed my sheepe.

sonne of Jonas
17 *He sayd unto him the third time, Simon †Joanna,† lovest thou me?
*Peter was †sory,† because hee sayd unto him the third time, Lovest thou me? And
grieved
*hee sayd unto him, Lord, thou knowest all things, thou knowest that I love thee. Jesus
*sayth unto him, Feed my sheepe.

yoong
18 *Verily, verily I say unto thee, when thou wast †yoonger,† thou girdedst thy selfe,
*and walkedst whither thou wouldest: but when thou shalt be olde, thou shalt stretch
*foorth thy hands, and another shall gird thee, and cary thee whither thou wouldest
*not.

This
19 *†Thus† spake he, signifying by what death he should glorifie God. And when
*he had spoken this, he sayth unto him, Follow me.

Then
20 * Peter turning about, seeth the Disciple whom Jesus loved, following, which
*also leaned on his breast at supper, and said, Lord, which is he that betrayeth thee?

Peter seeing him, and what shall
21 *†When Peter therefore saw him, hee† sayth to Jesus, Lord, †what shall

this man <u>doe</u>
*he do?†

that he
22 *Jesus sayth unto him, If I will †have him to† tarie till I come, what is that
*to thee? Follow thou me.

23 *Then went this saying abroad among the brethren, that that Disciple should not
*die: Yet Jesus sayd not unto him, He shall not die: but, If I will that he tary

*till I come, what is that to thee?

This is the Disciple
24 *†The same Disciple is he† which testifieth of these things, and wrote these
*things, and we know that his testimony is true.

And
25 * There are also many other things which Jesus did, the which if they should
that even the world it self
*be written every one, I suppose †the world† could not
*conteine the books that should be written, Amen.